REAL
BEAUTY

REAL BEAUTY

Eddy M. Zemach

The Pennsylvania State University Press
University Park, Pennsylvania

Library of Congress Cataloging-in-Publication Data

Zemach, Eddy M.
  Real beauty / Eddy M. Zemach.
        p.   cm.
  Includes bibliographical references and index.
  ISBN 0-271-01638-8 (cloth : alk. paper)
  ISBN 0-271-01639-6 (pbk. : alk. paper)
  1. Aesthetics.   I. Title.
BH39.Z444   1997
111'.85—dc20   96-23182
                                                              CIP

It is the policy of The Pennsylvania University Press to use acid-free paper for
the first printing of all clothbound books. Publications on uncoated stock satisfy
the minimum requirements of American National Standard for Information
Sciences—Permanence of Paper for Printed Library Materials, ANSI Z39.48-1992.

Contents

Acknowledgments

Some parts of this book are based on previously published work. I thank the editors and publishers of the journals who were its first hosts for their kind permission to rework and reuse the the following articles: "Why Prescriptivism in Aesthetics Is Wrong," *Metaphilosophy* 7 (1976): 191–205; "Nesting," *The Monist* 73 (1990): 296–311; "Real Beauty," *Midwest Studies in Philosophy* 16 (1991): 249–65; "The Ontology of Aesthetic Properties," *Iyyun* 42 (1992): 49–66; "Existence and Nonexistents," *Erkenntnis* 39 (1993): 145–66; "Emotion and Fictional Beings," *Journal of Aesthetics and Art Criticism* 54 (1996): 41–48.

My first teacher of aesthetics was Pepita Haezrahi, who kindled my interest in aesthetics and encouraged me to pursue my own way in it. I remember her with affection and gratitude. I also thank her memorial fund for monetary help in preparing this book. In graduate school I worked in aesthetics under the guidance of Paul Weiss, an original thinker, a wonderful teacher, and a wise adviser. For many years I discussed philosophy with my very dear friends Menahem Brinker, Eric Walther, Ed Erwin, John Bacon, Alan Goldman, and David Widerker. Michael Krausz, a great friend, aesthetician, musician, and painter generously helped in getting this book published. The love and support of these friends, and of my two brothers, Heruth and Meir, made a life of struggling through thorny abstract problems a splendid adventure for me. I cannot thank them enough. Finally, I think of my children, Ariel, Eden, and Ella: I hope they find real beauty in their lives.

Introduction

I ask you to help me choose new tiles for my kitchen. We enter the store, examine the specimen on display, and you say: "Take number 15; it is sturdy, not fragile like most other tiles." That is, you give me a *practical* reason why tile number 15 is good. I look at that tile, turn it over, read the inscription on the reverse, and yell: "See where it was made? That country's export products are manufactured by prisoners; one should not support slave labor." That is, I give you a *moral* reason why tile number 15 is not good. Thus one feature of the tile (sturdiness) supports, from a practical point of view, one normative description of it ("It is good!"); a feature predominantly used in that way I call 'a practical property.' Another feature of the tile (being made by prisoners) supports, from a moral point of view, another normative description of it ("It is not good!"); a feature predominantly used in that way I call 'a moral property.'

In that innocuous way things can be said to have many normative properties, for example, economic properties (we say, "This tile is good: it is cheaper!"), safety properties ("This tile is good: it protects against fire!"), military properties ("This spot is bad: the enemy can see us here!"), health properties, sentimental properties, religious properties, erotic properties, nutritional properties—and aesthetic properties. An aesthetic property is, then, a feature of a thing that is predominantly used to justify a normative description of that thing from an aesthetic point of view. If you say that tile number 15 is pretty, you give an aesthetic reason for saying that it is good; if you say it is ugly, you give an aesthetic reason for saying that it is not good. Prettiness and Ugliness are, then, aesthetic properties, and the predicates 'pretty' and 'ugly' that name them are aesthetic predicates.

Aesthetic predicates are very common and very useful. If you want to see a movie tonight, you will do well to consult the paper for what the critics have to say. You will find that some pictures are referred to as 'excellent,' 'a must,' 'superb'; others are called 'a bomb,' 'dismal,' or 'dull.' Often, movies are graded on a scale: five stars are given to the best movie, and one star or no stars to the worst. What does this tell us? Is a movie called 'superb' because it has remarkable security features, or a great religious merit, or an excellent nutritional value? Surely not. Critics inform us of the aesthetic properties of the movie. You want to know how good the movie is *aesthetically*, and the movie critic tells you which aesthetic predicates apply to it.

In *aesthetic sentences* the subject of the sentence is qualified by an aesthetic predicate. What is an aesthetic predicate? We need not have the answer now, since, when a word is uttered in an actual context, we know which, and what kind of, predicate is expressed by it. For instance, we recognize economic predicates, though in other contexts the same words (e.g., 'a bull market,' 'a recession') refer to different properties (a place where bulls are sold, a filing out of clergy after service). We know when 'pretty,' 'ugly,' 'gaudy,' 'dramatic,' 'lyrical,' etc. are used as aesthetic predicates, though in some contexts they express nonaesthetic predicates (e.g., "That was an ugly thing to do" is a moral, not an aesthetic, sentence). On the other hand, words like 'great' ("Klee is great"), 'weak,' 'big,' 'small' (as in 'small voice'), etc. often serve as aesthetic predicates. No type-word expresses a predicate; only token-words, that is, occurrences of type-words in contexts, do. When we learn our language, we learn to distinguish those contexts and to identify the predicates expressed in them.

The problem in aesthetics that people are most concerned with, a problem that bothers many of us and may have led you, too, to aesthetics in the first place, is not how to identify an aesthetic sentence. That you can do well enough. What people want to know is whether aesthetic sentences, however identified, describe matters of fact, that is, whether they can be objectively true and, if so, what makes them true, that is, what their truth conditions are. Earlier I introduced aesthetic properties, in an ontologically innocuous way, as whatever it is we refer to when we wish to support aesthetic sentences we utter. May we, however, take this notion seriously, maintaining that there really are aesthetic properties and aesthetic facts in nature and that they determine whether a given aesthetic sentence (e.g., "Klee is great") is true or false? I say yes. I argue for realism in aesthetics, that is, the view that aesthetic sentences have genuine truth-values: they are true if and only if the aesthetic properties they ascribe to things really characterize those things. Coupled with metaphysical realism this view goes against the grain of our time (in past centuries it was common sense). Today, metaphysical realism is unpopular even with respect to science; the position that aesthetic sentences, too, are true or false depending on whether they correspond to reality, is scoffed at by the postmodernist laity and philosophers alike. Aesthetic sentences, they mostly say, have no truth value (or else are true in a special nonrealistic sense, either disquotationally[1] or internally,[2] that is, relative to practices assumed warranted in a given community).

The most radical of those philosophers are the noncognitivists, who hold that aesthetic sentences are not used to describe anything at all but serve an altogether different purpose. Let me examine that radical view first and ask, what do aesthetic sentences *mean*?

1. For such a notion of truth, see, e.g., Paul Horwich, *Truth* (Oxford: Basil Blackwell, 1990).

2. Cf. Crispin Wright, *Truth and Objectivity* (Cambridge: Harvard University Press, 1992), chaps. 2–3. Of the antirealistic theories of truth the most complete ones are, I think, Michael Dummett's and Simon Blackburn's.

1

NONCOGNITIVIST AESTHETICS

1.1. Attitudes and Commendations

The meaning of a sentence may be, not a statement that something is the case, but a question whether something is the case, or an order that something be the case, etc. Often, the grammatical form indicates the kind of meaning a sentence has. "Excuse me!" "What time is it?" "Do you hear me?" "Get off the roof!" "No smoking!" "Long live the king!" "Damn you!" "Thank you!" "Help!" etc. usually express questions, requests, orders, greetings, curses, etc., rather than statements; thus, they have no truth-value. "Excuse me!" is neither true nor false; the ordinary meaning of that sentence is a request, not a statement, and requests are neither true nor false. An indicative sentence such as "Abraham is older than Sarah" has a statement as its meaning: it states that Abraham is older than Sarah and is true or untrue depending on whether Abraham is older than Sarah; but a sentence that has no statement as its meaning can be neither true nor false in that way.

Aesthetic sentences seem to express statements: "This tree is lovely" has the same grammatical form as "This tree is an elm," and the latter sentence is certainly used to make a statement. Yet some philosophers, the *noncognitivists*, maintain that here grammar is misleading. They hold that the sentence "This tree is lovely," as commonly understood, is more like "Excuse me" than it is like "This tree is an elm"; it expresses no statement. The noncognitivists say that an aesthetic sentence is even less like an indicative sentence than are "Excuse me" and the other sentences above. Their reason is that the meaning of the sentences above includes a propositional element that identifies a state of affairs (my being excused, your getting off the roof, the king's living long, your being damned, your hearing me, there being no smoking here, etc.) whose existence is questioned, or ordered, or requested, etc. by using the above sentences. The meanings of such sentences include propositions, and propositions can (although in the above sentences they are not) be stated, that is, used to express statements. On the other hand, there are sentences whose meaning includes no propositional element whatsoever. When you sneeze, even an atheist may say, "God bless you"; when uttered in such circumstances, that sentence does not express a wish that God will bless you, and hence it includes no propositional element describing the state of affairs of God's blessing you. Similarly, despite its grammatical form, the sentence "How do you do?" is not used as a question, but as a greeting; the propositional content the words seem to have plays no role in its customary meaning. You will be amazed if, having said "How do you do?" to passersby, they stop to tell you how they live their lives. As we understand these sentences, they have illocutionary force (they are greetings, apologies, etc.) only. That is how noncognitivist aestheticians construe aesthetic sentences: their meaning, they say, includes illocutionary force but no propositional content.[1]

---

1. Frege distinguished between (1) a sentence, (2) its sense, (3) its force (sense plus assertive force is a statement; sense plus interrogative force is a question; etc.), and (4) an act it is used in: one can use a sentence to assert, to ask, etc.

My taxonomy is similar: (1) A *sentence* is a physical object: a string of sounds or ink marks; (2) its *meaning* consists of (a) a *content* that presents a state of affairs and (b) an *illocutionary force*: interrogative, assertive, optative, etc. The content, that-p, is a part of the meaning of a sentence whose whole meaning is a question whether p is the case, or a statement that p is the case, or an order that p be the case, etc. (3) A meaningful sentence can be used in a *speech act* such as ordering, stating, asking, etc.: we ask questions, issue orders, and make statements.

A content need not be coupled with illocutionary force. The content that snow is black presents the state of affairs, Black Snow, but asserts nothing; thus it is neither true nor false. The statement "Snow is black" has a content and assertive force; thus it is false. A statement may, but need not, be asserted: in using "If snow is black, I am a monkey's uncle" one uses the statement "Snow is black," which has a truth value, but does not assert that snow is black. Or one may use a question rhetorically, not asking anything. Usually, however, we use the statement "Snow is black" to assert that snow is black, and the question, "Is snow black?" to ask whether snow is black.

To ask whether snow is black one needs to use a question, say, "Is snow black?" that involves the content that snow is black but *not* the statement "Snow is black." To order that snow be black one must issue the order that snow be black, which involves the content that snow is black, but no statement or question.

What, then, do we do by uttering an aesthetic sentence? What is its illocutionary force? On this, noncognitivist aestheticians differ. *Emotivists* say that whoever utters an aesthetic sentence is emoting, that is, is giving vent to feelings. To express emotion in that manner is to perform an illocutionary act that involves no proposition, referring to no state of affairs. The emotivist holds that those who say, "X is beautiful," *describe* neither X nor their feelings; they give vent to their feelings. When John says, "What time is it?" he asks a question, but he *describes* neither the time nor his own questioning. To ask is not to describe a mental state of questioning. Likewise, when John says, "This tree is beautiful," he describes neither the tree (as realists hold) nor his feelings about the tree (as subjectivists hold). Rather, according to the emotivist, by uttering that sentence John vents an emotion, or expresses an attitude, toward the tree. The emotivist says that aesthetic sentences have an *emotive meaning:* their meaning consists of emotive illocutionary force only.

Another kind of noncognitivist, the prescriptivist, holds that aesthetic sentences are commendatory; their illocutionary force is to commend. Thus, in uttering an aesthetic sentence about an object or a situation X, one commends, that is, prescribes, some attitude or feeling toward X. Both emotivists and prescriptivists hold that aesthetic sentences have illocutionary force and no propositional content. The two views may therefore be combined; one may hold that aesthetic sentences are used to express an emotion or an attitude toward an object or situation X *and* also to commend that others, too, have that emotion or attitude toward X.[2]

That is the core of noncognitivism in aesthetics. It should be distinguished from another view, also held by noncognitivists, that in uttering an aesthetic sentence about X one evinces emotions that did actually move one when one viewed X. The latter view has a twin, the claim that by uttering aesthetic sentences about X one actually causes others to adopt one's attitude toward X. Both these claims (which parallel the view that a work of art expresses the feelings that were actually felt by the artist at the time of its creation and that the said work in turn causes its observers to relive those feelings) are, I think, not essential to noncognitivism, and noncognitivists may disavow them without forsaking their basic position. These latter claims are clearly indefensible, since a hypocrite or a conformist

---

2. That statement of noncognitivism is distilled from the writings of Charles Ogden and Ivor Richards, Charles Stevenson, Alfred Ayer, etc. and is rephrased to reflect later distinctions made in metaethics and in the philosophy of language.

may say, "X is sublime," thereby expressing (on the emotivist view) a certain attitude to X, although that attitude is not actually held by the speaker; similarly for the emotion evinced by that sentence: it may never have been actually felt by the speaker. One may also commend a positive attitude to X without that commendation's being actually espoused by the addressee. The perlocutionary effects of a commendation need not bear out the expectations of the speaker; they are irrelevant to the meaning of the sentence used.

Noncognitivism is not the view that in uttering an aesthetic sentence we express feelings regarding an object or a situation X, praise or scorn it, or exhort others to have similar emotions or adopt a similar attitude to it. That view is quite noncontroversial; a realist can hold it too. The sentence "This car attains a speed of 100 km/hr in 30 seconds" expresses a descriptive statement that is either true or false, yet a salesperson can use it to recommend the car. One may express a negative attitude and incite others to have that attitude to X by yelling, "X is a thief," a factual statement that is true or false. The difference between these and aesthetic sentences, according to the noncognitivist, is that these sentences *also* have propositional content, while aesthetic sentences have none.

A noncognitivist need not commit what John Searle has called "The Speech Act Fallacy,"[3] that is, the error that the meaning of all commendatory terms is exhausted by their commendatory function. Noncognitivists may admit that the meaning of some aesthetic sentences has a propositional component and thus can be used to make (true or false) statements. Consider sentences such as "X is flowery and verbose" or "Y is sentimental." I said above that a realist can agree that by uttering these sentences one expresses a negative attitude to X and Y and commends a negative attitude to them. On the other hand, emotivists and prescriptivists need not deny that some factual information is conveyed by these statements. If X consists of three words only and Y is the great pyramid, even a noncognitivist can agree that the above sentences imply something false. Noncognitivists may say, however, that such sentences have a composite meaning that is partly propositional and partly a pure emotive or prescriptive illocutionary force. Thus a noncognitivist need not deny that some aesthetic predicates contain descriptive as well as prescriptive or emotive components; some aesthetic predicates (say, 'beautiful' and 'ugly') are purely aesthetic, while others (say, 'verbose' or 'delicate') are compound, having an aesthetic (emotive

---

3. John Searle, *Speech Acts* (Cambridge: Cambridge University Press, 1969), 136–41.

or prescriptive) as well as a factual meaning. Noncognitivism may then be said to apply only to pure aesthetic predicates (PAPs); it is the meaning of PAPs that noncognitivists allege to contain no reference to matters of fact. A noncognitivist would then argue that an element of factual meaning may be added to pure aesthetic sentences (PASs); the meaning of the latter is exhausted by their emotive function and by their use to commend, denounce, or express attitudes and exhort others to espouse these attitudes as well.

Cognitivists in ethics have argued that ethical predicates are *not* composite, that the contention that they are is the Achilles' heel of ethical noncognitivism. Best known are Philippa Foot's arguments that ethical predicates such as 'coward' and 'honest' cannot be analyzed into purely ethical and purely factual components.[4] I am not convinced, however, that this strategy will work in aesthetics, and therefore I do not use it. Let us give noncognitivists the benefit of the doubt and leave the claim that some aesthetic sentences are compounds of PASs and "factual" sentences unchallenged. From now on, let us distinguish PAP from other aesthetic predicates and PAS from other aesthetic sentences. Economic predicates are predicates predominantly used to discuss situations and objects from an economic point of view; legal predicates are those mainly used in discussing legal aspects; and aesthetic predicates are those predominantly used to discuss objects and situations from an aesthetic point of view. PAPs are purely evaluative aesthetic predicates. Thus both 'baroque' and 'beautiful' express aesthetic predicates, but 'beautiful' also expresses a PAP, while 'baroque' does not. 'graceful,' 'gaudy,' etc. do express PAPs, but unlike 'beautiful' part of their meaning is also an aesthetic predicate that is not a PAP. I think this uncontroversial.

Another metaethical cognitivist argument I do not rely on is that PAPs occur not only in simple sentences (e.g., "X is beautiful") but also in complex sentences (e.g., "If X is beautiful, I'll buy it") that are not used to commend. Since the predicate 'beautiful' has the same meaning in both sentences, commendatory force cannot be all the sense that it has. Noncognitivists in aesthetics may reply that the embedded PAS is in fact mentioned and not used in complex constructions. (That would be similar to Donald Davidson's analysis of belief sentences; he says that the sentence 'p' is mentioned, not used, in "X believes that p.") Noncognitivists may analyze "If X is beautiful, I'll buy it" thus: "If I say, 'It is beautiful,' I will buy it." They may then

---

4. See, e.g., Philippa R. Foot, *Virtues and Vices* (Oxford: Basil Blackwell, 1978).

continue to argue that a PAS contributes nothing to the descriptive meaning of the sentence in which it occurs, for one may condition a future behavior on one's readiness to utter some merely evaluative or expressive sentence.

The noncognitivist holds that PASs are purely evaluative; they are used only to emote, praise, or berate. Yet what feeling and what attitude do PASs (according to the emotivist) express or (according to the prescriptivist) exhort others to have? Not ordinary emotions such as shame, anger, or fear; those are evinced in other ways (blushing, clenching a fist, hiding, etc.); uttering PASs is clearly not a way to express them or to commend them. So what feeling or attitude is disclosed or mandated by using a PAP? One answer is Hume's: the attitude is approval or disapproval. Hume argued that fact and value are distinct, and any fact can be either approved or disapproved of. Moore (in his attack on naturalism) accepted this view, and so did Wittgenstein in the *Tractatus*: according to it, the world is exhausted by facts; thus value, the acceptance or rejection of facts, is transcendental. One answer to our question is, then, (a) that PAPs express approval or disapproval. Another answer is that PAPs express and/or exhort to adopt (b_1) a unique aesthetic attitude to X or (b_2) a unique aesthetic experience caused by X. Option a lends itself better to the noncognitivistic approach because approval and disapproval need not have phenomenal aspects. Advocates of (b_1) and (b_2), on the other hand, find it more natural to hold that PASs not only express an aesthetic experience caused by X and/or advocate taking an aesthetic attitude to X, but also refer to that (phenomenally describable) experience and/or attitude. In order not to discuss (a), (b_1), and (b_2) twice, once as brands of noncognitivism and once as brands of subjectivism, I follow a time-saving policy: Chapter 1, on noncognitivism, discusses option a, and Chapter 2, on subjectivism, discusses options b_1 and b_2.

To investigate (a) we must know what the object of approval or disapproval is. I see four options. That which is commended or condemned can be (1) the object or situation X referred to by the grammatical subject of the aesthetic sentence; (2) an aspect or property of X; (3) a use of X or a goal achieved by using it; (4) a kind of behavior toward X. Let us check all these options and see whether any of them is cogent.

Let me use 'A+' as a shorthand for all positive PAPs and 'A–' as a shorthand for all negative PAPs. Then all positive PASs have the form "X is A+" and all negative PASs have the form "X is A–." Now let us investigate: are PASs used (as emotivists say) merely to evince, or (as prescriptivists say) merely to commend, positive and negative attitudes toward any of the candidates 1 through 4 above?

1.2. Of an Object

I begin with candidate 1, an object or a situation: the *Mona Lisa*, the Alps, Caruso's singing, etc. Now, is it true that one who says that X is A+ expresses thereby a positive attitude toward X or recommends that others adopt such an attitude? Certainly not. Had that been so, a man who says, "X is beautiful, but I do not recommend it," would have pragmatically contradicted himself, just as it is a pragmatic contradiction to say "p, but I do not believe that p." To utter the above sentence would have been, *per impossibile*, to commend X by making a statement that condemns it. The sentence "X is A+ and p," where 'p' is a sentence condemning X, would have been as paradoxical as "I do not believe that the pitcher is broken, but the pitcher is broken." Yet the sentence "This pitcher is beautiful, but I do not commend it" (because it is unhealthy, or too heavy, etc.) is not paradoxical at all.

Similarly for the emotivist: if I think that beautiful Dina is wicked, I may say, without contradicting myself, "Dina is beautiful, but my attitude to her is negative." Yet if by uttering "Dina is beautiful" I express a positive attitude to Dina, then I express both a positive and a negative attitude toward Dina at the same time (since, for sure, to say "my attitude to X is negative" is to express a negative attitude to X). I therefore am an acute case of split personality and urgently need psychiatric treatment. That is the case whenever one disapproves of a thing about which one has a positive aesthetic evaluation. The sentence "This painting is beautiful but morally corrupt; I disapprove of it" is not self-contradictory. Beauty is not the only consideration that determines our attitudes. I may find an aesthetically excellent novel socially dangerous or religiously blasphemous and therefore disapprove of it, urging others to condemn it too; if the novel is aesthetically good, I may find it even more objectionable because it is more dangerous; my condemnation of it would then be all the more vehement.

How can noncognitivists account for these cases? They may accuse me of lack of sensitivity to the grammatical structure of the sentences I used as counterexamples. These sentences, they may say, do not have the form "X is A+ and p"; rather, they have the form "X is A+ but p": two clauses conjoined by the word 'but.' Since 'but' indicates a reversal of the sense of the antecedent clause, and since the clause following 'but' expresses a negative attitude, my examples are not counterexamples to noncognitivism; actually, they prove it. They show that "X is A+" commends X, expresses a positive attitude to it. In sum, the noncognitivist may answer: "In all your examples the antecedent clauses serve to express a positive attitude to the object. Then by the word 'but' the speaker indicates that despite that initial positive attitude, his or her ultimate attitude to the object is negative. The fact that the speaker needs to say "Dina is beautiful *but* my attitude to her is negative" shows that the antecedent clause does express a positive attitude to Dina. That is why the speaker needs to use the word 'but': in order to explain that the speaker's ultimate view of Dina is not what the antecedent clause would lead us to believe.

For the sake of argument let us grant that 'but,' or another word to the same effect, must appear in every sentence that both expresses a negative attitude to X and says that X is A+.[5] Yet that does not imply that "X is A+" is a contentless device used *only* to express a positive attitude to X. After having taken a positive attitude to X, one *may* change one's mind and take a negative attitude to X, but that is not the case here. If noncognitivists are right, the speaker expresses a positive attitude to X, and then goes on, in the same sentence, to express a negative attitude to X. Such behavior is psychotic. Yet one need not be mentally deranged in order to say "X is beautiful, but my attitude to it is negative." I therefore conclude that noncognitivism of the first kind is wrong.

So why do we use the word 'but' in the above sentences? The realist need not deny that by means of sentences of the form "X is A+" we express a positive attitude to X. The question is whether that is all that we do in uttering such sentences, whether "X is A+" does not also describe X, explaining *why* we have a positive attitude to it. It is the noncognitivist, who denies that PAPs also contain a description of X, who cannot account for the function of the word 'but' in such sentences: no one in his right mind will say, "My attitude to Dina is positive, but my attitude to Dina is negative." As the noncognitivist interprets it, the reasonable sentence "Dina is beautiful, but she is wicked, and therefore my attitude to her is negative" takes this absurd form: "p, but q, therefore not-p."

The first type of noncognitivist (who holds that aesthetic sentences mean a commendation of objects and situations) may try to defend himself by weakening the commendatory force of the antecedent clause of complex aesthetic sentences. That clause may be said to express, not one's established attitude to its subject, but rather one's prima facie attitude to it. On this

---

5. This grants too much. Suppose that beautiful things depress you or give you pain. If I know that beautiful things cause you dire pain, I may say to you, "X is A+, and *therefore* I do not recommend it to you." A similar statement may be made by those who believe that beauty is the work of the devil, intended to tempt us to sin. They will hold that the beauty of X is itself a reason to evaluate X negatively.

suggestion we should interpret sentences of the form "X is A+ but p" thus: "Prima facie, my attitude to X is positive [prescriptivists may add: "and I urge you to adopt a similar attitude"], but p." Yet that interpretation is not viable either. Suppose that Reuben, a moral man who is also endowed with a delicate aesthetic sensitivity, considers producing the play X. At first he is struck by the morally damaging nature of the play, and so his initial attitude to X is negative. Yet Reuben is impressed by the beauty of the play, and that consideration wins; he finally decides to produce X after all. Reuben may report his deliberations thus: "Initially, my attitude to X was negative, but X is so beautiful that in the end I have taken a positive attitude to X after all." This is a perfectly reasonable report, and none of us would suspect Reuben of being insane. Interpreting that sentence according to the above suggestion of the noncognitivist, however, making it explicit, we get a ridiculous statement: "Initially Reuben's attitude to X was negative; but initially Reuben's attitude to X was so positive that in the end Reuben has adopted a positive attitude to X after all." This interpretation of Reuben's clear and plain statement is nonsense. The reason for that interpretative failure is obvious: one may initially like X for reasons other than its aesthetic merit. For instance, X's reasonable price may incline me initially to favor it; yet later, when I realize how very ugly it is, I change my attitude to it. To identify an initial positive attitude to X with a positive aesthetic valuation of X may be absurd.

Another suggestion that a noncognitivist of the first variety may bring up is that "X is A+" expresses, not a positive attitude to X, but readiness to have one. Thus "X is A+, but my attitude to X is negative" does not mean "my attitude to X is positive, but my attitude to X is negative"; it means, rather, "I was inclined to have a positive attitude to X, but my attitude to X is negative." Yet that suggestion too leads nowhere; it cannot explain how the following sentence can be informative: "I was initially inclined to a positive attitude to X, but X is so ugly that my attitude to it became negative" (it surely does not mean "I was initially inclined to a positive attitude to X, but I was initially so inclined to a negative attitude to X that my attitude to it became negative"!). By saying "X is beautiful" one does *more* than express an initial inclination to have a positive attitude to X.

At this point it is clear what is required. To say "X is A+" is not merely to express a positive attitude to X. Those who say, "Dina is beautiful," do not merely express a positive attitude to Dina nor merely commend her. They express a positive attitude to, or commend, a *property of* Dina. That adjustment takes care of all the problems I have hitherto raised; a thing can be appealing in one respect and unappealing in another. A good scientist may be poor company, or clever but dishonest; X may be commended in one respect but not in another. One may say, without contradiction, "I approve of this property of Dina but not of that one." However, to hold that "X is A+" expresses a positive attitude to X or commends X *in some respect* is to abandon the first variety of noncognitivism, for what is now said to be commended by the aesthetic sentence is not X *simpliciter* but an aspect of X. That is already the second variety of noncognitivism, presented at the end of section 1.1. I therefore leave the first variety of noncognitivism, finding it hopeless, and turn to the second candidate.

1.3. Of an Aspect

The second noncognitivistic candidate for the subject of approbation and commendation by aesthetic sentences is an aspect or property Y of X. That option has two variants: it is one thing to commend this wine for its bouquet and another to commend the bouquet of this wine; the latter commendation is implied by the first, but it does not mean all that the first means. A commendation of X for its Y can therefore be either a commendation of the aspect Y of X or a commendation of X because of Y and insofar as it has Y. Let us see whether aesthetic sentences mean any of these things.

Needless to say, noncognitivists cannot claim that by uttering "X is A+" one commends the aesthetic properties of X, since, being antirealists in aesthetics, they hold that there are no such properties. Therefore noncognitivists must hold that those who seem to commend the aesthetic aspect of X in fact commend some other (nonaesthetic) property of X, say, its adherence to an accepted artistic model, its faithfulness as an icon of its subject matter, its survival value, or whatever. Fortunately, we need not examine each of the purportedly commended nonaesthetic properties separately. Call the reductive property (i.e., the real property of X that an utterance of "X is A+" allegedly commends), whatever it may be, 'P.' Noncognitivists of the second variety hold, then, that "X is A+" is an expression of a positive attitude to, or a commendation of, the P of X or a commendation of X because of its aspect P and insofar as it has P. Is this an adequate account on the meaning of PASs?

No. Noncognitivism of the second kind suffers from all the ills of noncognitivism of the first kind. In a variation on Moore's famous argument, I claim that one may hold that the P of X (be it what it may) is beautiful while having an overall negative attitude to that P, and to X because of P and insofar as X possesses P. And vice versa: one may take X's P to be ugly and yet have a positive attitude to P and/or to X on P's account. Adapting my conclusion in the previous section, aesthetic approbation is not merely a commendation of X's P, for *any* P that is not simply X's aesthetic properties (whose existence noncognitivists deny).

Let P be X's coloration. Is saying that X's coloration is aesthetically good tantamount to commending it? Not at all. Suppose that the transportation department holds a contest for designing a new traffic sign. An artist designs a traffic sign X whose color pattern P is aesthetically superb; the contest judges admit that readily. However, they think that using the said pattern for a traffic sign is a bad idea. The committee's report may read thus: "We do not commend P, because it is too beautiful; an aesthetically superb color design may distract drivers and cause accidents." The committee likes the aspect P of X from the aesthetic point of view, but they do not recommend it. Thus to utter "X is A+" is not to commend the P of X.

For another example, let P be resemblance to reality, and let the reductive theory be that to praise a work of art aesthetically is to praise its resemblance to the subject it depicts. Let Reuben be an orthodox Jew, raised in a tradition that forbids a realistic depiction of human figures, who is asked to recommend an embroidered cover for the holy ark in the synagogue. Reuben also adheres to the said reductive theory of beauty, that is, that beauty in art is faithful representation of the depicted subject. Of one curtain, X, Reuben says: "X is beautiful, but I do not recommend it, because its embroidery represents a human figure, and hence it is unsuitable for us." This response is not at all strange, but if we interpret it as the second variety of noncognitivists would, we obtain this odd remark: "Reuben recommends the curtain because of its property P; however, he does not recommend the curtain because of its property P." Clearly, something has gone awry here, not in Reuben's mind but, rather, in the theory that gives such an odd interpretation to his perfectly coherent comment.

1.4. Of a Perceived Aspect

One theory of the second kind I need to examine separately, for the reductive property P that it chooses evades my above refutation. The property chosen is the appearance of X, that is, X as seen or otherwise observed. On that theory what aesthetic sentences express is approval or commendation of X's appearance. The originator of that theory may have been Saint Thomas

Aquinas, whose dictum "Beauty is what pleases Sight" is sometimes interpreted to mean that "X is beautiful" does not describe X, it only expresses one's pleasure at the sight of X. I examine the version of that theory suggested by J. O. Urmson.[6]

Urmson begins by saying that if X is good in one respect or from one standpoint (moral, aesthetic, economic, religious, etc.), there are criteria for evaluating objects in that respect or from that standpoint. These considerations are relevant to evaluating objects in that respect and differ from considerations relevant to the evaluation of X in other respects. Thus far, I agree. Which considerations are relevant, then, to aesthetic evaluation? What criteria gauge aesthetic merit? Urmson's reply involves a reductive noncognitivism of the second kind: the relevant aspect is the way objects are present to the senses.

Taken verbatim, that view is open to an obvious objection: it implies that all empirical judgments are aesthetic, for they all depend on the way things appear to the senses. Surely not every moral, economic, and military evaluation is aesthetic? Consider these dialogues:

QUESTION: What do you like about this picture?
ANSWER: The way it looks; it reminds me of mother.
or
QUESTION: What do you like about these flowers?
ANSWER: Their scent; it repels mosquitoes.

These evaluations are not aesthetic, since the criteria used in the evaluations are not aesthetic criteria; yet both answers rely on the way the evaluated object appears to the senses.

Urmson, however, is not guilty of that mistake; after all, his aim was to find a criterion that is specific to aesthetic judgments. His view is that a preference for X is aesthetic if and only if its justification by reference to the way X appears to the senses is *final* and does not rely on additional reasons. In the above two dialogues the preference for the particular way the given objects appear to the senses is based on further reasons that explain why those particular appearances are preferred (it reminds one of mother;

6. J. O. Urmson, "What Makes a Situation Aesthetic," *Proceedings of the Aristotelian Society*, supp. vol. 31 (1957): 75–92; reprinted in *Philosophy Looks at the Arts*, ed. Joseph Margolis (New York: Scribner's Sons, 1962), 13–26. Page references in the text are to the Margolis volume.

it repels mosquitoes). These judgments are not aesthetic, since the reason for which the painting and the flowers are preferred is not their sensory appearance *as such*. Were the respondent only able to justify his preference for the painting and the flowers by the way they appear to him, not invoking any other reasons, his preference (Urmson holds) would have been aesthetic.

In all the objections to noncognitivism raised in the previous section I tried to show that a positive aesthetic evaluation of a property P of X need not be a commendation of that property P of X (or of X insofar as it has P); one may like X's P aesthetically without commending it *tout court*. Urmson avoids that difficulty: according to him the commended property is the way X appears to the senses, when it is used as a final justification of the commendation. Those who commend (or condemn) the way X appears to the senses for ethical or religious or economic reasons can further justify why they do (or do not) approve of X's appearance, but those who judge X from the aesthetic point of view cite the way X appears to the senses as their *only* reason for the evaluation of X. They cannot justify their preference for X's particular appearance to the senses any further. Urmson's definition must then be this: an approval or disapproval of X is aesthetic iff (1) the property of X that serves as ground for evaluation is X's appearance and (2) there is no way to justify why that particular appearance is a reason for approval (disapproval). Urmson puts it thus: "Objects have qualities which are given to sensation and which cause us to evaluate them either positively or negatively without any further justification."[7] "X is good from the aesthetic point of view" therefore means "X is commendable for its appearance"; that is, X is aesthetically good if and only if X's appearance is approved of as such. Here the term 'as such' is here an excluder: no further facts beyond X's P are needed for it to be commendable. Thus Urmson says that the way a poem sounds is a test of aesthetic excellence if that sound as such is the basis for preference.[8]

Is that true? Is a preference that is exclusively grounded in the way X appears necessarily aesthetic? We may define it so, as Kant did,[9] but that definition does not agree with common usage. Consider Jones, who likes hard-core pornography. He enjoys looking at detailed depictions of female private parts; there is nothing else that he does with these pictures except

7. Ibid., 23
8. Ibid., 22.
9. Immanuel Kant, *Kritik der Urteilskraft* (Berlin and Liebau, 1790), 224–26 (henceforth *KdU*).

look at them; hence what he likes is the way they appear to his senses.[10] Yet Jones may deny that those pictures look beautiful to him. He may even say that they are sordid but that some sordid pictures are fun to look at. So, if Jones may enjoy looking at X and yet think that X is ugly, his preference is not aesthetic; liking X's appearance is not the same as liking X aesthetically.

Smith is an avid stamp collector who loves to look at rare stamps. She goes to stamp exhibitions and is thrilled to look over the stamps for hours, showing great interest in every detail of their appearance. In that case too, the only thing she does with the stamps is look at them, so it is their appearance that she enjoys; yet she need not call them beautiful. On the contrary, Smith may say that many precious stamps are crude and ugly. Her preference for their look is therefore not aesthetic, and so it is not true that what is beautiful is simply that which we like to look at. One need not find X aesthetically attractive in order to enjoy observing it. Most people like to look at their photographs; is that because we all find ourselves good-looking?

There is a Kantian way to block these counterexamples. In all the cases above, preference was not based on appearance alone. Knowledge of ambient facts was essential to X's attraction. The enthusiastic observer is keen to look at X because some *external* facts, beside X's mere appearance, are true of X. Had these facts not been true of X, then, sameness of appearance notwithstanding, one would not have been interested. The voyeur would not have shown any interest in the picture had he not known that it depicted human genitalia. Had he believed that it was a picture of, say, a flower, he would not have been fascinated by it. The same goes for the stamp collector, whose fascination with old ugly stamps depends on the unobservable fact of their rarity and great monetary value. These facts, and not the stamps' appearance, attract Smith; she would not look at visually indistinguishable pieces of paper that she knows are not stamps; she would not have looked at these stamps had she not known of their history and market value, or had these very stamps not been rare and precious. Thus, one can rebut my objection by postulating that aesthetic preference is preference exclusively based on the way things appear to the naked eye, independent of any knowledge of unobserved background facts.

That definition is, however, arbitrary and cannot be accepted. First, as any textbook on the psychology of perception points out, there is no

---

10. Some writers (e.g., James Joyce, in *A Portrait of the Artist as a Young Man*) argue that a pornography fan likes not X's look but the sensations it causes him to have, but that is incorrect: he may enjoy pornography even in the absence of such sensations.

such thing as sheer appearance to sense, unmediated and unadulterated by background knowledge. One cannot look at X with a naked eye, stripped of all associations and significance that X has for one. What one knows modulates what one sees in every case. Aesthetic preference cannot be preference based on what naked eyes see, for there are no naked eyes. Second, even if it were possible for us to inspect a sheer sensory given, the said definition would exclude as nonaesthetic paradigm cases of aesthetic appreciation. In the aesthetic appreciation of art the observer is never content with X's immediate appearance, but proceeds to interpret the symbols in X so as to see it in its relation to the relevant facts in its ambient world, for example, in comparison with other works of art.

The same is true of the aesthetic observation of nature. What we aesthetically appreciate is tinged with background information. We know which shapes and colors are signs of health and life and which of death and decay; that difference is not a matter of raw appearance, yet it influences aesthetic appreciation. Knowledge of X's provenance also modulates our judgment: Kant noted that we enjoy the song of the nightingale, but the same sound produced by a human singer is ludicrous.[11] His conclusion was that our appreciation of art is not purely aesthetic,[12] but if all preferences that rely on prior knowledge are nonaesthetic, we cannot aesthetically appreciate anything. Limiting the grounds of aesthetic judgment to sense data only makes aesthetic appreciation impossible for intelligent beings.

Suppose that Jones strongly disapproves of a certain killing; when asked for his reasons he gives a detailed description of the outward appearance of the scene, using this as his only reason for disapproval. Is his evaluation aesthetic? We do not know. In the absence of further clues this evaluation is unfathomable. Were Jones to say that the blood does not match the color of the rug, we could classify his evaluation as aesthetic. But if his sole ground for condemnation is the presence of some nonaesthetic phenomenal properties ("the knife is about ten inches long, the rug is blue and square," etc.) and he does not tell us what is wrong with them, his evaluation is not based on any known system of evaluative criteria.

The appearance criterion turns aesthetics into an *asylum ignorantia*: if there is no reason for preference, the preference is aesthetic. But aesthetics is not a trash can for all arbitrary and inexplicable preferences. People whose preferences are aesthetic *do* give reasons, aesthetic reasons, for their

---

11. *KdU* 302.
12. *KdU* 311.

preferences. Arbitrary preference is not aesthetic preference. Later I argue that there is some grain of truth in Urmson's position, but as a noncognitivist aesthetics, proposing a property the commendation of which is an aesthetic judgment, it does not work. Brute preference for some appearance P need not be aesthetic; it may be a whim or a habit.

Urmson's distinction between systems of evaluative criteria is a move of a realist. How, then, does he end as a noncognitivist? Perhaps it can be explained thus: in his well-known article "On Grading" Urmson shows the difference between the evaluative label 'good' and the criteria for being a good F.[13] He shows that (early emotivism to the contrary) the word 'good' in "X is a good apple" does not differ in meaning from the word 'good' in "X is a good knife"; the *criteria* for being a good apple differ from the *criteria* for being a good knife, but the word 'good' has the same meaning in both contexts. So, if aesthetic judgments have the form "X is a good aesthetic object," there must be special criteria for being a good aesthetic object, that is, for being aesthetically good. In that I think Urmson is right. At this point, one step away from realism, Urmson turns his back on his original view[14] and endorses Kantian noncognitivism instead. Why? I think the answer is this. The criteria for being a good knife or a good apple are derived from our reasons for using knives or apples. Purpose determines criteria for being a good F: once you know what a particular kind of thing is good for, you can figure out what a good thing of that kind would be. Aesthetic evaluation, however, seems different, for it is hard to see what aesthetic objects are good for or what purpose they serve. Finding no purpose by which to evaluate aesthetic objects, romanticism makes this alleged lack of purpose of aesthetic objects (objects evaluated from the aesthetic point of view) into their hallmark. It defines aesthetic evaluation as an evaluation that makes no reference to any purpose or function. Thus, romantic aesthetics cleverly converts the problem of the apparently missing purpose into a solution, defining aesthetic preferences as precisely those preferences that lack grounding. The noncognitivist's P of X we commend (or, the P in whose name we commend X, insofar as X possesses P) becomes X as it appears, X's pure appearance, not considered under any concept. In that way Urmson and others come to believe that preferring X's look is an aesthetic preference iff one has no reason for preferring it.

13. J. O. Urmson, "On Grading," *Mind* 59 (1950): 145–59.

14. Cf. the note added by Urmson to his article in the Margolis volume (*Philosophy Looks at the Arts,* 26), also in his book *The Emotive Theory of Ethics* (London: Hutchinson, 1968), 98ff.

I argued that aesthetic preference cannot be identified with unjustified preference. It is true that aesthetic preference is based on direct observation, but the directly observed properties are aesthetic: Gracefulness, Gaudiness, Harmony, etc. That is the grain of truth in Urmson's view: aesthetically good objects are good to observe. Aquinas's definition of beauty (*id quod visum placet*) can be given a similar realistic interpretation: beauty is that which makes things good to observe (I elaborate later). Urmson came close to that view, but instead of the realistic interpretation he endorsed noncognitivism of the second variety, which I trust has now been disproved.

1.5. Of Suitability to a Purpose

According to the third strain of noncognitivism, "X is A+" commends some use of X. The only meaning of an aesthetic sentence is commendation of the aptness of a given object for some special goal and/or persuasion of others of that object's use for attaining that goal. Many such goals were proposed in the history of aesthetics as the desiderata whose attainment aesthetically good things are supposed to facilitate. These include cleansing the soul in pity and fear, synaesthetic perception, symbolizing morality, intuiting the thing-in-itself, communicating feeling, disseminating religious truth or class ideology, world making, emotional education, empathy with inanimate things, production of aesthetic experiences of great magnitude, and many others.

Luckily for us, we need not examine each proposed goal in order to dismiss the third kind of noncognitivism. First of all, however, note how odd is this view of aesthetic predicates. A special slate of commendatory terms to praise or denigrate the use of objects for one goal is an incredible linguistic profligacy. We have no special praise and censure terms that commend and discommend an object for catching fish, playing ball, making love, keeping the peace, getting rich, or any other of our goals. So why should there be a special vocabulary just to commend a thing for, say, cleansing the soul in pity and fear?

Let us designate the alleged goal, whatever it may be, 'G.' A noncognitivist of the third variety believes, then, that in uttering "X is A+" one advocates using X for G. Aesthetic sentences are like slogans, promoting the use of a product for some purpose. According to the noncognitivist, PASs make no factual statements; they have emotive meaning only. Yet if "X is A+"

means that X is good for attaining G, it must be possible, at least in principle, to *verify* whether it is. The usefulness of X in attaining G may be hard to verify or refute, but even so, it is either true or false that X is an effective tool for achieving G. That means that "X is A+" is a factual statement after all, alleging that X is good for achieving G, which can be confirmed or disconfirmed to a certain extent by facts. A *pure* aesthetic sentence turns out to be true or false; but that is what the noncognitivist denies.

One may hold, for example, that the sentence "Campbell's Soup is good soup" does not express a statement; it says nothing that is true or false but has emotive meaning (commending Campbell's Soup) only. That position cannot be maintained, however, if it is also held that what "X is good" means is that X can bring about some desideratum G, say, preventing cancer. Those who hold such a view must admit that if Campbell's Soup is carcinogenic, then the sentence "Campbell's Soup is good soup" is *false*. That is precisely the error against which Urmson has warned the emotivist, and it shows that the strategy of the third type of noncognitivism is self-defeating. If "X is A+" recommends that X be used to attain G, G being a goal whose attainment can be ascertained, then PASs make a factual claim (that X is conducive to, or detrimental to, achieving G). The view that aesthetic sentences are neither true nor false is then abandoned.

Noncognitivists may take a different tack: they may hold that aesthetic sentences say nothing about the utility of X in achieving G; all that these sentences do is urge the addressee to use X to achieve G; that is what emotive meaning amounts to. "X is A+" only exhorts one to use X for attaining G, with no factual statement implied. But in suggesting that emendation noncognitivists cease to uphold the third type of noncognitivism and move on to the fourth. They no longer claim that "X is A+" ascribes to X an ability to facilitate G; rather, what they now suggest is that to utter a PAS is to commend to those who wish to get G a behavior that involves X. That suggestion parses "X is A+" roughly as "I use X to attain G; do likewise!" that is, as commending some G-seeking behavior (for G, use X!). To say that is to forgo the third kind of noncognitivism and offer the fourth one instead.

1.6. Of a Form of Behavior

The fourth and last strain of noncognitivism I discuss here construes aesthetic sentences as exhorting us to engage in (what Wittgenstein calls) some "fine shades of behavior."[15] On that view aesthetic sentences are used to advocate a certain kind of behavior, usually an "attentive" behavior, toward the object named by the subject of the aesthetic sentence. Sentences of the form "X is A+" express a recommendation that we behave with respect to X in the way that people usually behave when they are in museums, when they attend concerts, when they face a scenery they call 'beautiful,' etc. To call X 'ugly' or use similar aesthetically negative terms is, therefore, to advocate the opposite kind of behavior with respect to X, that is, roughly, not to attend to it reverentially. Emotivists may say that by aesthetic sentences we give vent to our tendency to behave in some such way; prescriptivists may add that by uttering "X is A+" and "X is A–" we commend that behavior to others. PASs have no meaning other than this; uttering them is a speech act of commending, or of expressing readiness to engage in, such behavior toward X. Call that alleged behavior toward aesthetic objects 'B+' when it is positive (advocated by a sentence of the form "X is A+") and 'B–' when it is negative (advocated by "X is A–").

The idea is alluring; but are there really such typical ways of behaving, B+ and B–, which we manifest toward aesthetically considered objects? I think not. There are indeed typical ways of behaving toward objects that we like and typical ways of behaving toward objects that we do not like, but there is no special way of behaving toward objects that we *aesthetically* like or dislike, that is, things that we like or dislike for aesthetical reasons. Take, for example, what Wittgenstein says about Lewy's landlady:[16] she often dusts a picture hanging in her drawing room. Suppose that she also provides special lighting for it, contemplates it often, points it out to guests, etc. Record everything that this lady does with regard to that picture; could you then say whether her behavior is of the kind B+? No. That behavior is not specific to objects that the said lady finds aesthetically good. She would behave in that way with respect to *every* object that is dear and significant to her for any reason, aesthetic or nonaesthetic. If the picture is a portrait of her late husband, then even if she does *not* think it aesthetically good and cherishes it only as a sentimental memento, she may behave toward it in the same way. Let L behavior be our typical liking behavior, and L(X) our way of treating an object X that we like. We can establish, then, that Lewy's landlady behaves L-ly with respect to the said picture; but is her L behavior of the kind

15. Ludwig Wittgenstein, *Lectures and Conversations on Aesthetics, Psychology, and Religious Belief* (Oxford: Basil Blackwell, 1966).
16. Ibid., 11.

B+? No piece of behavior, save uttering aesthetic sentences, can determine whether her L behavior is B+ or not. An L behavior may be due to many reasons, and the L behavior itself does not say whether it is aesthetically motivated or not.

We thus obtain three reasons to reject the fourth kind of noncognitivism. First, we behave L-ly not only toward things we like aesthetically but toward things we like in general. Jones looks long at his sick mother's face not because he finds her so beautiful but because he loves her. We behave L-ly toward all that is near to our hearts, be it a dog, a doll, or a stamp collection. There is no special B+ behavior, so the noncognitivists' claim that "X is A+" is a recommendation to act in way B+ is false. Second, in saying "My bride is beautiful" Jones certainly does *not* urge others to behave toward his bride as he does; it will offend him greatly if they do! Third, we have different reasons for behaving in any given way, including L. That two people behave in the same way toward X does not mean that they do so for the same reason; one may be aesthetically motivated, the other not.

Partisans of the fourth strain of noncognitivism may look for a difference between aesthetically and nonaesthetically motivated L behavior that is not apparent at the time of behaving. A difference may be found in the etiology of the behavior: for example, if Jones's L behavior toward X is sentimentally, rather than aesthetically, motivated, we shall find that he was previously attached to X. If Jones behaves L-ly both toward an X that is aesthetically attractive to him and toward a Y (to which he is, say, sentimentally attached) that he does not find aesthetically attractive, we may find that he had a former relation to Y but not to X. Former attachment is necessary for sentimentally motivated L behavior, but aesthetically motivated L behavior does not require it; it may be spontaneous. If that is so, then a B+ behavior may be defined as L behavior that is not caused by the observer's prior attachment to the object.

That attempt to brace the tottering thesis is futile. The suggested condition is not necessary, because a work of art, too, may require prior acquaintance in order to be aesthetically appreciated; unless one is familiar with the work, no L behavior will occur. The condition is not sufficient, either, since aesthetic appeal is not the only cause of L behavior toward unfamiliar objects. Compassion, hunger, and greed can cause it too. These and other interests may cause immediate L behavior toward objects that are attractive to us for such nonaesthetic reasons. Noncognitivism of the fourth kind relies on there being *behavioral* differences between aesthetically and nonaesthetically motivated L behavior; but no such differences exist.

Some people like birds, others like fungi. Jones may be watching birds, not because they are beautiful or because he is sentimentally attached to them, but because that is his hobby. Asked why he watches birds, Jones may answer that this is what he likes to do; he need not have a reason for liking. Perhaps we like to watch animals because it gratifies our vanity to watch those who are inferior to us; the reason is not aesthetic. Smith, the stamp collector, behaves L-ly toward her stamps: she looks at them often, spends money on their upkeep, treats them with care, thinks and talks about them. She need not have a financial or sentimental or aesthetic motive in order to devote time, effort, and money to her stamps. She likes to tend to her stamps; others like to play games, jog, work in the garden, fight, or smoke. Nonaesthetically motivated L behavior is common: Moliere's miser displays L behavior toward his gold; he likes to look at it, touch it, roll in it, hoard it. Jones looks at the nameplate that attests to his success ('A. Jones, President') in the same way that Smith looks at a Rembrandt. Take the case of hard-core pornography again: millions buy these pictures, store them carefully, and look at them repeatedly. Aesthetic preference has nothing to do with that (probably innate) interest. X fans need not find Xs aesthetically attractive in order to behave L-ly toward Xs.

Fred collects foreign coins; he considers most of them ugly, yet his attitude to coins is similar to that of an art lover to an original Rembrandt: careful contemplation and attention to details (which both find worthwhile and gratifying). A fan shows L behavior vis-à-vis his or her object of interest, whatever it may be. Observe how Jones reads a poem that appeals to him aesthetically, and compare that with his reading an important piece of news in the paper. Jones scrutinizes both pieces carefully, with sensitivity to nuances; he reads them over and over again, clips and saves them, shows them to others, and commits them to memory. The difference in the reasons for the L behavior is not reflected in the behavior itself.

Moreover, the very same item X, a description of a football match, for example, may elicit L behavior for different reasons. Abe behaves L-ly toward X because he is a fan of the winning team; Beth, because she loves football; Connie enjoys the style of the article; Dan derives pleasure from strife and violence; Evan is the team's owner and profits from its victory; Fred is a player who enjoys reading about his own exploits; Greg is the reporter himself. All of these people, and many others, exhibit L behavior toward the article in question. They all are interested in it, albeit for totally different reasons. Their behavior shows that they hold X valuable, but what that value is cannot be gleaned from their behavior alone. To identify the one who values the article for its aesthetic merit we must elicit verbal reports. Noncognitivists, however, cannot benefit from these reports, at least not from the one that gives aesthetical reasons for liking, since they would reduce its meaning to advocating the L behavior observed. We ask the fourth kind of noncognitivists *why* one L-behaves toward X, but they cannot answer that, for their notion of B+ and B– behavior is bogus. Therefore, their view is untenable.

2

SUBJECTIVIST AESTHETICS

2.1. The Aesthetic Experience

Unlike the noncognitivists, subjectivist aestheticians hold that aesthetic sentences have a propositional content; unlike the realists, they deny that "X is A" attributes the aesthetic property A to the object X. Instead, they hold that "X is A" states that as a result of having observed X one undergoes a special experience: the aesthetic experience. A variant of this view is that "X is A" means that only a well-trained or ideal observer can undergo that experience upon encountering X. Some aestheticians have gone further to conclude that the real object of appreciation, the true work of art, is not X but the aesthetic experience that X occasions. What experience that is, is again controversial: on some views each person's experience upon observing X is a veritable artwork; others say it is the typical aesthetic experience of observers of X; other views stipulate that it is a structure of funded experiences of select observers, or the best experience of an ideal observer, or an experience identical with the experience of the artist. I shall not discuss that plethora of subjectivistic aesthetic suggestions, which range wide from Geiger to Ingarden, from Croce to Pepper, from Dewey to Lukacs, and from Green to Scruton. For my purposes it is enough to examine their common assumptions only; if these assumptions are unacceptable, all systems based on them are discredited, regardless of difference in detail.

The surface grammar of aesthetic sentences suggests that they attribute aesthetic properties to public objects, but subjectivists hold that surface grammar is misleading, for material things in the external world have no such properties. The true subject matter of aesthetic statements, they say, is the experiencer: PASs are about the experiences one may have. PASs do not seem elliptical, but the subjectivist insists that they are. Monroe Beardsley explains that although "X is A+" is, after a fashion, about X, what it says of X is that it is a good tool for generating aesthetic experiences. Beardsley uses that assumption to explain why people often disagree in their aesthetic judgments: given the considerable psychological differences between people, it is natural that a tool effective for Smith will not work for Jones, and a tool that affects Jones, causing great aesthetic experiences in him, will be unsuitable for Smith. Beardsley's *instrumentalism*, the view that artworks are instruments for generating aesthetic experiences of considerable magnitude, is a semantically sophisticated version of traditional subjectivism.

The common basis of all subjectivist theories in aesthetics is, then, the following semantic thesis: "X is A" means that X can (or did or would) cause one to have an aesthetic experience. What *is* that experience? Some subjectivists say it is a kind of pleasure, aesthetic pleasure; others hold that it is a unique experience that is phenomenologically distinguishable from all other experiences. Let us examine both suggestions.

2.2. Aesthetic Pleasure

The subjectivist who believes that there is an aesthetic kind of pleasure holds that one can introspectively distinguish between several kinds of pleasure, one of which is the aesthetic. I argue that pleasure is not a feeling, and hence there can be no phenomenologically distinguishable types of pleasure. It is untrue that when we enjoy a specific activity or state, it is accompanied by a specific kind of pleasure appropriate to that activity or state, a pleasure that goes together with it and it alone. Further, it is untrue that there is a kind of pleasure that we recognize as the aesthetic one by noting that it feels different from other kinds of pleasure, for instance, those that accompany playing chess or making love. The very idea that one kind of pleasure *feels* aesthetic is odd: how can a kind of sensation, introspectively examined in isolation from its cause, disclose what occasioned it? We do not recognize a special "gardening pleasure" or a "monetary-success pleasure"; it is thus hard to believe that there is a phenomenally identifiable sensation of aesthetic pleasure. We do not discern distinct sensations of pleasure that accompany distinct kinds of pleasurable activity or distinct pleasurable states.

Furthermore, pleasure is not, and cannot be, a sensation. The taste of wine is indeed qualitatively different from the touch of silk, and both are different from the experience of listening to Bach; but it is not true that each of the aforementioned feelings is accompanied by an additional, distinct feeling of pleasure. Rather, the feelings above are themselves pleasurable; that is, we like to have them. "X is pleasurable" does not mean "X causes a feeling of pleasure"; it means "X is a nice sensation; we prefer having X to having any Y that is not so nice." Gilbert Ryle was right, therefore, to insist that "to enjoy X-ing" cannot mean "to have a feeling that *accompanies* one's sensation of X-ing."[1] To like ice cream is to like the ice-cream taste, not to like *another* sensation, a pleasure sensation that accompanies the said taste. Swimming and kissing are pleasurable, not because *another* feeling, pleasure, accompanies the feelings of swimming or kissing, but because we like these feelings themselves.

The mistake is conceptual, for the relation between pleasure and its object is intentional and not, as the subjectivist has it, causal. If you like to play chess, it is engaging in that activity that you like; otherwise, if what you like is some sensation that playing chess causes in you, then you do not really like to play chess. Were the pleasure of playing chess itself a feeling, it could be generated in me, say, chemically. But no sensation can be such that, having it, I enjoy playing chess, even though I neither play chess nor believe that I play chess! This argument has a stronger modal version: if chess pleasure is an independently identifiable feeling whose connection to playing chess is contingent, it might have been generated by another activity, say, taking a shower. So, it is possible for one to have all the normal feelings of taking a shower and yet have the pleasure of playing chess! That is absurd.

Were pleasure a feeling, it would be a feeling we like to have, one that we enjoy having. If enjoyment is itself a feeling, that implies that pleasure causes a feeling of pleasure in us; call it 'pleasure$_2$.' Since we would also like to have pleasure$_2$, it must be causing a third kind of pleasure, pleasure$_3$, and so on; an infinite series of pleasures is generated. To avoid the regress we have to explain our preference for pleasure by saying that we just like pleasure; we prefer having it to not having it. If that explanation makes sense, however, we can employ it from the start to explain our preference for the taste of wine or the feel of silk. We need not postulate another feeling,

1. Gilbert Ryle, *The Concept of Mind* (Chicago: University of Chicago Press, 1984), chap. 4. See also his *Dilemmas* (Cambridge: Cambridge University Press, 1962), lecture 4, and "Pleasure," *Proceedings of the Aristotelian Society*, supp. vol. 28 (1954).

pleasure, which pleasant sensations give rise to and for the sake of which we indulge in them. I conclude that "X is pleasurable" cannot be interpreted as "X is accompanied by the feeling pleasure."

Even if there were such a feeling as aesthetic pleasure, it could not explain our love for art. Art lovers want to observe artworks, not to have a feeling that is conceptually independent of any such observation, the feeling aesthetic pleasure. That feeling could be induced by injection, without one observing or believing oneself to be observing any art. Surely, we would not call those who take the pleasure injection, instead of listening to music, art lovers? Art lovers insist on observing art and would not settle for that injection. This shows that what art lovers like is not the feeling of aesthetic pleasure (even if it were to exist).

If the intensity of our aesthetic pleasure is the criterion by means of which we determine which objects have high aesthetic value (i.e., are beautiful), that pleasure must be identifiable in itself, without reference to the objects that cause it. We must identify the sensation of aesthetic pleasure and gauge its intensity, and only then dub the object that causes it 'beautiful.' Aesthetic pleasure must therefore be an independent feeling that is only contingently related to observation of beautiful things. So, in some possible world aesthetic pleasure *is* generated by, say, putting one's shoes on. That is as logical as playing chess to enjoy tennis. We have here a *reductio ad absurdum* of the view that aesthetic pleasure is a feeling. I conclude that a subjectivist who holds that "X is A+" means "X is causally responsible for producing aesthetic pleasure" postulates an entity for whose existence we have no introspective evidence, that makes motivation logically impossible, and that, even if it were to exist, can have nothing to do with our love of art and other beautiful things.

Beardsley, whose subjectivism hinges on the notion of aesthetic experience, sensibly defines the difference between the various types of pleasure not by their phenomenal traits but by the type of object that induces them, defining aesthetic pleasure as enjoyment of perfectly organized wholes.[2] Abandoning the attempt to identify the aesthetic pleasure by introspection is, indeed, a step in the right direction, but Beardsley cannot afford it, for once you take that step, the concept of aesthetic pleasure becomes redundant. If we need to know whether our pleasure was caused by a perfectly organized whole in

2. Monroe Beardsley, "The Discrimination of Aesthetic Enjoyment," *British Journal of Aesthetics* 3 (1963): 291–300; see esp. 299.

order to know whether it was aesthetic, aesthetic pleasure is not a feeling at all. What kind of feeling is that whose identification requires a knowledge of its cause? Feelings are introspectively identified; you would not reclassify a dire pain as a light tickle if you found out that it was caused by a feather. If aesthetic pleasure is subject to such reclassification, it is not a feeling.

2.3. Aesthetic Attention

A second option for a subjectivist is to say that on observing certain objects (different objects for different people) one gets a characteristic experience that one introspectively identifies as the aesthetic experience. "X is A+" describes X only indirectly as that X which causes (or should cause) aesthetic experiences. I argue that no such experience exists, that its postulation is based on a conceptual error, and that, even if it existed, it could not do what subjectivist aestheticians expect it to do.

I cannot examine here all theories of aesthetic experience; let me, then, discuss only the most influential theory of that variety, the one Monroe Beardsley advocated in his *Aesthetics*. Beardsley says he opposes subjectivism, yet as 'subjectivism' is defined above he is a subjectivist.[3] The following famous formula summarizes his view: " 'X is a good aesthetic object' means, 'X is capable of producing good aesthetic experiences (that is, aesthetic experiences of fairly great magnitude).' "[4] Beardsley holds that "by acute introspection" one can identify a special, aesthetic way of attending to objects, which he identifies with the aesthetic experience: "First, an aesthetic experience is one in which attention is firmly fixed upon heterogeneous but interrelated components of a phenomenally objective field—visual or audio patterns, or the characters and events in literature . . . The experience differs from the loose play of fancy in daydreaming by having a central focus: the eye is kept on the object and the object controls the experience."[5] Is that

3. Even in "The Discrimination of Aesthetic Enjoyment," which is friendlier to realism than is *Aesthetics,* Beardsley insists that the only valid characterization of aesthetic value criteria is this: properties providing aesthetic satisfaction. Aesthetic satisfaction is again primary; aesthetic value (hence aesthetic value judgment) is defined by means of it.

4. Monroe Beardsley, *Aesthetics: Problems in the Philosophy of Criticism* (Harcourt, Brace & World, 1958), 530.

5. Ibid., 527. In this passage Beardsley defines "X is a good aesthetic object," not "X is aesthetically good," but I do not think that, for Beardsley, there is a difference between them.

mental set typical to observing what looks aesthetically valuable? I think
not. Beardsley's description suits a detective or a researcher much better; a
biologist observing a microbe through a microscope is not daydreaming; his
"attention is firmly fixed upon heterogeneous but interrelated components"
of the preparation he examines. A hunter fixes his attention (his life depends
on it!) more firmly on his phenomenal field than a tourist, whose interest in
the forest is merely aesthetic. A pedantic proofreader scans a page's visual appearance in minute detail; surely, his experience is nevertheless not aesthetic?
One interested in matters aesthetic pays attention not to all "heterogeneous
but interrelated components" in, but to the aesthetic properties of, the item
observed.

    Beardsley's second hallmark of the aesthetic experience is that it is "an
experience of some intensity": "The concentration of the experience can
shut out all the negative responses . . . by marshalling the attention for a
time into free and unobstructed channels." That experience is "bound to its
object": "we pay attention *only* to what we are seeing or hearing, and ignore
everything else."[6] But ignoring interfering stimuli is not typical, and often
not even true, of aesthetes. The researcher, the hunter, and the race driver are
much more likely to keep their attention fiercely fixed on what they observe,
ignoring side stimulations, than a visitor to a museum. Music lovers do
not usually sit through a concert without a stray thought ever crossing their
minds. Intelligent readers *never* behave in the manner described by Beardsley:
while reading they may think of the present work's relations to other texts,
stop to look up a word, go back to an earlier passage, etc.

    The third feature of Beardsley's aesthetic experience is that it "hangs
together, or is coherent, to an unusually high degree." But what is a coherent
experience? A drunk or drugged person may have incoherent experiences,
but when in full possession of one's senses one's experiences are, usually,
coherent. To illustrate what he means Beardsley gives some examples, such
as this one: "Stop the music because of a mechanical problem or the ringing of
a phone, but when it is started again, two bars may be enough to establish the
connection with what went before and you are clearly in the *same* experience
again."[7] Such ability to remember where one was, reorient oneself quickly,
and regain concentration is undoubtedly desirable; people endowed with it

---

He explicitly identifies "X is a good aesthetic object" with "X is aesthetically valuable," and
the latter expression is synonymous with "X is aesthetically good."
    6. Ibid., 528.
    7. Ibid.

can easily resume a conversation, a game of chess, or the writing of an essay, after a break, as if it did not occur. Blessed are those who have it. But how is that gift related to aesthetics? Interrupted by a telephone conversation when listening to music, I, for one, cannot after hearing two bars "establish the connection with what went before." My memory is not that good, and I am afraid mine is the typical case. Beardsley adds that a resumed experience is "the *same* experience again" as that which has been interrupted. Indeed, you would recognize the unity of what goes on now with what went on before the interruption, but that is so with conversations, games, or lectures. There is a grain of truth in this description, but it is shrouded in dense subjectivistic fog: *works of art* are indeed highly unified wholes, but the subjectivist, speaking of unified *experiences* instead of unified *works*, buries this important fact under misleading pseudopsychological circumlocutions. To say that the experiences (rather than the experienced objects) are coherent is to obfuscate the issue.

The next trait of the aesthetic experience is said to be this: "Fourth, it is an experience that is unusually complete in itself. The impulses and expectations aroused by elements within the experience are felt to be counterbalanced or resolved by other elements within the experience, so that some degree of equilibrium or finality is achieved and enjoyed."[8] The description best fits the experience of skiing or having sex or a good massage. Such an experience may indeed be "complete in itself," and "impulses and expectations aroused by elements" in it "are felt to be counterbalanced or resolved by other elements" in it. None of that is typical to reading *War and Peace* or to listening to Bach's B Minor Mass. Those experiences are *not* complete in themselves; they draw on prior experiences and require rich background beliefs. Nor do such experiences end when the reading or the concert are over; on the contrary, they linger for a long time, reverberate in our minds, and may resurface on occasion. Again, there is a grain of truth here: Beardsley's description is true of the artwork, but it grossly misdescribes the experience we have of it, that is, the effect it has on us.

The question, What do you experience when you observe works of art? means something like this: How do works of art affect you?; and the answer to that question is that not all works of art affect me in the same way. Some amuse me and others shock me; some depress me and others elate me; no one feeling accompanies all works of art.

8. Ibid.

Why, then, do the subjectivists take an accurate description of art and inappropriately apply it to our response to art? The reason is their naturalism. Subjectivists apply aesthetical descriptions to mental events because (perhaps under the influence of Locke or high school science classes) they think that aesthetic predicates cannot be true of reality: material things are really square and soluble in water, but not really graceful and dainty. Naturalism requires that physical things be described by physical predicates only, yet we feel that aesthetic predicates do describe something. What can that be, if not physical things? Subjectivism has a bright idea: apply aesthetic predicates to feelings! Thus, subjectivists say that "X is A" describes not X itself but the experience we have when exposed to X. For that gambit to work, there needs be a unique feeling, felt by all and only those who observe a thing of beauty; the trouble is that no such feeling exists.

A subjectivist may react by disowning Beardsley's description and still cling to the notion of aesthetic experience. "Having had an aesthetic experience," the subjectivist may insist, "I know it exists; I am personally, introspectively acquainted with an experience that I undergo when and only when I examine great works of art." The only way to rebut such testimony is to show that it cannot be true; if the very notion of an aesthetic experience is flawed, no one *could* have had it. In the next section I show this, and also show that, even if such experience were possible, it could be of no use in aesthetics.

2.4. The Impossibility of Aesthetic Experience

There are two reasons why the aesthetic experience cannot be what aesthetic sentences are about. The first reason is that the aesthetic experience is supposed to be a *positive* feeling generated in sensitive souls by great art. Clive Bell writes: "The starting point for all systems in aesthetics must be the personal experience of a certain feeling. All objects that cause such a feeling we call works of art."[9] That feeling is an internal indicator of goodness in art: a good artwork is whatever causes it. Such an experience warrants uttering a sentence of the form "X is A+." But what about sentences of the form "X is A–"? Negative aesthetic judgments are aesthetic judgments too; to say that X is clumsy, cacophonous, crude, and ugly is to judge that X is bad from

---

9. Clive Bell, *Art* (London: Arrow Books, 1961), 21.

the aesthetic point of view. If "X is A+" expresses an aesthetic statement, so does "X is A−." Yet if an aesthetic statement reports an aesthetic experience, then both "X is pretty" and "X is ugly" report that an aesthetic experience has taken place (or should take place). Surely it is false that both "X is beautiful" and "X is ugly" report the *same* experience and hence have the same meaning.

The instrumentalist theory of the aesthetic experience lacks equivalent referents for the contraries 'A+' and 'A−.' The only opposites Beardsley has are "X is likely to bring about an aesthetic experience of considerable magnitude" and "X is unlikely to bring about an aesthetic experience of considerable magnitude." The latter phrase fails, however, to capture the sense of "X is A−": by "X is ugly" we do not mean that X does not impress us aesthetically. Finding X ugly *is* being aesthetically impressed by X—negatively so. That negative aesthetic appraisal subjectivists cannot explain. Proponents of the aesthetic experience cannot solve the problem by reducing the difference between positive and negative aesthetic evaluations to difference in the intensity of the alleged aesthetic experience, taking all aesthetic sentences to be of the form "X is A(i)," where 'i' is the intensity of the experience. That is a bad ploy, for even a low-intensity aesthetic experience would be a *positive,* not a negative, aesthetic experience. As described by Clive Bell, the aesthetic experience may be big or small or may not occur at all, but it cannot be negative. So how can anything be ugly? According to descriptions of the aesthetic experience 'a negative aesthetic experience' is a contradiction in terms. Yet aesthetic sentences come in a negative as well as in a positive form; hence, aesthetic experiences cannot be what they are about. No semantics is adequate that interprets only positive predicates and has no interpretation for negative predicates of that kind.

My second objection to the subjectivists' notion of aesthetic experience is that (unlike the notion of aesthetic pleasure) it involves a *petitio principii.* An aesthetician who wishes to avoid a realistic interpretation of aesthetic sentences can say, without begging the question, that these sentences report an experience of great magnitude, provided that the said experience is described in the vocabulary of psychology. Such "grounding" of the aesthetic experience was attempted by I. A. Richards and, in a more sophisticated way, by Beardsley, who tried to turn aesthetics into a branch of empirical psychology. For that project to succeed, the aesthetic experience must be described in nonaesthetic terms. That constraint was carefully observed by Kant, but Beardsley neglects it. He uses aesthetic terms to describe the aesthetic experience: it is identified as a unified, coherent, and rich experience. These are *aesthetic* predicates; to use them unreduced to the vocabulary of empirical psychology is to espouse realism in aesthetics. In *Aesthetics* Beardsley hurtles between a Scylla of inadequate psychologistic descriptions of the aesthetic experience and a Charybdis of aesthetic, nonnaturalistic descriptions of it, which are adequate but subvert his original goal. In later writings he favors the second alternative; answering George Dickie,[10] Beardsley says that his attribution of coherence and unity to experiences does not replace the attribution of these properties to external objects, but supplements it.[11] Aesthetic experience is a chain of unified, complex, harmonious experiences; a sequence of psychological events can be mutually connected like, and even with, external objects. Experiences can fit each other, and they also can fit a painting that causes them. Yet if a chain of experiences is aesthetic if and only if it has *irreducible* positive aesthetic features (unity, coherence, etc.), the subjectivist's notion of aesthetic experience loses its raison d'être. If you maintain that an experience is aesthetic iff it has certain irreducible aesthetic properties, you cannot maintain that to attribute aesthetic properties to X is an indirect way of saying that X gives rise to aesthetic experiences. If "X is an aesthetic experience" means "X is an experience that has positive aesthetic properties," then it is not possible to reduce "X has positive aesthetic properties" to "X causes aesthetic experiences."

Subjectivists introduced the notion of the aesthetic experience so as to avoid interpreting the sentence "X is A+" realistically, with 'A+' naming an irreducible aesthetic property of X. Instead, they interpret it as "X can produce aesthetic experiences of great magnitude." But if the term 'aesthetic experiences' is in turn defined as 'experiences that are aesthetically good,' then the notion of the aesthetic experience is idle. If 'an aesthetic experience' is defined as an experience that has positive aesthetic properties, it cannot replace the realistic notion of aesthetic properties.

2.5. The Aesthetic Attitude

In section 1.1, I said that the notion of the aesthetic attitude has several uses. Noncognitivists use it to interpret my uttering "X is A+" as indicating that

10. George Dickie, "Beardsley's Phantom Aesthetic Experience," *Journal of Philosophy* 62 (1965): 129–36.
11. Monroe Beardsley, "Aesthetic Experience Regained," *Journal of Aesthetics and Art Criticism* 28 (1970): 3–11.

I have taken an aesthetic attitude to X and/or as exhorting others to take that attitude to X. The subjectivists use that notion to interpret "X is A+" as describing an experience caused by taking an aesthetic attitude to X and/or as saying that X is such that it is worthwhile to take an aesthetic attitude to it. The subjectivistic reading is straightforward and more intuitive, so I discuss the aesthetic attitude, in this chapter, as a brand of simple or instrumental subjectivism.

In his article "The Myth of the Aesthetic Attitude" Dickie has done a great deal to destroy the myth that there is a special aesthetic manner of attending to objects.[12] The aesthetic realism of the present essay is as opposed as can be to Dickie's own view, yet I think that his rejection of the notion of the aesthetic attitude is eminently correct. I have little to add to Dickie's debunking of the alleged aesthetic attitude; instead, I show how antirealism foisted that unhappy notion on Kant and other romanticists.

Aestheticians spoke of an aesthetic attitude long before Kant, but Kant was the first to put it at the heart of aesthetics. Kant recognizes three mental faculties: a cognitive faculty subject to the concepts of the understanding, a faculty of desire subject to the principles of reason, and a sentiment of pleasure and displeasure subject to the reflective judgment. To perceive aesthetically, Kant says, is to attend to X without conceptually categorizing X (it is irrelevant what kind of thing X is) and without making X an object of desire (it is irrelevant whether X is real or not). Instead, we approach X via our capacity for pleasure and displeasure: it pleases us not qua such and such and not qua potential satisfier of desire, but in itself. To take an aesthetic attitude toward X is, then, to observe X in a way that is (1) practically disinterested (seeking no gain to the observer) and (2) nonabstracting and nongeneralizing (not apprehending X as instantiating a concept), thus (3) to regard X as self-explanatory, as a kind unto itself.

Trait 1 of the aesthetic attitude,[13] disinterested interest, is entirely bogus; the argument for it is a clever sleight of hand. Saying that Smith does something without concern for her own interest, we mean that she is altruistic: she sacrifices her own gratification for the sake of others. But in watching a play or reading a novel, one does not sacrifice one's interests for the sake of others; to engage in these activities is to indulge one's own

12. George Dickie, "The Myth of the Aesthetic Attitude," *American Philosophical Quarterly* 1 (1964): 5–65.

13. Heralded by contemporary Kantians such as Francis Coleman or Jerome Stolnitz.

interests. The sleight of hand is to *call* every interest (economic, sexual, etc.) that motivates self-serving action, except the aesthetic interest, 'interested' and then "discover" that the aesthetic interest alone is disinterested! Thus a new monster, disinterested interest, is born. The "disinterestedness" of the aesthetic interest is based on mere verbal prestidigitation. To have culinary or sexual interests is to wish to engage in certain activities, suffer if one is denied them, be ready to give up other satisfactions in order to have them, and so on. The same is true of our aesthetic interests. Aesthetic needs are no different from needs for love, power, or food. Some people like to play music or read poetry even when they are not compensated for their effort. We often forgo satisfaction of other needs so as to satisfy aesthetic needs; we suffer when we cannot pursue our aesthetic interests. It is entirely disingenuous to classify as self-serving all human interests except the aesthetic interest alone, which is glorified as "disinterested."

If you listen to music for its own sake, that does not mean that you do not listen to it for your sake, for by listening to it you satisfy yourself, not the music! I may attend a concert for your sake, but not for the concert's sake; the concert gains nothing by my attending it. Therefore, to listen to music for its own sake is not to have a "disinterested interest" in music (whatever that means); it is to have genuine interest in music. I do not listen to music in order to attain some other end, for example, to please you, but listening to music itself satisfies me, just as eating, having sex, playing with my children, and meeting friends are activities that satisfy me in and of themselves. To engage in an activity for its own sake is to be genuinely interested in it, not the opposite, as Kant has it.

The notion of the aesthetic disinterested interest is perhaps one aspect of the great romanticist attempt to secularize European culture, with art as a substitute for religion. Romanticism has tried to model art on religious institutions, and to a great extent it has succeeded: we dress for the opera as we would for church, assume an attitude of reverence toward art and artists as was traditionally accorded God and his ministers, treat art as lofty and spiritual, etc. Now religion teaches that it is wrong to worship God in order to serve one's own interests. God should be worshiped because he deserves to be worshiped; it is sacrilegious to treat worship as a profitable transaction. We are supposed to love God for what he is, and love is unselfish. Aspiring to replace religion, romanticism needed a new selfless interest that transcends mundane interests. Thence the "disinterested interest." But that is a hoax; art lovers engage in self-gratification, not in worship. Aesthetic enjoyment is no less mundane and self-serving than any other enjoyment.

Feature 2 of the aesthetic attitude gave rise to Bullough's theory of the aesthetic distance, that is, a putative midpoint between excessive interest (underdistancing) and a loss of interest (overdistancing) in the observed object. Allegedly, if you distance an object properly, ignoring the practical interest that propels you to it or away from it, it is perceived in its individuality. I agree with Dickie, however, that all this psycho-geometry is a myth. Overdistancing and underdistancing are not modes of attention at the opposite ends of a continuum whose midpoint constitutes a third, aesthetic mode of attention. The first two are merely two causes for *not* paying attention, and aesthetic distance is just attention. If you are attacked by a leopard, you do not examine the charging animal with "underdistanced" attention; you are just too busy saving your life to pay attention to the pattern of patches on the leopard's back. If you are preoccupied with other thoughts when you pass by the leopard's cage in the zoo, you miss its pretty pattern not because you contemplate it with "overdistanced" attention but because you fail to pay attention to it.

Aesthetic-attitude theorists illustrate underdistancing by the famous scene where Don Quixote "saves" the heroine of the puppet show from her "cruel kidnappers." That example is supposed to show that excessive involvement with the object (underdistancing) gets in the way of seeing it as art and precludes aesthetic appreciation. A much better description of the said example, however, is that Don Quixote fails to appreciate the play because he attends, not to the aesthetic features of the scene, but (mistaking it for real life) to its ethical features. Indeed, attention to ethical features *may* (rightly!) distract one from attending to aesthetic features, but Don Quixote's failure to recognize the fictionality of the scene has nothing to do with his failure to appreciate it aesthetically. Let us suppose that Don Quixote is right: the scene is not fictional, a princess is really abducted. He still has the option of ignoring the ethical aspects of the scene and tending to its aesthetic features only, or attending to its ethical significance and rescuing the princess, never attending to the aesthetic merits of the scene. The question is which features one chooses to attend to.

Not all nonaesthetic interest is detrimental to aesthetic attention: an understudy's attention and sensitivity to aesthetic features of a play is heightened, not dulled, if that person expects to replace the lead; a financial interest (deciding whether to invest in the play) may also sharpen one's sensitivity to its aesthetic details. External, nonaesthetic interests may either enhance or distract one's attention to aesthetic details, but there is no "overdistancing" or "underdistancing" for them to cause.

Kant, via Edward Bullough, influenced Benedetto Croce, R. G. Colling-wood, Pepita Haezrahi, and Eliseo Vivas, who also take the aesthetic attitude to be a complete, undivided, unwavering attention to an object. Vivas gives this example: really to see a deer is to see it aesthetically; if your interest is practical—say, you see it as game—you see it only partially. Vestiges of Kant's distinction between concepts of the understanding and nonconceptual syntheses of intuition[14] influence T. E. Hulme, Jacques Maritain, and Martin Heidegger, for whom aesthetic observation is pure contemplation free of the Procrustean bed of concept formation. In the beginning, we all see aesthetically: we see the object as a unique particular, a being in its own right, not as a member of some kind (e.g., as a table, a chair, or a deer). We see an individual *this* in a nondiscursive way. The aesthetic attitude is perception of an individual essence.

I contend that the above version of the aesthetic attitude theory is worthless. Nonretarded adults cannot look at a chair, a table, or a deer and *not* see it as a chair, a table, or a deer. No seeing is uncategorized: for aesthetic appreciation one needs to be aware of sizes, shapes, and colors, yet these are categories too. If you could rid yourself of concepts and categories and observe the world as a baby does, your aesthetic sensibility would be nugatory. To appreciate a tree in fall you need to know about death; to see the beauty of a deer you need to know what the function of eyes and legs is; to see the Alps as sublime you need to know how high most hills are.

If the aesthetic attitude is undivided attention, it is neither necessary nor sufficient for observing aesthetic features. I noted earlier that were total attention a sufficient condition for having an aesthetic attitude, a scientist who observed a bacterial culture with complete concentration, and a hunter who examined the landscape, noting every detail, would manifest an aesthetic attitude par excellence. Were undivided attention to an observed object a necessary condition for having an aesthetic attitude to it, you could not see that a person passed in the street or a landscape seen through a train's window is beautiful. Yet that is surely false; if a quick glance at a snow-crested mountain cannot be an aesthetic observation of it, how many days must one spend staring at it—and how many details of it does one need to note—before one can be said to have aesthetically observed it?

Haezrahi's example of aesthetic attitude is engrossment in the fall of a single leaf, noticing the rustling sound it makes as it detaches from its branch,

---

14. Immanuel Kant, *Kritik der reinen Vernunft* (Riga, 1781), A 95–114.

its shining golden color as it passes through the sunlit air, the semicircular arc of its fall, etc.[15] These details are indeed aesthetically impressive, but they are not "all the immediate plenitude of its [the object's] concrete sensual attributes";[16] there are many perceptible details that the rapt aesthete need not note, for example, the number of spots on the leaf, its diameter, the velocity with which it drifts, or the direction its tip points at each second while falling. Haezrahi's choice of features that the aesthete attends to is highly selective; hence it refutes, rather than supports, the doctrine that aesthetic attention is an unselective, total attention to an object. Like Schopenhauer, Croce, and Green, Haezrahi holds that when you aesthetically observe the leaf, "[t]here is a pause in time. The chain of your thoughts is severed. The red and golden tints of the leaf, the graceful form of the arc described by its descent fill the whole of your consciousness, fill your soul to the brim . . . if you had other preoccupations and other purposes you have forgotten them. You do not know how long this lasts."[17] This is a pretty myth, but nonetheless a myth, not a description of a real event. One may admire the falling leaf while being very much aware of a toothache or a pinch in one's shoe, while knowing full well how long this fall lasts and that one has a bus to catch in two minutes. On the other hand, one may entirely forget one's real circumstances when engulfed in a poker game. Total absorption is neither sufficient nor necessary, nor even typical, to aesthetic interest.

Kant held that there is only one kind of phenomenon: aesthetic attention is the first stage in the process by which our cognitive mechanism constructs *all* phenomena. Neo-Kantians demur, holding that there are several kinds of phenomena, constructed by us in distinct ways (according to Ernst Cassirer, by using distinct symbolic forms). V. C. Aldrich holds that the plurality is perspectival, not ontological; for example, an aesthetic attitude makes us see a thing as an aesthetic, rather than as a physical, object.[18] But how do aesthetic objects differ from physical objects? True, we do not discuss a Rembrandt and a galaxy in the same terms, but that does not show that they are constructed in distinct ways.[19] The properties that we look for in ships are not those on account of which we are interested in shoes, but that does

15. Pepita Haezrahi, *The Contemplative Activity* (London: Allen & Unwin, 1954), 25–36.
16. Ibid., 27.
17. Ibid.
18. V. C. Aldrich, *Philosophy of Art* (Englewood Cliffs, N.J.: Prentice Hall, 1963), 6–55.
19. See Nelson Goodman, *Ways of Worldmaking* (Indianapolis: Hackett, 1978), 1–40, 91–140.

mean that ships and shoes are not physical objects in exactly the same sense. A discussion of an object from a scientific point of view and a discussion of it from an aesthetic point of view call for different predicates, but that is no evidence for Neo-Kantianism. Examining a nation from an economic point of view you pay attention to features different from those you tend to when you examine it from a military point of view, but that does not mean that you have examined two nations, one economic, the other military. That is true of objects in general. Naturalists must deny that physical things can have irreducible nonnatural (e.g., aesthetic) properties, but others have no reason to deny it. Nelson Goodman and Hilary Putnam to the contrary, the properties Square and Pretty are compatible and may characterize the same object in the same world.[20]

Kantians who stress feature 3 (and also 1) above of the aesthetic attitude define it as attending to phenomenal objects. Whether the object exists is immaterial for the aesthetic attitude, they say. In this the aesthetic attitude differs from mundane attitudes like the cognitive and the practical, where the existence of the object matters a great deal. Beardsley also regards the aesthetic object as essentially *phenomenal*. I submit that this is false; aesthetic evaluation is often conditional upon the object examined being real, not make-believe. Would your excitement in watching the performance of an acrobat or a ballet dancer not be considerably diminished were you to learn that these were not real people but computer-generated images? Will you still enjoy the opera if you discover that the singing is prerecorded, not produced by the people on the stage?

---

20. In several articles, and in his book *The Many Faces of Realism* (Peru, Ill.: Open Court, 1987), Putnam gives the following example to prove the incompatibility thesis. Rudolf Carnap postulates a world containing exactly three objects. A Polish logician objects, saying that if a, b, c are in w, there are seven objects in w: a, b, c, and the mereological wholes ab, ac, bc, abc. These descriptions of w are incompatible at the most basic level, so there is no description of w to which both Carnap's and the Polish logician's descriptions can be reduced.

I answer that the two logicians use 'object' in different senses: Carnap requires objects to be distinct (not overlap); the Pole does not. Let 'ibject' denote objects that may overlap others and 'ubject' objects that may not. Now both logicians must agree that there are seven ibjects and three ubjects in w.

The number of ibjects can differ from the number of ubjects in a world only if it instantiates Overlap. Thus, if you take numbers to be sets of sets, you need fewer ubjects to model a number than if you do not construe numbers as containing other numbers as elements. Once you take a position you can say how many ibjects, and how many ubjects, you need to model a given number.

Furthermore, the notion of an object only the phenomenal properties of which count is murky. All practical human interests involve phenomenal properties only. You have no interest in the reality of your house if it gives you all the visual, auditory, tactual, etc. sensations you expect from a real house. If all that is given, what do you care if the house is real or not? Beardsley's requirement reminds one of Wittgenstein's "selling" Malcolm a lamppost, provided that Malcolm is not to tamper with it in any way. Beardsley says that for aesthetic experience only a phenomenal field is needed, but that field should have all the visual and acoustical properties.[21] Visual structures need to be three-dimensional, for to appreciate a sculpture one must see it three-dimensionally. Now, tactual properties are also needed, and in some works of art smell and taste play a role too. Every sense quality may be relevant for aesthetic appreciation: no detectable property is ruled out a priori as candidate for aesthetic relevance. Thus, the merely phenomenal nature of the aesthetic object turns out to be a sham.

2.6. The Aesthetic Attitude Again

Many aestheticians combine aesthetic-attitude with aesthetic-experience theory. To illustrate that ploy I use R. F. Racy, who defines the aesthetic attitude as attending to "intrinsic" (as opposed to "external") properties of the object and, like Beardsley, conflates aesthetic attitude with aesthetic experience:

> Suppose I look at a tree. I may look at it to estimate how much fruit it will bear or to consider chopping it up as firewood or as a suitable anchor for one end of a hammock. So long as I look at it in any of these ways I am interested in its utilitarian qualities. I may, on the other hand, look at it *in a quite different way*. I may look at it *because* I am interested in its structure or shape, or the color of the leaves, or the texture of the bark, or for the dappled effect of its shadows on the grass. In looking at it *in this way* I am not interested in its utilitarian qualities but in the qualities which belong to the tree itself—its form, color, texture, and so on. In

21. Beardsley, *Aesthetics*, 530.

other words, I am interested in its intrinsic qualities. We may call
this, for convenience, "intrinsic perception" and *this is precisely
the aesthetic experience*—perception of an object for its intrinsic
as distinct from its instrumental qualities.[22]

There is a threefold confusion here between (*a*) looking at X for certain
reasons, (*b*) looking at X in a certain way, and (*c*) having a certain experience
as a result of looking at X. These, however, are logically independent of each
another. I may run the marathon for bad reasons without running it badly
and not have a bad experience as a result. Yet for Racy, having an aesthetic
reason for observing a tree is the same as observing it in an aesthetic way,
and that is the same as having an aesthetic experience.

Racy's distinction between intrinsic and practical features of objects
exemplifies the absurd romanticist tenet that aesthetic interest in an object
excludes attention to its practical uses. Consider this reasoning: growing
apples is an intrinsic feature of trees, so perceiving it is intrinsic perception,
and experiencing it is an aesthetic experience. But we have a practical
interest in apples, so growing apples is an instrumental property of the tree,
perceiving it is extrinsic perception, and experiencing it is not an aesthetic
experience. The absurdity is obvious. In fact, aesthetic attention to the tree
is often sensitive to the tree's significance for us and its impact on our lives.
We see the tree as bountiful, calm, serene, a source of life and hope, because
we see it as that which spontaneously feeds us. We hope it will bloom again
after the winter; hence it embodies a promise of overcoming difficulties. It
looks permanent and strong because it lives longer than we do and is taller
than we are. These are "external" features of the tree; yet to bar them from
molding perception is to see the tree with dead eyes. Objects shorn of their
human meaning lack aesthetic interest.

The division of properties into intrinsic versus practical is like Jorge
Luis Borges's classification of animals into (*a*) those belonging to the Emperor, (*b*) embalmed, (*c*) trained, (*d*) suckling pigs, . . . (*n*) those that from
afar look like flies.[23] If a relation to us is always a practical property, then
Tall is a practical property, since trees are tall in relation to us. Typically,
for romanticists, Racy holds that interest in the color or shape of the tree is

---

22. R. F. Racy, "The Aesthetic Experience," *British Journal of Aesthetics* 9 (1969): 345–
52; emphasis added.
23. Jorge Luis Borges, "The Analytical Language of John Wilkes," in *Other Inquisitions*
(New York: Washington Square Press, 1966), 108.

always aesthetic, while an interest in the tree's commercial use is utilitarian, hence not aesthetic. That is wrong. My interest in the commercial use of trees may be purely aesthetic: I aesthetically admire the delicacy and power of the vibrant timber trade. A botanist's interest in the tree's color may be entirely utilitarian, while a retired person's idle interest in its commercial use may be entirely nonutilitarian (but nonaesthetic also!).

Yet, for the sake of argument, let us grant the romanticist that scientific, social, economic, etc. interests are practical, and define aesthetic interest as an interest that is *not* practical. (Obviously, this is wrong; scientists need be no more practically minded than aesthetes.) For this definition to work we need to know when an interest is not practical. Perhaps, if all my desires and needs are checked and none of them is found to motivate my interest in X, I may conclude that my interest in X is not practical. So, until I examine all my desires, I cannot tell whether my interest in X is aesthetic: I must first verify that no practical need of mine motivated my interest in X. That task is almost infinite. Further, not all my desires are known to me, or to anyone else, so the task can never be completed. The absurd result is that I can never know whether my interest in X is aesthetic.

Perhaps God knows all our desires and which is active in any time, so although we never know whose interest is aesthetical, God does. But even this meager consolation has to be denied the subjectivist. We often do things for no reason at all. Which desire motivated me to move my finger right now? None; I just did it. Surely it is wrong to conclude that, therefore, I did it for aesthetic reasons! Aesthetic-attitude theorists make it impossible to distinguish between doing something for no reason and doing something for aesthetic reasons. Thus, the subjectivist's attempt to give content to the notion of the aesthetic attitude fails. I conclude that there is no aesthetic attitude; no aesthetic mode of cognition, or attention, exists. That remnant of the medieval psychology of faculties and cognitive powers must be relocated to the wax museum of still-born philosophical fictions. There, in the company of square circles and married bachelors, it may rest in peace.

2.7. Relativism in Aesthetics

Relativism is perhaps the most widely held view in aesthetics. Most people who express an opinion on the subject profess a version of it. To many it seems self-evident: they do not think of it as a philosophical theory but as plain common sense.[24] In this section I present the main features of the theory, and in the next one I show that it is necessarily false: no variation or emendation can save it, for its basic conception of the issue is thoroughly erroneous.

The phenomenon that the relativist in aesthetics attempts to explain is the fact that, when it comes to aesthetic questions, people are not all of the same mind. Jones says that a given painting is good, Smith denies that, and there is no accepted way to determine who is right and who is wrong. More likely than not, those who disagree remain in disagreement. Thus, many aestheticians believe that there is no place for arguments in aesthetics.[25] Controversy, they say, can be total and radical; members of different cultures may entirely disagree in their aesthetic judgments. Even in the same society people may have radically different aesthetic taste: what I find beautiful is ugly in your eyes, and there is no way to adjudicate the matter.

Relativists explain these alleged data by taking aesthetic properties to be phenomenal and subjective ways in which objects appear to observers. The logic of 'gaudy,' they say, is different from that of 'triangular.' With regard to the latter we distinguish between being triangular and looking triangular: something can be triangular without looking triangular and vice versa. According to relativism, that distinction does not hold for aesthetic predicates; to claim that X is gaudy is to claim that X *seems* gaudy to one. X can appear pretty to Jones and ugly to Smith, but there is no sense in asking whether X is really pretty, since, for aesthetic properties, to be is to be perceived. People say, "It is ugly to you but not to me," and that ends the discussion. Relativists are phenomenalists in aesthetics, taking aesthetic predicates to denote ways in which things appear, as distinct from ways in which things are. They treat aesthetic predicates as phenomenalists treat sensation words: when I say, "X is A," I make the statement that X appears A to me, as "It is hot" really means that I feel hot. Like "It is hot," what I say is to a high degree incorrigible, since it describes an internal event with

24. For an elaborate version of that theory, see I. C. Hungerland, "The Logic of Aesthetic Concepts," *Proceedings and Addresses of the American Philosophical Association*, October 1963, 43–66; reprinted in *Philosophy of Art and Aesthetics,* ed. Tillman and Cahn (New York: Harper & Row, 1969), 595–617; see also her "Once Again, Aesthetic and Non-aesthetic," *Journal of Aesthetics and Art Criticism* 26 (1969): 285–95.

25. The classical exposition of that view is in three articles in W. R. Elton's influential anthology, *Aesthetics and Language* (Oxford: Oxford University Press, 1954): J. A. Passmore, "The Dreariness of Aesthetics," Arnold Isenberg, "Critical Communication," and Stuart Hampshire, "Logic and Appreciation."

respect to which I usually am the final authority. Just as my belief that I am hot decides the question whether I am hot, so does my belief that X appears A to me decide the question whether X appears A to me. Thus there is no arguing about matters of taste: *de gustibus non est disputandum*. If "X is A" said by me means that X appears A to me, there is no sense in arguing about it, just as under normal circumstances there is no room to question my belief that I am in dire pain.

In order to examine this view, consider the situation it was meant to explain: a dispute between Jones and Smith on whether X is gaudy. Aesthetic relativists say that their dispute is spurious: Jones and Smith do not disagree, since they talk about different things. They only think they disagree, because the grammatical form of "X is A" misleads them, creating the impression that both are talking about X. In fact, neither of them talks about X: Jones is talking about the way X looks to him and says that it is gaudy, while Smith speaks about the way X appears to her (a different sense datum) and says that it is not gaudy. It is as if Jones were to say that his aunt lives in Miami and Smith would demur because her aunt lives in Rome: if Jones and Smith have different aunts, there is no difference of opinion between them. The problem is dissolved by showing that disputes about aesthetic matters are misdirected: there is no dispute; hence there is no difficulty.

Aesthetic relativists claim that arguments in aesthetics are spurious because the parties speak about different things. These relativists do not claim, however, that the argument is spurious because the parties speak about different *properties*. They think that both Jones and Smith refer to the same property, say, being gaudy. Relativists do not say that Jones or Smith or both do not know what gaudiness is and thus talk about two altogether different properties. (That would be as if Jones claimed that cats like cheese and Smith demurred, saying that her aunt lives in Miami.) On the contrary, the relativist holds that the apparent controversy between Jones and Smith is resolved by showing that they attribute the same property, gaudiness, to different things: Jones attributes gaudiness to an object that is private to him (his feeling or way of seeing X), and Smith declines to attribute it to an object that is private to her (her sensation or way of seeing X).

So we must ask the relativist, how is it that Jones and Smith both understand the term 'gaudy'? If all aesthetic predicates apply to private objects, then Jones has never seen or otherwise examined any object to which Smith ascribes any aesthetic predicate 'A,' and vice versa. No one has ever examined an object to which someone else ascribed an aesthetic predicate. In that case, how can one know which property is being ascribed by others when they use the term 'A'? How can we tell whether we refer to the same property or not? How can children learn to use aesthetic predicates if it is impossible to show them an example of what an aesthetic predicate applies to? If I have never known, or can know, anything to which some adjective is applied, how can I learn what it means?

That argument is attributable, of course, to Wittgenstein, who used it to show that a private language is logically impossible. To work in aesthetics, however, it must be radically altered. Relativists in aesthetics hold that aesthetic predicates describe phenomenal items, so by uttering an aesthetic sentence one does make a meaningful statement that is either true or false. I argue that if relativism is right, aesthetic predicates can have no meaning, certainly not a meaning that both disputants are familiar with. I claim, therefore, that relativism in aesthetics is self-contradictory.

Unlike Wittgenstein, I believe that there are three good ways to learn the meaning of predicates attributable to internal items only. One way is by analogy from common external stimuli. We all use the phrase "It hurts" in similar circumstances, so I assume that what you feel when your arm is pricked by a pin is similar to what I feel when that happens to me. The second way is by analogy from common reaction: behavior is a criterion (in Wittgenstein's sense: a justifier barring counterindications) for mental events. We learn how to use the predicate 'pain' because a certain kind of reaction is our prima facie criterion on how to apply that predicate. It is analytically true that, unless counterindicated, whoever behaves in a certain observable manner is in pain. The third way is by analogy from predicates that do apply to publicly observable objects. That is Hume's famous example of learning about a new shade of blue by looking at specimens of somewhat darker and somewhat lighter shades of blue.[26] That way opens up quite a few possibilities: comparison, contrast, ratios (A, the new predicate, is to the predicate B as C is to D), and so on. Can a relativist use any of these ways to assign meaning to aesthetic predicates?

2.8. The Impossibility of Relativism

The first way, analogy from stimulus, is closed by the basic assumption of relativism in aesthetics. The relativist insists that there need be no agreement

---

26. David Hume, *An Enquiry Concerning the Human Understanding* (London, 1748), chap. 3.

between our aesthetic judgments, since it is possible for the same external stimulus to appear via radically different aesthetic properties; there need be no similarity in our aesthetic reactions to public objects. The relativist assumes that radically different internal objects may be generated in different people by the same external object. Therefore there is no reason to believe that when you and I use an aesthetic term in an encounter with the same external object, we use it to convey the same meaning. The fact that in these cases we emit similar sounds is no evidence that we refer to the same property. Only if it is assumed that we usually make similar aesthetic judgments in similar circumstances does it follow that we probably, in those cases we utter similar sounds, refer to the same property. Relativists, however, reject that assumption, since in their view the same stimulus can bring about radically divergent internal states in different people. So the internal state you call 'gaudy' may be radically different from the internal state to which I apply the same term when stimulated by the object X. You cannot describe your internal state to me either: to do that you must use aesthetic terms, but those I cannot understand, for I know not to which internal objects you apply them! Thus I cannot know what you mean by any aesthetic term that you use.

The second way, fixing meaning by behavioral criteria, is also blocked, for, as argued above, the presence of no aesthetic property evokes a specific behavior that is typical to it alone. One cannot learn what 'gaudy' means from the way people behave with respect to objects they call 'gaudy.' We have characteristic pain behavior, but there is no seeing-as-gaudy behavior that is typical to people in general or even within the same culture. One cannot describe a seeing-as-gaudy behavior as an aversive or avoidance behavior either, for in many cases one is interested in an item that one thinks is gaudy. Jones may buy a picture that looks gaudy to him as a gift to a friend who has poor taste, or for a child, or as a joke, or because it is the latest rage and he wants to be *au courant*, or because the painter is his friend and he does not want to insult him, or in order to give the impression that he has no taste, etc.

Even if Jones is attracted to objects to which he applies one aesthetic predicate and repulsed by objects to which he ascribes another aesthetic predicate, that cannot indicate what Jones takes these predicates to signify, because (as I argued in Chapter 1) there is no *aesthetic* aversion behavior and *aesthetic* attraction behavior. No behavior is specific to *aesthetic* attraction or repulsion; explicit avowal constitutes the only evidence that Jones likes X aesthetically and not for another reason. Smith, in buying a dress, may be doing that for many different reasons. Her reason may be that her mother will like it (or not like it), that the dress makes her look thinner (or younger, or older, or more serious, or extravagant, or anything else), that her friend has (or does not have) a similar dress, that it reminds her of something or other, that she has already tried on other dresses and is tired of choosing, that it is (or is not) comfortable, that the price is fair (or exorbitant: she wants to annoy her parents), that it is gaudy (she wants to be provocative), that it is ugly (she wants to punish herself), that though it is plain it goes well with her wardrobe, that it is easy to wash, etc. Various interests intersect in daily life, and no piece of behavior carries a tag to tell which interest is motivating it, so aesthetic interest cannot be described in terms of a behavior it motivates. Concepts may be roles in a social game, but if an object X plays several roles, a behavior directed toward X does not disclose in which role of X it is directed to X.

Davidson argues that we must assume that people are intelligent and benevolent; otherwise, given Smith's behavior B, we cannot learn about her desires unless we know her beliefs, and we cannot learn about her beliefs unless we know her desires. Let us make these assumptions, then; given behavior B and the object X that occasioned it, we can now tell what Smith's beliefs and desires are. But the relativist claims that the object X that evoked B is unobservable by us. Assuming that Smith is intelligent and benevolent, we can tell which unobservable X causes B if we know her desires and beliefs, and we can tell what her desires and beliefs are if we know which X prompts her to B. But B alone is insufficient to advise us both of X's identity and of Smith's desires and beliefs. Thus, relativism implies that we can never understand Smith (i.e., anyone), and we cannot understand what her words mean.

The third strategy, analogy with other predicates, also holds no promise for relativists in aesthetics. One may learn the meaning of one aesthetic predicate, say, 'gaudy,' by comparison and contrast with other predicates. Dictionaries define 'gaudy' by other aesthetic terms ('cheap,' 'has sharp contrasts,' 'tasteless,' 'irritating,' 'vulgar,' 'unnecessarily conspicuous,' 'immodest'), yet to define *all* aesthetic predicates in that manner is to try pulling oneself up by tugging at one's own bootstraps. A new aesthetic predicate may be explained to me by using others that I already know, but if all aesthetic predicates are unknown to me, that explanation will not help me in the least. I am not any wiser if a word that I do not understand is explained to me in a language that I do not speak. At most I learn a syntax: that these incomprehensible terms are related to each other in ways whose significance I cannot surmise.

Can nonaesthetic properties be used in the analogy? Explaining aesthetic properties by nonaesthetic ones is like explaining what colors are by acoustic analogues. The reason for the impossibility of such explanations is *not* the often made claim that a nonaesthetic description of X can neither entail nor increase the probability that a certain aesthetic predicate applies to it. This position of Arnold Isenberg, Mary Mothersill, Frank Sibley, and others is demonstrably wrong; later, I argue that nonaesthetic predicates must be inductively related to aesthetic predicates. Nonaesthetic sentences can therefore support the *truth* of aesthetic sentences, but they cannot explain their *meaning*. Aesthetic properties, like phenomenal ones, must be observed to be known: it is impossible to explain the meaning of aesthetic predicates to those insensitive to aesthetic qualia. Frank Jackson's Mary, a blind physicist who has all the appropriate instruments, can establish by indirect means that her garment is red without knowing what the phenomenal property that 'red' refers to is.[27] Similarly, one who knows that X has the nonaesthetic property P may be able to infer *that* X has the aesthetic property A, but not *what* A is. Those acquainted with no aesthetic property cannot learn the meaning of aesthetic predicates by analogy; if you tell them how gaudy things look, using nonaesthetic predicates only, the best they can do is construe Gaudy as a property in a sense modality they are acquainted with, for example, color, and surely that is misleading. To understand the term 'aesthetic' one needs to be acquainted with at least some aesthetic properties.

Relativism in aesthetics makes aesthetic predicates necessarily incomprehensible; hence, they have no public meaning, and no one can understand what is being said when aesthetic predicates are used to describe objects. Now, the fact remains that relativists have set out to explain disagreement on aesthetic matters. Disagreement is a situation where two people who understand a predicate do not agree on its application. If aesthetic terms have no meaning, there can be no disagreement, because neither party can understand the other, that is, what quality others assign to X by saying that it is A. Thus, if relativists are right to assume that radical disagreement on aesthetic matters is possible, it follows that disagreement in aesthetics is conceptually impossible. Relativism in aesthetics is therefore self-contradictory.

Relativism tried to explain *radical* disagreement. However, if disagreement on aesthetic matters is partial and limited to few cases, there is no need for relativism. Realists about aesthetic properties have no difficulty there, for occasional disagreement about observable properties is common: if there

27. Frank Jackson, "Epiphenomenal Qualia," *Philosophical Quarterly* 32 (1982): 127–36.

is a basic agreement on observables, there can be disagreement on difficult, new, and marginal cases. If aesthetic matters allow radical disagreement, aesthetic properties are entirely unlike observable nonaesthetic ones, and we need relativism to explain the difference. We saw, however, that if relativism is true, aesthetic terms are meaningless and there can be no disagreement on aesthetic matters. Hence either there is no disagreement on aesthetic matters, or else relativism is false. We do disagree on aesthetic matters; therefore, relativism in aesthetics is false. We therefore have a reason to believe that radical disagreement in matters of taste is logically impossible.

There can be radical disagreement on the application of a set of theoretical predicates, for the entire set can be explained by means of other, observational predicates. Undefined observational predicates can be given meaning only ostensively; hence there can be no radical disagreement on their application. To disagree about application the parties must understand the applied predicate, so no family of observational predicates can lack standard application. Relativists admit that the aesthetic predicates are observational, denoting observable properties that are irreducible to nonaesthetic ones. Thus, at least some aesthetic predicates must be learned by ostension, noticing to what objects these predicates are applied. It follows that at least some aesthetic predicates denote observable properties of public objects, to which they are correctly applied. The moral is that since aesthetic judgments sometimes differ, these judgments can only be about matters of fact, attributing to a public thing X properties it either has or lacks, and whose presence in, or absence from, X can be empirically established.

3

AESTHETIC REALISM

3.1. Observation Conditions

If we disagree on aesthetic matters, I argued, our disagreement cannot be radical: those states are mutually exclusive. If there is a controversy on whether an aesthetic predicate 'A' applies to X, 'A' must have standard application conditions or else be explainable by aesthetic predicates that have standard application conditions. Otherwise 'A' can have no meaning, and there can be no dispute on whether "X is A" is true, for "X is A" is meaningless. Yet if aesthetic terms have a standard application, why do we disagree on their application so frequently? If aesthetic terms are like color terms, whose meaning we learn by ostension, why is it that we almost never disagree on whether X is red, but we do disagree on whether X is gaudy?

Things look different when we observe them under different conditions. Descartes was so impressed by the fact that a piece of wax feels hard when it is cold and soft when it is hot that he thought it best not to attribute such sense properties to things at all.[1] Although one can see what Descartes meant, that radical measure is excessive. When there are standard observation conditions (SOC) for observing a kind of thing, say, wax, we may attribute to it those phenomenal properties that we observe it to have under those conditions. Let us define: conditions C are SOC for a property F and a thing X iff, when X is observed as F in C, then X is F. For instance, if in

---

1. René Descartes, *Meditations on First Philosophy* (1641), Meditation 2.

daylight, at a distance of few yards, when you are awake and not drugged, your eyes open and your eyesight good, you seem to see X kissing Y, that is the best reason to believe that X kissed Y; but if, when your eyes are shut, you dream that X is kissing Y, that observation is not a good reason to believe that X kissed Y. X's appearing red attests to X's being red only if it so appears under standard conditions; an observation having the same content made under other conditions may be poor evidence for X being red. Descartes made his point: observations conflict; so if observation can teach us about the properties things have, some conditions must be *standard* for examining X (and other things of its kind) for F-ness (and other properties of its kind). If observation conditions are nonstandard, X may look red and be blue, observed circular and be ellipsoid, etc.

SOC are needed not only for "secondary" properties like color, but for "primary" properties too. For instance, measured distances between points on X's circumference and its center may all come out equal, but X is circular only if the conditions of measurement are standard (e.g., the system is at rest). I seem to see a ship gradually decrease in size, but whether that observation indicates that a ship is moving away from me depends on the conditions under which the observation is made, that is, on whether those conditions are SOC for the object and property observed. If I am drugged, dreaming, if what I see is not a ship but a collapsible toy, my observation does not prove that a ship is moving, for observations conducted under nonstandard conditions do not disclose the true properties of the objects examined. Observational error occurs when we observe as if p, but the observation conditions are nonstandard for checking the truth of 'p' and its ilk. Sense properties are often observed under nonstandard conditions: green things look black in red light, square things look round when spun, straight things look broken when dipped in water, moving things look stationary in stroboscopic light. Observing that X is F when we are dizzy, drunk, or dreaming is no evidence that X is F. For there to be objective knowledge, observation predicates need SOC.

Realists in aesthetics are therefore under no obligation to hold that if X is gaudy then it would look gaudy to everyone, under all observation conditions. In nonstandard conditions objects are seen as having aesthetic properties that they do not really have. Aesthetic properties are in that respect like all other observable properties: what is beautiful may look ugly when observed under nonstandard conditions.[2] Indeed, what looks gaudy to you

---

2. I first suggested the notion of aesthetic SOC in "A Stitch in Time," *Journal of Value Inquiry* 1 (1967–68): 223–42, and used it in my books *Analytic Aesthetics* (Tel Aviv: Daga,

may look dramatic and not gaudy to me, but (relativism to the contrary) that is not the end of the matter. That X looks A+ under condition C, and under condition D looks A–, is precisely what we should expect if A is an objective, publicly observable property of things. Invariance under variable observation conditions would have impugned its objectivity, not the other way around.

SOC are not (as is often said) the conditions that generally prevail or are more common than others. Even in a northern country where the sun shines only for a few hours a day SOC for color call for sunlight. A dress is red, not gray, even if it is most often seen in the dim light of bars, where it looks gray. SOC for bacteria do not usually prevail; they require expensive instruments, as well as long professional training in techniques of observing through microscopes, with which laymen are not familiar. SOC for the taste of wine require natural skills: not all of us can become, even after long study, wine tasters. Both native talent (perfect pitch) and training are required for identifying a key in music. Some pictures appear as such only when illuminated by laser beams; others need polarized light to be seen. The distance needed to detect sadness in a face is larger than the distance optimal for detecting tooth decay; to determine the grade of meat you need skills different from those needed to determine the quality of perfume.[3]

Second, J.J.C. Smart to the contrary, SOC are not conditions in which more distinctions can be made than otherwise. Smart says: "Let me introduce the concept of a normal percipient. One person is more a normal percipient than another if he can make color discriminations that the other cannot. For example, if A can pick a lettuce leaf out of a heap of cabbage leaves whereas B cannot though he can pick a lettuce leaf out of a heap of beet root leaves, then A is a more normal percipient than B."[4] This definition has much to recommend it: indeed, experts observe differences where laymen see none; yet, as it stands, it is quite unacceptable. A person who makes a vast number of distinctions that have no basis in theory and that no one else observes is an aberrance and not the most normal percipient, who sets the standard for correct classification. Smart's definition implies that all statements of the form "Smith seems to see a difference between X and Y, where there is none"

1970) and *Aesthetics* (Tel Aviv: Institute for Poetics and Semiotics, 1976). Philip Pettit takes a similar approach in "The Possibility of Aesthetic Realism," in *Pleasure, Preference and Value*, ed. Eva Schaper (Cambridge: Cambridge University Press, 1983).

3. See my "Seeing, 'Seeing,' and Feeling," *Review of Metaphysics* 23 (1969): 3–24.

4. J.J.C. Smart, "Sensation and Brain Processes," in *The Philosophy of Mind*, ed. V. C. Chappell (Englewood Cliffs, N.J.: Prentice Hall, 1962), 166.

are logically false, since, if Smith seems to see a difference that others do not see, she is, by definition, more normal than they are; she sets the standard. Thus, no allegedly observed distinction can be challenged. Surely that is wrong. Conditions under which a record number of distinctions is made need not be standard; he who registers the highest number of observational distinctions may be plainly mad.

Third, one may erroneously think that statements of the form "C are SOC for F" are analytic, being an integral part of the meaning of 'F.' The argument for that view is that you cannot claim to know what 'red' means unless you can distinguish between red and nonred things, and that ability presupposes knowing whether the given conditions are right for that observation. But that is not generally true: you may understand the predicate 'red' without knowing that red things do not look red under blue light; that is, you need not know what observation conditions are standard for it. Our ways of telling when a person is dead were not available to our forefathers, yet it is foolish to say that they did not understand the word 'dead' or that death is unobservable. SOC may be revised: for example, an old way of checking whether X is gold (biting it) is now considered inadequate, yet the meaning of 'gold' did not change. True, most of the stuff that passed the old test for being gold also passes the new chemical test, but that need not have been so; a new test may disqualify most of the stuff that passed the old one and yet be considered a precisification of the SOC for gold and not a change in the meaning of 'gold.'[5] Thus, I define SOC as conditions in which we see things aright. Formally, C are SOC for F properties of K things iff an x of kind K looks F_i under C iff $F_i(x)$.

That definition sounds disappointing and uninformative: first I say that to see things as they are, you must observe them under SOC, and then, when you search for those SOC, I say that they are those conditions in which things look as they are! Is this not circular? It is. I plead guilty, but claim that circular definitions can be useful. Reflective Equilibrium, the process of mutual adjustment between theory and observation, is circular, yet it is the best method we have. By that method, theory rules which observations are

5. In "Naming and Reference" (*Journal of Philosophy* 70 [1973]: 702), "The Meaning of 'Meaning' " (in his *Mind, Language, and Reality* [Cambridge: Cambridge University Press, 1975]), and other writings, Hilary Putnam does require water to have the same nature as *most* of what is called 'water' by members of our linguistic community. But that claim is incompatible with his other thesis, that X is water iff it has the same nature as the sample *originally* dubbed 'water': *its* nature may be shared by only a few samples of what we (mistakenly) came to call 'water.'

admissible, and observations rule which theory is acceptable. That is circular but highly fruitful: what we do is tentatively use both our observations of things as F and our theory on what things are F, playing them against each other, trying to find such C that, if it is SOC, then our basic beliefs and basic observations are veridical. As we shall see, the two work in tandem.

Both external conditions (the observed stick is half-immersed in water, the light is tinted or dim, etc.) and internal conditions (the observer is hypnotized, insane, ignorant, etc.) of observation may be nonstandard. Under such conditions things do not look as they are, so these conditions induce *illusions*.

A *caveat* is now due. Saying that things observed under SOC look as they are does not commit us to naive realism. A shortsighted or astigmatic Kantian may complain that he is not seeing things as they are; he may tell his optometrist, "At night, bright things look to me bigger than they are," without having by that relinquished his Kantianism. He does not mean that, with spectacles on, he will see the noumenon, the *Ding an sich* itself. Twenty-twenty eyesight, he may explain, reveals phenomena, items in the transcendentally constituted phenomenal world, and his complaint is that he is not seeing *them* as he knows they are.

Naive realism is not a live option in metaphysics. We know that the human sensory system is activated by only very few of the physical features of our environment; we are sensitive to only a tiny segment of the electro-optic radiation (sight) and air vibration (sound). Our mental representation of these stimuli is specific to our species; furthermore, we are animals whose evolution is geared to maximizing survival, not truth. To believe, as naive realists do, that the human parochial image of nature is an accurate replica of the real world as it is in itself is quite unreasonable. We have a reason to believe that organisms equipped with different sensory mechanisms sense different qualia and that what they sense has to do with what contributes to their survival. In the future we may have implanted transducers sensitive to other features of reality, so our present sensory image of nature will seem myopic, pathetic in its lack of sensitivity to the world. I therefore conclude that 'X as it is' may refer to X not as it is in reality but as it is in our common phenomenal world. 'Real' is used in two senses: the metaphysical sense refers to the *Ding an sich*; the popular, to the phenomenal world of common sense.[6]

6. Cf. my "Look, This Is Zeus," in *Interpretation, Relativism, and the Metaphysics of Culture,* ed. Michael Krausz and Richard Shusterman (New York: Humanities Press, forthcoming).

3.2. Observation and Theory

Let me recapitulate. SOC are defined as the conditions in which things appear as they are. How things are (in any world) is stated by our theory, so what are SOC for objects of kind K with respect to F-ness depends on what our theory says about Ks. If our theory says that Ks are F then their SOC are those in which they look F. That seems circular, for theories are confirmed and refuted by observation; observation tests the theory, so how can theory say which observation is veridical? My answer is that observation and theory are interdependent: SOC emerge by a mutual adjustment of theory to observation and observation to theory; reevaluation takes place on both sides. Theory is guided by observation; observation is validated by theoretical considerations; neither side is independent of the other.

Looking F, I said, is no evidence that X is F if C are not SOC for F-ness; it may even be that appearing F under C shows that X is non-F. Yet no empirical inquiry can detect SOC, for observation provides us only with facts of the above type: Y appears G under D, Z appears H under E, etc. Suppose that we wish to know what X's weight is. We put it on a scale and the dial seems to point at the figure 7. Now, if it does point to 7, we have a reason to believe that X weighs seven grams. But does it point to 7? If conditions are nonstandard (say, we look at the dial sideways, or are in a hypnotic trance), its looking so does not settle the matter. The claim "If X appears F in C, then X is F" cannot be due to induction; inductive support for that claim must take this form: "In the past, when X seemed F under C it really was F, so probably whenever X looks F under C, it is F." Yet if we do not know which objects are F (we only know that they appear F), we have no inductive support for the claim that if X seems F under C, it really is F.

Therefore, some C must be adopted as SOC by a decision that X's seeming F in C is a prima facie good reason for holding that X is F. That also applies to the observation conditions: we cannot check whether conditions that appear C indeed are C, for that results in infinite regress. For empirical testing to be possible, we need to assume, a priori, that whatever seems F is indeed F. We start by taking all observers as standard and all observations as equally veridical. (Thus, when Jones says, "To me it is gaudy," he is not avoiding, but proposing, an objective verdict, for at this egalitarian stage the best possible reason for holding that X is gaudy is that Jones sees it so.) Then, to adjudicate between conflicting observations, theory confers privileges of standardhood; only when conducted under the privileged conditions is an observation deemed to establish fact. Attributing an observational property (be it Red or Gaudy) is therefore a theoretical verdict; it is based on observation, but is not exclusively decided by it.

When a theory matures, its SOC become complex and include tools and training; those who have the training and are adept at using the tools are *experts*. Experts regiment the application of predicates: their verdict brings some debates (whether Earth is round, whether Shakespeare is a good poet) to an end. The process may be slow, punctuated by fierce debates based on scant theory, but at the end of the day experts do emerge. That happens because, unless there are community-wide standards on how to apply observational predicates in that field, no communication about it, hence no disagreement about it, is possible. We therefore accept the verdict of experts and the theory on which it is based. Their talent, training, and tools set the standard.

SOC for some features (e.g., color) can be attained by nearly everyone; for other features (scientific and aesthetic ones) only experts attain the required SOC. These can, and do, change: schools and movements in art, and also in science, suggest new SOC and train experts to observe under the new conditions.[7] Others rely on, and defer to, experts (scientists, art critics) in applying these *observational* predicates; we learn that our observation of X as F may be illusory, for the conditions under which it was made may have been nonstandard.

That rule is similar to the principle Hilary Putnam called the "Principle of Division of Linguistic Labor."[8] Putnam applies it to ordinary substance terms: according to him, the application of these terms ('gold,' 'water,' 'fish,' 'bird,' etc.) is not determinable by laypeople; decision is relegated to experts in the relevant field. Whether or not that principle is true of substance terms (I have argued that it is not),[9] there is little doubt that it is used with respect to many observation terms. Consider the following exchanges:

—Look: a butterfly!
—It is not a butterfly; it's a moth.

—Do you hear the guitar?
—It's a lute, not a guitar.

7. That description is originally attributable, of course, to Thomas Kuhn (*The Structure of Scientific Revolutions* [Chicago: University of Chicago Press, 1962]).

8. See note 5 above.

9. Eddy Zemach, "Putnam's Theory on the Reference of Substance Terms," *Journal of Philosophy* 73 (1976): 116–27.

—I'll take the pink and green dress.
—It is magenta and cyan.

—There is a pretty picture.
—You mean that nauseating, sentimental monstrosity?

—What an expressive scene!
—You mistake histrionics for expressiveness.

How can the first speakers' observations be wrong? Because they are not in the SOC for making them. Aesthetic observations are like that: observers who do not attain the SOC for making those observations may be wrong; the work does appear to them as expressive, gaudy, or whatever, yet they are wrong, because, by the theory we have good reasons to accept, their viewpoint is not the SOC for such observations.

Having set the ground rules, let us now get to work: show the objective reality of the aesthetic properties. The arguments in this chapter are of two kinds: one set of arguments for scientific realists and the other for metaphysical realists. I do not argue for realism in general; that subject falls outside the scope of the present essay. What I wish to do is prove that *if* you subscribe to any kind of realism, scientific or metaphysical, aesthetic features are a part of it. That is, if *any* predicates correctly describe objective reality, aesthetic predicates are among them.

3.3. Empirical Adequacy

Scientific realists hold that the best scientific theory is probably true and that the entities it posits really exist. One theory is better than others if it satisfies the methodological constraints on theories to a higher degree. A good theory is more empirically adequate than its rivals; that is, it accounts for more data. It is simpler; that is, it explains the data by fewer laws, postulates fewer kinds of entities, and uses more intuitive calculi. It is more elegant in not including irreducibly ad hoc and phenomenological local laws, and it provides more true, nontrivial, and surprising predictions than the other theories.

We have a vast body of data about the activities, beliefs, and pronouncements of people who create art, collect it, consume it, and review it; these data are routinely integrated and explained by aesthetic statements based on aesthetic theory: statements such as "In her work the artist confronts the prevalent manneristic, courtly style of her era by executing her paintings in a rough way, omitting details, thus achieving a dramatic effect that is striking for her age" or "The pianist plays Beethoven mellifluously, gently; she highlights his debt to the tradition rather than his romanticism; she does that by . . . [followed by a list of facts about the way the pianist plays, all explained by their desired aesthetic effect]" or "Jones will not like Pinter; Pinter is much too poignant for one who adores clever, well-made plays and sees Shakespeare as a magnificent barbarian; take him to see Wilde or Shaw instead."

These statements, which essentially use aesthetic predicates, do enormous explanatory work. By citing a certain work of art's aesthetic character, they explain why it has the features it has. They make sense of the overt behavior of artists and their audiences, of what they do and of what they do not do, in terms of the aesthetic results of their actual and counterfactual actions. They integrate otherwise dissimilar phenomena (say, in music and in painting) under aesthetic descriptions and use aesthetic generalizations to predict the future behavior of consumers and artists. These explanations abound because they are so successful, which in turn vindicates the theories on which they are built. The said theories are tested and corroborated many times each day ("Put it lower; it is less menacing that way"; "I bet Smith will be the best-dressed woman tonight; she has such impeccable taste") and are subject to rigorous tests in the academia, where artworks are described and analyzed in terms of their aesthetic features. That, too, shows that aesthetic theories are successful at both tasks: they make sense of past phenomena and predict future ones.

We cannot achieve these results (explain preferences, actions, and reactions) without using aesthetic predicates; yet we cannot "translate" aesthetic terms into physicalistic terms.[10] Some thinkers believe that in principle psychological terminology must replace the aesthetic (cf. the materialists' hope of explaining action without the belief/desire vocabulary), but since we have no idea how it can be done, we must regard that belief as no

---

10. In his charming "Music Lessons" (in *Puzzles About Art,* ed. Margaret Battin et al. [New York: St. Martin's Press, 1989], 123–26), Stanley Godlovitch writes of a student of the guitar in the distant future who looks for physicalistic equivalents he can accurately follow to the verbal performance instructions that come with the old scores. For that purpose, he uses various metronome-like devices of increasing complexity, but gives up when he cannot find a suitable "affectometer" that will translate into physicalistic terms the instructions in the last movement of Ponce's *Sonatina Meridional: "violento, destacado con humor, robusto, con dulzura, ironica, con calor, lenjano y humoristico, apasionado."*

more than an article of faith. I. A. Richards, who, in his theoretical work,[11] claimed that aesthetic terms are reducible to psychological ones, never had such reductions in his practical work.[12]

Aesthetic theories are empirically tested; therefore, they can be empirically adequate. To buy a friend a present, you want to know what aesthetic features that person identifies and appreciates; you need an aesthetic theory in whose terms a gift can be described and matched with the friend's aesthetic taste. If your theory is empirically inadequate, you will get to know it, and regret it, by your friend's reaction.

Art has a history. A theory that successfully explains the said history is *beliefworthy*. The theories that explain that history with any degree of success essentially use aesthetic terms, while naturalistic theories neither give *reasons* for what is done in art nor predict its course. We understand developments in the history of each art form, relations between the arts, and connections between art and events in the world at large in terms of aesthetic concepts (contrast, harmony, intensification, tension, influence, protest, etc.). We need them to account for the very existence of art and its role in human history, how it shapes our ideals and desires. Naturalism cannot explain even controversy in art, for example, why X appears lyrical to Jones, while to Smith it looks bland and dull. Abjuring aesthetic properties, naturalism cannot even predict what *words* one will use to describe X, for no ordinary nonaesthetic predicate is coextensive with an aesthetic one.

An aesthetically sensitive person distinguishes the Tender from the Effete, the Dramatic from the Bombastic, etc. Such differences have no use outside aesthetics, so naturalists must regard those who readily make such distinctions (that is, most of us) as psychotics, subject to perceptual delusions. An artist, who monitors aesthetic distinctions and uses them as indicators on how to go on in his work, would then be a hallucinating lunatic, relying on figments of rabid imagination. Surely that is false. Aesthetic predicates are routinely used to impart information (German autobahns inform motorists when a beautiful view, *schöne Aussicht*, lies ahead); we will be very upset if none of it is true! As scientific realists we should believe a good, empirically adequate theory that ascribes aesthetic properties to things. Which aesthetic theory should we believe? The best; then, if "X is A" is a theorem of that theory, one has a good reason to believe that X is indeed A.

11. I. A. Richards, *Principles of Literary Criticism* (London: Routledge & Kegan Paul, 1924).

12. I. A. Richards, *Practical Criticism* (London: Routledge & Kegan Paul, 1929).

Like all theories, an aesthetic theory may be supplanted by others; its justification may expire. We may revise our view on the aesthetic properties of X, and thus on the SOC for being A. Yet preferring one theory to another is not arbitrary. Take a straight stick that appears bent when half-submerged in water. We have good reasons for saying what I have just said, namely, that the stick is straight and that viewing it half-submerged in water is not the SOC for it. It is unwise to consider semisubmergence in water as SOC and then explain why that stick misleadingly appears straight when taken out of the water. The theory on which that stick is truly bent is incompatible with much evidence; to maintain it we need radically to overhaul physics. Such unwieldy results make it silly to believe the theory that requires them. It is better to explain our data by saying that the stick is not bent, though we do see it as bent. The better theory, which is more worthy of acceptance, will adopt other SOC for molar things, and it will follow from it that sticks are not seen as they really are when observed in a state of half-submergence in water.

The same considerations apply to aesthetic theories. Aesthetic predicates are assigned to objects by critics who rely on theories. When theories T and T* conflict, it often makes more sense to accept one rather than the other, endorsing the SOC it proposes for the aesthetic properties it deals with. A theory that explains why a baroque oratorio would seem boring to a teenager who lacks musical education, though the oratorio itself is not boring, is methodologically superior to a theory according to which the said oratorio is really boring. Surely the first theory has a greater explanatory power; it is simpler, more concise, and it connects with other good theories better than its rival. A theory that takes as standard the observation conditions of a teenager who cares only for rock music must explain the mechanism through which people who have had some exposure to classical music fall victim to a pernicious illusion that the oratorio is graceful and profound. It must show how a monotonous drone (as the oratorio is if the teenager's observation conditions are SOC) causes an elaborate hallucination of fictitious (since unperceived by that teenager) properties. It needs to expose the hallucination-inducing properties of the oratorio that cause not otherwise delirious adults to be so deluded that they seem to perceive rich emotional and spiritual meanings in a dull whir. Perhaps those adults are not deluded but perpetrate a monumental hoax, a worldwide conspiracy against the young. Such a theory, like other colossal conspiracy theories, requires evidence of such a malicious plot, a proof of the cynical intentions of the cabal that hatched it. Since we have no such evidence, the music-conspiracy theory is methodologically inferior to the rival theory. That theory can explain, in great detail, why that oratorio, while possessing beauty and great inner richness, would seem monotonous and boring to teenagers unfamiliar with the musical language and tradition in which it has been conceived. It will predict that kids who wish to be overpowered by elementary rhythms, whose sense of hearing has sustained irreparable damage by the loud music they usually listen to, will not perceive these positive aesthetic features, at least not on first hearing.

SOC are chosen by methodological considerations. For example, a theory implying that the stick is truly straight but appears bent when half-submerged in water meets the methodological constraints much better than its rival, the theory that the stick is really bent but misleadingly appears straight in air. The latter theory is neither simple nor elegant, it has little predictive power, and it is not conservative (it fails to interface with other theories we accept); hence it is epistemically unjustified, and it is unreasonable to believe it. Similarly, a theory that chooses as standard those conditions under which Bach's work appears aesthetically good is much more simple and elegant than its rivals and has more predictive power. It predicts that Bach will sound boring under observation conditions that do not include an ability to follow a melodic line, notice tonal variations, identify the key, perceive the structure of parts, hear polyphonic nuances, and understand a spiritual meaning. The rival theory has to pass over in silence questions such as, how will the musically educated respond to certain variations in the performance of that work? On the other hand, the theory on which Bach comes out aesthetically good explains why various performers play it as they do. It makes sense of behavior (say, decisions of judges in musical competitions) that its rival theory must describe as pathological, lacking any rationale. A theory, one consequence of which is the theorem that Bach's music is great, can explain Bach's relations to his predecessors and exactly in what he improved upon them. That theory can tie Bach's music to art-historical movements that precede and succeed it, and to historical events that serve as its foil. It can do the reverse too, that is, use art to explain historical and sociological phenomena (e.g., why romanticism is tied to progressive movements in the nineteenth century and to reactionary ones in the twentieth). Therefore, it is a better theory.

Not all assignments of SOC are equal, for not all of them can charitably explain the behavior of artists and art lovers and make that explanation converge on what we know about human culture from other sources. A theory that takes as standard the conditions under which Bach's work looks boring, full of clumsy flourishes lacking in taste and meaning, cannot do that. It cannot explain Bach's (and his performers') reasoning. As I said, one *may* hold that those who admire Bach are victims of delusion or else just pretend to admire him, passing off tin as gold (as in Andersen's tale *The Emperor's New Clothes*). Yet if those who listen to Bach were crazy or conniving crooks, they would manifest other symptoms of these conditions, but such symptoms are clearly missing. The said theory is weak, hence unworthy of credence.

3.4. Are Aesthetic Explanations Impotent?

Some scientific realists hold that aesthetic and moral theories should not be given a realistic interpretation, for value properties are explanation-wise impotent and theoretically odd; that is, they are poor predictors of phenomena and do not sit well with the rest of science. J. L. Mackie says that aesthetic and other value properties are not "part of the fabric of the world" in the way that mass and velocity are; thus, value predicates should be reduced to predicates of psychology and physics.[13] Gilbert Harman concurs; his premise is one I accept: "[S]cientific principles can be justified ultimately by their role in explaining observations."[14] He adds that we may posit protons because "facts about protons can affect what you observe," but we should not posit value properties, for "there does not seem to be any way in which the actual rightness or wrongness of a given situation can have any effect on your perceptual apparatus."[15] A good theory should explain why we make the judgments that we make and why we promulgate that very theory. A value theory, however, no matter whether it is true or false, fails that test: what the theory states is "completely irrelevant to our explanation" of why that theory was offered.[16] Why we observed the phenomena it deals with and why the theory is offered are explained by physical and psychological facts about us, and not by value properties of things.

That argument is unacceptable. To explain a specific value judgment one needs to explain why we endorse a certain content (not why we uttered

13. J. L. Mackie, *Ethics: Inventing Right and Wrong* (Harmondsworth, Middlesex: Penguin, 1977).

14. Gilbert Harman, *The Nature of Morality* (New York: Oxford University Press, 1977), 9.

15. Ibid., 8.

16. Ibid., 7.

certain words). Aesthetic terms do not occur in science; so a scientific explanation of an aesthetic judgment must present the content of that judgment in the vocabulary of natural science or else hold that aesthetic judgments lack content. However, we saw in the first two chapters that both strategies fail. Noncognitivism is false, and there is no way to report value judgments in value-neutral terms. Structuralist, psychoanalytic, Darwinian, Marxist, and biopsychological attempts to substitute naturalistic terms for aesthetic ones are notoriously inadequate. Reductions of aesthetic properties to naturalistic ones have a poor record; they were popular in the nineteenth century, but were abandoned long ago. Many aestheticians are still convinced that a reduction ought to be possible, but no one tries to carry it out.

Typically, Mackie and Harman do not offer reductions of value properties and would probably agree that previous attempts to do so have failed. Yet they do not give up hope: naturalistic reduction of aesthetic and ethical judgments must be possible *in principle*, so science will provide it in the future. Can such a reduction be carried out? I think not. It is not enough to provide necessary and sufficient conditions for the application of value terms: that only means that (as a realist may believe anyway) value properties supervene on physical ones. Mental events may supervene on physical events and yet not be reducible to them, and similarly, irreducibly aesthetic properties may supervene on nonaesthetic ones.

Science cannot explain our aesthetic observations: Why does this lied seem delicate? An aesthetic explanation, say, "because it is delicate," is unavailable to science. Science may predict that we will utter the *sentence* "This lied is delicate," but not that this lied will look delicate, for the term 'delicate,' like all phenomenal terms, is not a scientific term. Why do we sense qualia? Why do we see X as white, straight, or ugly? Facts about the brain say nothing about what it is like to experience X as red or gaudy. Science cannot explain that, for it lacks the concepts *red* and *gaudy*, and these cannot be reduced to concepts science has, say, of brain-cell spikings. No description of cells can make you understand how Red differs from Blue and Gaudy from Delicate, what each of these phenomenal features is. The conceptual resources of science as we know it are unfit for that task.

The only explanation we have for our experiencing phenomenal properties is the one given by Aristotle: the experience of sensing F-ly is an observation of an object X that is F. The basic concept in that explanation is *observation*: we can be *aware* (be acquainted with) the delicate nature of the lied. Science has no place for that relation; there is no physicalistic way to say what we want to say, to wit, that to observe X as F is to become acquainted with the property F. Some philosophers (most notably, Paul

Churchland)[17] suggest that we do away with such phenomenal terms and use science's terms instead to report data. Eliminating phenomenal terms from our language will, however, result in its *losing its ability to express science*. "My C-neurons fire!" cannot replace "I see red!" because, unlike the latter statement, the former statement does not specify my *evidence* for holding that my C-neurons fire. The information that my ground for that opinion is my sensing red is lost.

"I hear wailing music" and "I see red" are mode-specific: they are empirical grounds for believing that my C-neurons fire. I derive the conclusion that my C-neurons fire from the fact that I sensed thusly. Otherwise, "My C-neurons fire" is for me a dogma; if I cannot say what my reasons are for holding that my C-neurons fire, then it is a self-evident truism for me, a nonempirical dogma for which I need no evidence. Empirical belief is based on sensation. How, then, did I sense that my C-neurons fire? Did I smell the firing? Did I see it? Did I taste it? Did I hear a voice saying that? There are many ways for me to reach the opinion that my C-neurons fire, and only one of them is by seeing red. Merely to insist obstinately that my C-neurons fire (having lost my mode-specific evidence for it) is to express a dogma to which I just happen to adhere.

To forgo aesthetic and other phenomenal terms is to give up science too. Unlike other stories, science is based on experience; so, if we cannot report the qualia we experience, science becomes a fairy tale, a legend with no empirical support. We then lack the means to distinguish empirical observation from idle opinion. By eliminating phenomenal terms one therefore eliminates science. Moreover, that elimination cannot be justified, for one needs sense evidence that the elimination works (merely to say that will not do!), that the brave new scientistic lingo adequately reports our sensory experience. To cite the evidence of the senses, however, is to reinstate the expurgated phenomenal terms. Phenomenal terms cannot, therefore, be expunged from a scientific account of the "fabric of the world." If the charge against aesthetic theories is their essential use of phenomenal aesthetic terms, it fails. Phenomenal terms are ineliminable from any empirical account of reality.

We may grant Harman and Mackie that ethics and aesthetics are, indeed, isolated from the sciences. There are connections between acoustics

---

17. See, by Paul Churchland, *Scientific Realism and the Plasticity of Mind* (Cambridge: Cambridge University Press, 1979); *Matter and Consciousness* (Cambridge: Cambridge University Press, 1988); "The Direct Introspection of Brain States," *Journal of Philosophy* 35 (1985): 8–28; *A Neurocomputational Perspective: The Nature of Mind and the Structure of Science* (Cambridge: MIT Press, 1989); *The Engine of Reason* (Cambridge: MIT Press, 1995).

and musicology, geometry and art theory, linguistics and literary criticism; some explanations combine elements from ethics, biology, psychology, and aesthetics; yet these relations are not as strong as those between, say, botany and zoology. However, it is a folly to discard a successful theory if it impinges only marginally on other theories; you do not give up a theory just because it does not satisfy *all* your desiderata. Unifying all explanations is a regulative ideal, but its satisfaction is not guaranteed a priori.

3.5. The Primacy of Aesthetic Properties

My final argument intended for scientific realists is this: Scientific realists hold that the best theory is probably true. The best theory is one that passes the methodological tests with flying colors: it is highly coherent (internally and with other theories), simple, powerful, elegant, and dramatic (we prefer a theory T that successfully predicts events to a theory T* that only postdicts them; these theories explain the data equally well, but T is more *dramatic* than T*). Now, all these are aesthetic properties. All theories must have aesthetic properties, since those are what we judge them by. Elsewhere I have argued that these properties are the *only* constraints on theories.[18] As Willard Quine did see (and Karl Popper did not), no theory is ever refuted by observation: prediction failures may only cost a theory its generality and elegance, for it may add rules or ad hoc stipulations to explain the apparent failures; such additions may make a theory inelegant, but it will stay unrefuted. Thus, given that science has to account for observations, whose content makes up its data, scientific realism comes to this: ugly accounts are probably false. An account that is rich, powerful, dramatic, elegant, coherent, and simple—that is, beautiful (*unity in variety* is the oldest definition of Beauty)—is probably true.

To repeat, *given* that a scientific theory has to explain why we have the sensations we do have, it is evaluated by the degree to which it negotiates the methodological desiderata. These are all aesthetic features, so what they amount to is a demand that theories be beautiful, that is, have a high degree of unity in variety. A theory should be elegant yet powerful, rich yet simple, dramatic (predictive) yet conservative, total in scope yet limited in means.

18. Eddy Zemach, "Truth and Beauty," *Philosophical Forum* 18 (1986): 21–39.

Scientific realism thus amounts to an injunction to believe that scientific theory which has the highest aesthetic value.

Against that view, which I expressed in previous writings, it was argued that if science abides by aesthetic constraints, why is there not a multiplicity of styles in science as in art, why is there no postmodernist science, impressionistic science, and rococo science? Why must science be simple rather than baroque?[19] I answer that the form of a total, world-encompassing system that unites nature under mathematical laws must suit its content. It cannot be the form of a trio or a symphony, works limited in scope that do not aspire to embrace all possible phenomena. A poem or a painting may be pretty, lovely, playful, cute, even frivolous, but science cannot have that kind of beauty. Frivolous mathematics is repulsive; lyrical physics is atrocious. Science, the greatest common endeavor of all humanity throughout time is majestic; hence the style that becomes it is simple and austere. An old woman can be no less beautiful than a young woman, but not through being nubile or pretty, not by having a smooth skin and a nicely curved body. An old woman trying to achieve aesthetic excellence by acquiring such aesthetic virtues is monstrously ugly. Each sort of thing has its own way of attaining beauty; it can excel in aesthetic features that are appropriate to it. Science can be beautiful only through being monumental, sublime, strikingly simple, coolly elegant and powerful. Physics cannot be lovely as a tree, but then a tree cannot excel in awesome grandeur. Thus, a baroque science with millions of local pretty theoretical curlicues would be ugly, due to its enormous scale; in a manner of speaking, science can be beautiful only in the Egyptian style. It can aesthetically excel by providing fundamental wide-ranging harmonies, stark symmetry, high drama, and total scope; the kind of aesthetic excellence proper to it is dictated by its content.

If a methodologically excellent theory T posits the existence of electrons, that is, according to the scientific realist, a good reason to believe that there are electrons; if T is beautiful, it is probably true. And what about the statement that T is beautiful? Is *it* true? If it is not true, because 'beautiful' fails to denote, then T is not beautiful; a scientific realist would conclude that therefore it is probably not true. In that case there is no reason to believe it, and hence one should not believe that there are any electrons in reality. Thus, if we should believe that there are electrons (or any other statement of

19. Ramon Lemos and Alan Goldman have raised that objection in many conversations we have had on this issue.

science), we should also believe that 'beauty,' 'drama,' 'elegance,' and other aesthetic predicates are satisfied in reality and truly describe our science. Put it differently: suppose that the theory T is true. Since T is true, it is beautiful. If T is beautiful, the aesthetic theory AT, which says that T is A+, is true. If AT is true, its basic predicates denote features of the real world. Therefore, aesthetic properties are features of the real world.

A related argument shows that aesthetic properties cannot be unreal. Suppose that there is a theory T demonstrating that there are no aesthetic properties in reality, say, that 'elegant' and 'gaudy' should not be given a semantic interpretation. Now, if T is true, it too must pass muster and possess the required aesthetic virtues. We should believe that there are no aesthetic properties only if T (the theory that there are no aesthetic properties) is beautiful. Yet if "T is A+" is true, then there are aesthetic properties after all; ergo, it is logically impossible to disprove the reality of aesthetic properties. Belief in the reality of aesthetic properties is therefore required by all beliefs, since they are necessary for justifying them. To sum up: it is justifiable to believe *that p* (according to scientific realism) iff one believes that T, the theory implying *that p,* is beautiful. If T is beautiful, then Beauty is real. Believing the reality of Beauty is therefore a precondition for justifiably believing anything whatever.

There is a serious objection to the above argument. One may grant that to adopt a reductive theory T of aesthetic properties we must find it beautiful. However, once we adopt T, we have a world-picture where there is no place for aesthetic properties; instead of Beauty we have the property to which T reduces Beauty, say, Causing Brain-State N. So we may deny the existence of aesthetic properties after all, for we can describe our justification for adopting T in the vocabulary of T itself, saying, instead of "T is beautiful," "T causes brain-state N."

My answer is that the property Causing Brain-State N has no *justificatory power*. Why should the fact that T causes N justify the belief that T is true? Why should we prefer a theory that causes brain-state N to theories that do not cause N but cause M or L or any other brain-state? Having a methodologically perfect science is a natural desideratum of rational beings. The concept *causes brain-state N,* which replaces *beauty* in T, does not have that connection to rationality and perfection. We want our theory to be unified, powerful, and coherent, since these are *value* properties; it is good to be beautiful: the connection between beauty and goodness, or perfection, is conceptual, that is, a priori. On the other hand, Causing N has no such value. Epistemic justification is linked to Beauty; we like beautiful things, so it is an advantage for T to be beautiful. If it is not beautiful (if nothing is really beautiful), its special distinction is lost. That T causes N—and Causing N is the property we previously misdescribed as Beauty—is irrelevant to the truth of T; Causing N is not special, Beauty is.

Consider an example: There is a conceptual link between the concepts *witch* and *magic powers*, but the concept *eccentric woman,* which replaces *witch* in a modern theory, has no such link to *magic powers.* Suppose I believe that Mary is a witch, but later find out that there are no witches; what I wrongly described as witches are eccentric women. Since an inference from "Mary is a witch" to "Mary has magic powers" is valid, may I derive "Mary has magic powers" from "Mary is an eccentric woman"? Certainly not. Beauty is a value and may mandate credence, but if T is not beautiful, if it only causes N brain-states, it deserves no credence. However, if T deserves no credence, we have no reason to believe that there is no Beauty in the world.

3.6. Proofs for Metaphysical Realists

None of the proofs discussed in the previous sections will be acceptable to realists who reject scientific realism. Metaphysical realists argue that methodological excellence, that is, beauty, has nothing to do with truth. For all we know, the world in itself may be ugly, so why believe an account that presents it as pretty? Why should a pretty theory have a better chance of corresponding to the world as it is? A beautiful model may nicely explain and integrate our experience and yet be false. If the world is not as the best model presents it, then the more pleasing explanation is incorrect; the uglier model may be the one that the world satisfies. Reality (*das Ding an sich,* the noumenon) is as it is, and we cannot assume that the theory that pleases us the most describes it more accurately than a theory that pleases us not at all.

Can we show the metaphysical realist, first, that reality has certain aesthetic features and, second, that our aesthetic descriptions of it are generally right? Nonrealists such as Michael Dummett and Hilary Putnam think that a methodologically impeccable theory, say, the one that ideally rational beings will choose, cannot be false, since they identify *truth* with *justified assertibility.* But metaphysical realists insist on their distinction: they hold that a justifiably assertible theory may be false. Can a metaphysical realist know whether things in reality have aesthetic properties?

Yes. Whatever else the world has, it has aesthetic properties. You may doubt the existence of electrons, quarks, gluons, and other entities postulated by science, but not aesthetic properties. Even if there is no color or sound in the world, even if motion, space, and time do not exist, even if reality satisfies no predicate of our science, it must satisfy the aesthetic predicates.

First, the real world has *some* nature, some structure, some features, so it is aesthetically valuable. Were we able to examine it, we would find it pretty or ugly, dramatic or monotonous, dainty or sublime. Every thing is amenable to aesthetic evaluation. If we shall never know the world as it is, we shall not know what its aesthetic features are; yet, even if we never know its aesthetical character, it has some; it is boring or dramatic, ugly or pretty, as we could verify if we knew it as God does.

Compare 'central,' 'spherical,' and 'gaudy': which is the most fail-safe predicate, the most likely to apply to real things? If space is Newtonian, it has no center, so nothing can be central; if space is Einsteinian, there are no equidistant spatial points, so nothing can be absolutely spherical. But things can be gaudy in any manner of space; even if (as Leibniz and Kant thought) space is unreal, nonspatial things can be gaudy. Ascribing aesthetic properties to things can never be a category mistake. Not every possible world is spatiotemporal, but every possible world has *some* features, and these may be dramatic, harmonious, or bland. Even a lifeless world has aesthetic features, to wit, those that *would* be ascribed to it by an expert observing it under SOC. We can imagine a world to which no predicate of our science is applicable, but we cannot imagine a world that is unamenable to aesthetic valuation. Therefore, whatever other properties the real world has, it has aesthetic properties too.

A metaphysical realist may doubt whether aesthetic sentences can be true of reality, because our aesthetic judgments are not about noumena: the features we aesthetically evaluate are all phenomenal. We see the world as it presents itself to our sensitivity, via our sense organs, and other beings sense it differently. Now, it is true that due to our sensory apparatus we see trees as green, while an alien sensitive to radioactive radiation, not to the wavelengths we respond to, may sense nothing similar. Nevertheless, even if the noumenon we see as a green tree is entirely unlike our phenomenal green tree, it may still be pretty, sublime, repulsive, or gaudy, as we could verify had God chosen to let us know the world as it is.

So far, I have shown that a metaphysical realist need not hold that our aesthetic judgments do not apply to reality. I shall now show that many of our aesthetic judgments *are* true. Even if in science error on a grand scale is possible, in aesthetics it is not. We can put greater trust in our aesthetic beliefs than in our scientific ones. Scientific theories rely on inference to the best hypothesis, but, according to metaphysical realism, that is unwarranted: neither empirical adequacy nor methodological merit is truth. Aesthetic judgments, in contrast, are based on direct observation, which, as I shall now show, is necessarily usually veridical; aesthetic judgment cannot be all wrong. My proof may remind one of Davidson's proof of the impossibility of massive error and incomprehensible languages[20] (which I do not accept: aliens may prove that they have a language that we can never fathom),[21] but the similarity is superficial: my argument applies to aesthetic predicates only.

I have argued that our theoretical constraints are all aesthetic: there are no other criteria for judging theories. A theory cannot be refuted, but it can be shown to be cumbersome, crude, and devoid of dramatic power. A theory can be shown to be ugly, but not false. Suppose now that we may err in our aesthetic judgments, just as it is possible that all our scientific beliefs are wrong. What we take to be ugly may in fact be pretty, and vice versa. That possibility, however, robs us of our sole reason for not *using* (not to be confused with *believing*) bad scientific theories. The metaphysical realists maintain that an ugly theory may yet be true, but they do claim to know that it is ugly. Yet how do we know that? If we are as likely as not to be wrong in our aesthetic judgments, we may be wrong in thinking that a theory is ugly; then, we may be mistaken in our belief that it is not empirically adequate—so we have no reason not to use it. Which theory shall we use, then, if a theory's empirical adequacy is as elusive as its truth?

If our aesthetic judgment that T is a beautiful theory may be doubted, it needs support. It is useless, however, to produce another theory, with arguments that buttress the claim that T does nicely meet the methodological constraints, for the new theory is no less suspect than the previous one. The

20. Donald Davidson, "On the Very Idea of a Conceptual Scheme," in *Inquiries into Truth and Interpretation,* ed. Donald Davidson (New York: Oxford University Press, 1984), 223–42, and idem, "A Coherence Theory of Truth and Knowledge," in *Truth and Interpretation,* ed. Ernest LePore (Oxford: Basil Blackwell, 1986).

21. Suppose that a spaceship lands here. Its nonhuman crew is obviously highly intelligent; they learn English in a matter of days and converse with us on a variety of topics. However, when we ask them to translate some of their writings into English, they explain that they cannot do so, for theirs is a language that we cannot understand. The reason is that while we have six senses, they have sixty. They show us the bodily organs for these senses and explain that the simplest word in their language refers to a determination of at least twenty different modes of sensation. The number of computations their brains can handle is many orders of magnitude higher than ours, so it is reasonable that there can be no English translation of even the simplest expression in their language. Surely that is not impossible. But Davidson would have us say that our galactic friends are not intelligent and that they cannot have a language!

new theory looks beautiful, but perhaps it is not! If our ability to tell a good argument from a bad one is doubted, it is impossible to quell that doubt by further arguments (it is useless to make one take an oath that one did not lie under oath). Those who can assess theories, including the skeptic's and the metaphysical realist's, can apply aesthetic predicates *correctly*. Any argument, including the argument that our aesthetic judgments may be wrong, is worth considering only if we trust our ability to distinguish a good argument from a bad one, that is, only if we believe that usually we apply aesthetic terms correctly, telling the beautiful from the ugly. Thus our aesthetic judgments cannot be coherently conceived to be mostly false, for if they can, we should not believe the reasoning that led us to believe that they can. We cannot go very wrong in aesthetic discriminations: that is the one area where we must, on the whole, be right.

Consider the following example: Can you have good reasons to believe that you are utterly mad? Not that you have some illogical spells, but that you are insane, a raving maniac who thinks in an irrational way and cannot tell a valid argument from an invalid one? No. If you are convinced by the argument, you should believe that you are mad, and thus distrust the reasoning that led you to be convinced by the argument. On the other hand, if your reasoning is valid, you must reject the argument because its conclusion, that your reasoning is invalid, is false. Thus, you should reject that argument anyway. Nothing should convince you that you are mad, or (which comes to the same thing) that your aesthetic judgment is so bad that you usually mistake the inelegant and ugly (including ugly arguments) for the flawless, in which event faulty reasoning may look good to you. It is pragmatically paradoxical to doubt our basic aesthetic judgments, for if we do, we should doubt that that doubt itself is well founded. If I think my thoughts are drivel, that thought itself is drivel, and thus I should not heed it. I should not accept any arguments that my reasoning is good, for I should accept these arguments only if my reasoning is good enough to distinguish good arguments from bad ones, in which event the argument is redundant. If I do not know immediately, by just considering it, that my reasoning is good, I cannot discover it to be good. Therefore, if our aesthetic judgment is no good, then what seems to be a good reason for thinking that our aesthetic judgment is no good is also no good. Thus it is never reasonable to believe that our aesthetic judgment is faulty: if that proposition is true, we should believe that it is false; if it is false, then of course we should believe that it is false. Therefore we should believe that it is false.

4

TASTE AND TIME

4.1. The Foibles of Fashion

Aesthetic taste, people say, is fickle: we scorn today what yesterday we admired. So how can taste be a sensitivity to objective properties of things? A realist in aesthetics maintains that the truth of an aesthetic sentence depends on the aesthetic properties of the object denoted by the subject of the sentence. Why, then, does it seem that aesthetic evaluation depends not at all on the object evaluated, but on the variable taste of evaluators? At different times, they ascribe different aesthetic descriptions to the same unchanged object; does it not show that such descriptions are not objective descriptions of things? In the 1950s we saw longer skirts as soft, graceful, and feminine, while short ones looked childish or vulgar. Then, in the sixties, miniskirts came into fashion and were seen as charming, sexy, and free, and the longer skirts appeared clumsy and homely. In the eighties longer skirts again looked urbane, liberated, and smart, whereas minis seemed unsophisticated and demeaning. How can realists explain a change in judgment where there is no change in the object judged?

Notoriously, changes of taste occur not only in fashion but in art too. Aesthetic revolutions demote established artists, remove their paintings from walls and consign them to oblivion, while the rejects of yesterday are lionized and become culture heroes. If we offer incompatible descriptions of the same thing and are not in the least embarrassed about it, perhaps aesthetic statements do not describe that thing at all but, as the subjectivists say, our own attitudes and emotions.

Changes in aesthetic taste and preferential behavior can be explained by sociological causes, but merely causal explanations do not justify a judgment. If aesthetic statements describe public objects, they should be cogently defensible, and the cause of Jane's making an aesthetic statement need not be identical with the reason she has for believing it is true. Yet what reason can Jane have to change her description of X from A+ to A− when she admits that X has not changed? One reason is believing that her previous judgment was wrong, but Jane is not saying that. So, do fashion, and the variant evaluations of the same artwork, prove the realist wrong? Do they show that aesthetic judgments are not factual reports, that beauty is in the eyes of the beholder?

A realist may say that if at time t_1 Jane says that X is pretty and at t_2 she says that X is not pretty, she contradicts herself, and only one of her statements can be true. By the law of excluded middle, a realist may insist, at least one of these statements is false, and Jane was wrong when she made it. So when did Jane err, when she said that X is A+ or when she said the opposite? Earlier I endorsed the realist's thesis, that aesthetic sentences express statements about properties of public objects; yet the conclusion that Jane must have made a mistake, because the judgment she made at t_1 contradicts the one she made at t_2, is unacceptable. The critics who in 1900 praised Byron and ridiculed Pope were no less competent than those who in 1960 ridiculed Byron and praised Pope; must we say that at least one of these groups of experts was radically mistaken? Could all members of that group have bad taste? On what ground can we dismiss the observations made by one group of experts and accept those made by another group?

We firmly believe that Bach and Shakespeare are great artists, but we cannot spurn the connoisseurs of previous eras who preferred C.P.E. to J. S. Bach and Racine to Shakespeare. Is it a stalemate, our word against theirs? Some aestheticians argue that we have a good reason to prefer our judgment to that of previous generations: our experience of art is wider than theirs. We know artworks they did not know, so our scope is wider.[1] Yet basing our claim to knowledge of value on our wide scope is self-defeating, for the scope of future generations dwarfs ours. The wider-is-better argument cannot support our beliefs about the greatness of Shakespeare and Bach, for if we must defer to wider-experienced progeny, we must hold all our

---

1. See Jerrold Levinson, "Artworks and the Future," in *Music, Art, and Metaphysics* (Ithaca: Cornell University Press, 1990), 179–214.

judgments in abeyance. Our problems and aspirations, and also our art and very art forms, may seem tediously insignificant to posterity, and if their judgment overrides ours, we cannot trust any of our aesthetic judgments. The scope of *each* expert is, however, puny in comparison to that of his successors; that discredits all aesthetic judgments. Surely that is not what descriptivists believe.

If an entire past generation saw beauty where there was none, and failed to see great beauty that stared them in the eye, then we should not trust our generation's taste either. We, too, may be hopelessly deluded, seeing in X features that are not there. Our own experts' opinion is, then, useless, and their work on aesthetic judgments a waste of time. I conclude that classical descriptivism backfires: it ends by espousing the same nihilism that it started by opposing. The objectivity it confers on aesthetic judgments is vacuous, for a judgment that dismisses all the tests that an entire generation can administer is otiose.

An indication that classical descriptivism misses the mark is found in the fact that we feel no embarrassment and do not recant when in talking about fashion we say at t_1 that X is A+ and then at t_2 that X is A−. We do not say that we have made a mistake, that our former judgment was incorrect. A woman who bought a miniskirt at t_1 does not think at t_2, when she rejects such skirts offhand, that at t_1 she had poor taste or was a victim to illusion. On the contrary, she says that the miniskirt was beautiful for its time, just as the longer skirt is beautiful for its time. We must respect these statements and not force them into a mold that they do not fit.

Realists may resolve the difficulty by forgoing the intuition that aesthetic properties supervene on nonaesthetic ones.[2] They may argue that since (1) aesthetic features are real properties of things, and (2) at t_2 we observe in X aesthetic features other than those we observed in it at t_1, and (3) a

---

2. J. Kim, "Causality, Identity, and Supervenience in the Mind-Body Problem," *Midwest Studies in Philosophy* 4 (1979): 31–50. "A family of properties M is *supervenient upon* a family of properties N with respect to domain D just in case for any two objects in the domain D, if they diverge in the family M then necessarily they diverge in the family N; that is to say, for any x and y in D, if x and y are indiscernible with respect to properties in the family N then necessarily x and y are indiscernible with respect to M" (41). Cf. his "Supervenience and Supervenient Causation," *Southern Journal of Philosophy*, supp. vol. 22 (1984): 45–56, and "Supervenience and Nomological Incommensurables," *American Philosophical Quarterly* 15 (1978): 149–56. For recent material, see E. E. Savellos and Ü. D. Yalçin, *Supervenience: New Essays* (Cambridge: Cambridge University Press, 1995).

thing that has different properties at different times has changed, and (4) X's physical properties did not change between t_1 and t_2, therefore (5) only X's aesthetic properties changed. Our aesthetic judgments are not in conflict: X did change, though the entire change was confined to its aesthetic properties. The skirt did not physically alter between 1950 and 1980, yet its aesthetic properties changed by themselves.

This answer is ontologically irresponsible. The statement that X was pretty in 1950 and by 1960 became ugly is incomprehensible if it is added that no change other than a transition from beauty to ugliness took place in X. Told that Jones lost his good looks, we wonder what physical changes he underwent; we would be baffled if told that this change, from handsome to ugly, was the *only* change that took place in Jones. We take it to be a necessary condition that if X has changed aesthetically, then some of its nonaesthetic properties have also changed. A shirt that undergoes no physical change between t_1 and t_2 may yet appear pink at t_1 and not appear pink at t_2, but it cannot be pink at t_1 and not be pink at t_2. We will not say that its color changed unless there occurred a chemical change in it. If we take it off the clothesline on the porch and hang it in the closet, we may say that now it looks purple rather than pink, but we may not say that now it is not pink but purple instead. You cannot make a pink shirt purple, a sad tone gay, or an ugly picture pretty, without changing their physical features.

Subjectivists, who maintain that aesthetic predicates describe attitudes or feelings of subjects and not physical objects, offer the opposite answer. They have no problem with Jane's saying "X is A+" at t_1 and "X is A−" at t_2, for by their lights Jane describes the changes in (say) her own feelings; that X has not changed between t_1 and t_2 is then irrelevant. In Chapter 2, I argued that this answer is wrong. Aesthetical statements are based on *empirical observation* (we *see* that X is graceful, gaudy, gross, fine, cute, or dull), and therefore empiricists cannot dismiss them, saying that they are not true observations at all. If a whole class of observational reports can be disenfranchised by decree just because we have some trouble integrating them with other observations, there is no stopping that practice. Every empirical datum could then be discarded if we were unhappy with it; that would be to supplant empirical science with a hallowed dogma. Aesthetic properties are observed in nature with no less perspicuity and assurance than are their cousins, the so-called secondary properties (Sweet, Scented, Hot, Loud, Soft, Red, etc.); these are the uncontested objects of all empirical observation and the source of all our beliefs about nature.

Those who deny that aesthetic properties are real must accept Descartes's and Locke's arguments that "secondary" qualities should also be construed as mere states of the perceiving subject. These philosophers, in turn, cannot stand against Leibniz and Kant, who argue that the "primary" qualities too (e.g., Motion, Shape, and Mass) are not properties of objects but human sensations, because space and time, on which they depend, are merely our own forms of intuition, the special human way of ordering sensations. Quantum mechanics rejects Newton's view that all things have both Location and Velocity; nothing has that. Are they, then, subjective properties of human observers? If that is unacceptable, then so is the view that aesthetic properties are private. Subjectivism is false because its reasoning applies to all empirically observable properties without exception.

A third answer is offered as a compromise between classical descriptivism and subjectivism, dividing the domain of aesthetic predicates between them. On that view, genuine artworks have an objective aesthetic value, while taste in other things (clothes, songs, food, landscapes) is subjective: no reasons apply there, only raw likes and dislikes. That at t_1 we like some cloths and at t_2 dislike them is not a reappraisal of real properties; these changes of taste only reflect shifting moods and feelings of observers and require no justification.

That compromise is beset with the problems of both sides and has the advantages of neither. If empirical observation detects Beauty as a property that objectively qualifies artworks, we cannot disregard observations of that very property in items of popular culture. The usual argument for a distinction between artworks and other objects of aesthetic evaluation is that methods of evaluation exist only for art; preference outside art is idiosyncratic and varies from person to person and from time to time. But that claim is untrue: people do argue about aesthetic merits of popular bands and fashionable clothes. Some youngsters talk of nothing else. Champions of high art are but a tiny minority; many popular items achieved during their short life spans a degree of aesthetic acclaim and consensus unparalleled by any work of high art. Furthermore, periodical changes of taste occur in high art too; many celebrated masterpieces were rediscovered, called back after a century or so from oblivion. The relative frequency of such turnabouts cannot be ontologically essential.

Even if it were true that only in art is aesthetic judgment based on reasons, the ontological significance of that would be doubtful. Suppose that we can explain why *Moses* is a good work of art, but are unable to explain our spontaneous attraction to landscapes and fashionable dresses to which we take immediate liking. Is this a reason for denying objective ontological status to their beauty? Many phenomenal predicates ('red,' 'hurts,' etc.) are such that we cannot justify our belief in their presence. It does not render these properties unreal; we sometimes do change our judgment regarding them, but the change is neither random nor arbitrary.

Moreover, not only high art admits of reasons; we cite both aesthetic and nonaesthetic reasons to justify aesthetic verdicts outside art. Asked, "What makes him handsome?" one may reply, "A high forehead, big blue eyes, black hair, and high cheek bones." These are neither sufficient nor necessary conditions for being handsome, but they are valuable indications, good, relevant evidence, for believing that he *is* handsome. These are not different from a critic's reasons for attributing an aesthetic property to a painting ("What makes it poised is its diagonal structure, painterly style, and long brush strokes").

The "middle" position holds that to distinguish great artworks from the flashes of fashion we should try to solicit reasons, and that if none are forthcoming, the preference is not objective. However, we often do justify our preference for clothes. Further, even if no reasons come to mind, that does not mean that there *are* no such reasons, for they may merely elude one. Again, one may be aware of the truth-makers of one's aesthetic judgment even if one is unable to articulate them (perhaps for lack of words). Also, unawareness of these truth-makers does not preclude becoming aware of them later, recognizing them as what motivated one's original verdict. The "middle" position is, then, no answer; the problem is still with us: how to account for the vicissitudes and foibles of fashion.

I summarize: descriptivists hold that *all* aesthetic judgments are about aesthetic properties of the object judged. Albeit based on laudable empiricism, that view leads to denying the supervenience of aesthetic on nonaesthetic properties, and that is unacceptable. Subjectivists take *no* aesthetic judgment to be about the object's properties. That move leads to regarding *all* empirical judgments as capriciously subjective; justifying the attribution of any sense property becomes impossible. The middle ground solution, that some aesthetic judgments reveal what the object is, while others only reflect a subjective response to it, is also unacceptable, for its data are wrong, and it implausibly denies that judgments of beauty in nature and in fashion are aesthetic at all.

A constraint on a solution must be the tenet that emerged in the course of the discussion above: that everything, be it a Rodin sculpture or a fashionable dress, is subject to aesthetic evaluation in the same sense—a report on its publicly observable aesthetic properties. The solution I offer is closer to descriptivism, taking aesthetic judgments to be right or wrong about the object judged. Yet we can avoid the pitfalls of classical descriptivism by adding on the idea that we may have perfectly good reasons to observe X under nonstandard conditions D, although we know that the SOC (standard observation conditions) for X are C and not D. If we are justified in doing so, and if X appears A under conditions D, then, although it is not true that X is A, we have a right to judge (erroneously) that X is A. Before I flesh out this solution, however, I need some stage setting.

4.2. Time-Sensitive Properties

Let me start with a few platitudes. To appreciate a painting one has to position oneself at a distance of about one to ten (not a hundred) yards from it and look at its face (not at its back); we may use eyeglasses, but not a telescope. To understand a poem one must be proficient in the language and know something about its literary tradition and social world. If these and similar SOC are not put in place, one cannot observe the aesthetic properties of these objects. One's prospect of properly appreciating jazz is greater if one has listened to that kind of music before and has some idea of its traditions; novices cannot usually appreciate it, for they do not know what to listen for. A background in classical music may not ensure appreciation of jazz, because the SOC for the latter are different from those for the former. If you look for the wrong things, the music may appear chaotic. SOC for distinct kinds of artwork differ, and only when observed under their own proper SOC can objects of a given kind be properly appreciated, that is, observed as they really are.

I now wish to propose a distinction between those properties whose SOC include an essential reference to the location of the observer in time and those properties whose SOC include no such reference. I call properties of the first kind 'time-sensitive properties' (TP) and properties of the second kind 'not-time-sensitive properties' (NTP). The distinction is not sharp, for all properties are TP to some degree; the difference is a matter of centrality more than a dichotomy. Nevertheless, it is an important distinction. Take, for instance, the property Blue. To see a blue shirt as blue certain SOC must obtain, but these do not include a proper positioning of the observer in time. However, to see something as original, as conservative, revolutionary, classic, surprising, conventional, etc., we must tacitly position ourselves in a certain historical time or use that time as a reference point. These properties assume a temporal standard from which to observe whether the said property applies to a given object.

To *observe* an object as having certain TP one must look at it from a particular point in time. Tom Paine's work looked radical in 1776, and since these are the right conditions for looking at it, he was a radical, though an undergraduate who considers him from the vantage point of 1997 will not see him as such. A 1997 perspective is therefore nonstandard for observing these TP of Tom Paine. SOC for observing Paine must therefore specify the temporal point from which the observation is to be conducted. In order for one to see an object as innovative, antiquated, fashionable, traditional, unprecedented, archaic, obsolete, secondhand, astonishing, daring, nonconformist, ordinary, etc., one must observe it from a specific historical location, a standard vantage point in time. Not in every era will a miniskirt be seen as daring and provocative. It is so seen only against a certain historical background, say, the 1950s, with the kind of clothing then prevalent and given other details about the social and political climate of that time. That temporal location is crucial, for what looks innovative and bold against the background of 1960 would not seem to have these properties if viewed against other backgrounds. In 1900 that skirt would appear either childish or wicked, but not innovative; in 1990 it would appear old-fashioned and politically reactionary.

One may *know*, in 1990, that in 1966 the skirt X was seen as new and exciting, without being able to *see* X in that way. To know that X is F is one thing; to see X as F is another. A blind man can know that his shirt is blue (he may trust the vendor), yet the shirt does not look blue to him. A historian may know in 2000 how miniskirts looked to 1965 observers, without seeing them in that way him- or herself. The latter feat is not impossible, however; one can see things as people of earlier generations and other cultures saw them. We all have a great talent for empathy: all art (especially literature) relies very heavily on our ability to see the world as others see it. Imagination can transport one to the world of 1965, suspending many beliefs acquired in later years, so as not to impair one's seeing X much as a 1965 person had.

To savor X as it was experienced in 1965 an observer may, but need not, be *aware* of the prevailing cultural, political, social, etc. conditions in 1965 that *caused* people at that time to see X as F. Imagining that those conditions that made people see X as F do obtain is not necessary for seeing X as F. Suppose that a way of behaving, B, strikes me as arrogant because another mode of conduct, C, is customary in my society. Seeing B as arrogant need not, however, be accompanied by an awareness that C is customary in my society. I directly perceive B as arrogant. Sociologists may explain that I see B thus because the accepted norm in my culture is C, but I need not know why I see B as arrogant. I may not even know that C is the norm in my society, just as I need not know about the cones in my eyes to see X as blue, although the existence of cones is necessary for my seeing X as blue.

The dependence of properties such as New or Extravagant upon historical time is self-evident, but the field of TP is much wider. When we perceive a phrase as flowery or terse, vulgar or stylish, rude or polite, candid or arty, we perceive it against a background of the language commonly used in a particular period. If we do not assume the right temporal standpoint, the plain may seem flowery, the revolutionary, conservative, etc. We are, then, unable to tell where the work goes on conventionally and where there are dissonant or unconventional elements, and so we misinterpret the work and miss its climax. Inversion of word order in a text is effective only when viewed against the background of a normal use where the word order is different; otherwise, the inversion goes unrecognized, and we miss its effect. The same applies to other inversions: inversion of accepted ideas, structural and narrational inversion, etc. All these presuppose familiarity with the uninverted, traditional use; Otherwise, the inversion cannot be seen as such. To see a parody or satire as funny we need a background that functions as a perspective from which one observes the world. Explicit identification of that background, however, is not necessary, and it is not sufficient either: a learned historian may know that a certain line was funny to its contemporaries, without feeling in the least amused by it. The same goes for tragedy: one is apt to see an incident as tragic only if one has the appropriate values. In Huxley's *Brave New World* the civilized London audience in the year 632 After Ford sees *Romeo and Juliet* as a piece of amusing pornography. The 632 AF values are that death is not tragic, love is pathological, sex has no emotional significance, and the bearing of children is a dirty and loathsome act. Under such observation conditions evidently *Romeo and Juliet* cannot be seen as a tragedy.

We often miss the role of the TP in generating aesthetic value, not because we overlook them, but because we fail to distinguish them from other properties that require some background knowledge to be properly appreciated. Such assimilation occurs, for example, in the following otherwise excellent discussion by Erwin Panofsky:

The re-creative experience of a work of art depends, therefore, not only on the natural sensitivity and the visual training of the spectator, but also on his cultural equipment. There is no such thing as an entirely "naive" beholder. The "naive" beholder of the Middle Ages had a good deal to learn, and something to forget, before he could appreciate classic statuary and architecture, and the "naive" beholder of the post-renaissance period had a good deal to forget, and something to learn, before he could appreciate mediaeval, to say nothing of primitive, art. The art historian . . . *knows* that his cultural equipment, such as it is, would not be in harmony with that of people in another land and of a different period. He tries, therefore, to make adjustments by learning as much as he possibly can of the circumstances under which the objects of his study were created.[3]

TP are indeed properties whose SOC involve a specific cultural background (from the perspective of another culture they may look grotesquely deformed), but they make up a special kind of such property. Even if the ambient culture is entirely unchanged, the very fact that objects having certain TP have existed in that culture for a very long time is sufficient to deny that they are still seen under the same observation conditions. TP tire without withering: their changing is due to perceptual saturation and aesthetic fatigue, so their demise need not have to be due to physical decay.

The aesthetic value of fashionable items (garments, tunes, etc.) depends almost entirely on their TP. They are artworks that use TP design, rather than sound design or color design, to achieve value. Their aesthetic value is due not to NTP like shape and color but to TP such as provocation, novelty, and risk. Note, however, that even though the aesthetic value of fashion-dependent objects is not due to stable NTP, they do *not* have a sui generis aesthetic value. Symphonies, dresses, roses, and mountains owe their beauty to different nonaesthetic features, but these features are responsible for the presence in the symphonies, dresses, roses, and mountains of the same aesthetic property. Most obviously, the property Beauty accrues to all of them: they all have unity in variety. In painting, the aesthetic function of background is expressed in spatial design. We say, "The blue area in

3. Erwin Panofsky, *Meaning in the Visual Arts* (New York: Doubleday, 1965), 16.

the right-hand corner stands in sharp contrast to the orange square in the center of the picture, creating dramatic tension." In objects whose aesthetic value is TP derived, these very same aesthetic properties are due to temporal design. We say, "The wide, careless line in this spring's collection reflects the modern freedom of the body; the gay colors invoke psychedelic motifs and sharply contrast with the conservative black-and-white tone of high fashion of the past, creating dramatic tension." The aesthetic traits that make up the beauty of fashion-dependent objects are thus the same as those that make any artwork beautiful—tension and release, rhythm, drama, harmony, and irony—only, for objects of fashion, these features derive from their TP, while their NTP play a secondary aesthetic role.

Fashion-sensitive items therefore have an objective aesthetic value that can be perceived by empathically adopting the temporal standpoint specified in their SOC; then one sees them as they are. Yet, for many, that effort may be excessive. Why go through the trouble of working yourself into the mentality of another age to see a certain dress as beautiful, when there are so many dresses that you may see as beautiful in your present state of mind? The effort is not cost-effective, given the modest value of the dress even when seen as it should be. Moreover, investing so much energy to attain a shift of perspective may change your everyday preferences; you may be caught up in your game and come to prefer the clothing of another age. Those who do not invest considerable mental labor in that particular project will just see you as weird or as badly dressed. It takes too much time and effort to do aesthetic justice to one kind of past fashion; if that is your hobby, fine, but you cannot expect to do the same for every object under the sun. Life is too short for that. We therefore have a good pragmatic reason to assume the temporal standpoint of our own age and not bother too much about yesteryear's fashion.

There also is an aesthetic justification for disregarding SOC: Dante and Ovid may deserve our inculcating their SOC, but aesthetic considerations impose a limit on empathy. We are much more likely to make gross mistakes when adopting foreign SOC than when staying with our own. Anachronistic conditions of observation (that is, looking at the past with modern eyes) have yet another advantage over seeking the true SOC: the present-day idiom and way of looking come to us naturally and with ease, and it is not always wise to relinquish them for a hard-to-get truth. Thus there is no contradiction when in a lecture a historian says of some 1860 dress that it is very beautiful, but will never consider putting it on; a student moved by the lecture to don that dress will look ridiculous even to the lecturer. The same problem is prevalent in all the arts. I may know that a certain Greek play is beautiful, but not having at my disposal all the time needed to acquire the SOC that make me see it as such, I read a second-rate contemporary novel instead and enjoy it more. Such behavior is not irrational; aesthetically it is quite justified. I am aesthetically *justified* in discarding an old coat that is truly beautiful and will look beautiful when observed under its proper SOC. I simply cannot afford to see it as beautiful; there are greater aesthetic satisfactions I can acquire at a lower price (effort). The extreme difficulty of seeing the real beauty of the old coat from a distance of a hundred years is not more astonishing than the extreme difficulty of seeing a fine detail in a Brueghel painting from a distance of a hundred yards or knowing that a Chopin nocturne will not sound all that tender if played by a jazz band of six saxophones.

The question raised at the head of this chapter has now been answered. The true aesthetic properties of all things, fashion-sensitive articles included, are disclosed when they are viewed under their proper SOC; ascribing to X properties we observe it to have under nonstandard conditions is indeed a mistake. In essence, then, classical descriptivism is right: the old coat is beautiful, not ugly, since at the time specified by its SOC it looked beautiful. Yet classical descriptivism is wrong to imply that I have bad taste because I refuse to don it. My refusal shows neither stupidity nor bad taste: I have good reasons to look at the coat under today's nonstandard conditions. Aesthetic attractions are many, and I am under no obligation to make a correct appraisal of the aesthetic virtues of every thing. Unless you have a special interest in Hummel, there is no reason why your musical sensitivity should not be influenced by Romantic music, even though that influence will make you hear Hummel as clumsy (which he is not). If the SOC proper for Hummel are very hard to reinstate, it is silly to reinstate them to enjoy the rather limited charm of a minor composer.

If X is so valuable that the effort of re-creating its SOC is richly repaid when X is seen as it is, in its full glory, then it is rational to train young people so that they can, by imaginative effort, reinstate these SOC and observe X under them. That is what we do when we teach the classics. Then the effort is worthwhile, for these works are *really* great, as everyone who takes the trouble to assume their SOC can verify by direct observation. Education fights to save the classics' TP from the jaws of time. Consider Haydn's *Surprise Symphony*: to listen to it as it is, one needs to feel surprise when the famous chord sounds. Today, however, we do not tend to be surprised by that chord; a lot more is needed to surprise our jaded ears. To feel surprise one needs not only to know about, but to relive, the period. That can be done: people have a talent for empathy. We enjoy projecting ourselves by imagination into an alien world and feigning we are native to it. Without that talent we would not enjoy literature or the movies. Yet an accurate resurrection of a past world is a much harder project, and so we cannot see all things correctly. Since our time and energy are limited, we can take only a small number of classics. Nonclassics are usually viewed under nonstandard conditions; we see them not as they are but as they look under cost-effective conditions. That theoretical mistake is not a slip; it is irrational *not* to make that mistake with respect to *most* things.

Some classical works achieve their status nonstandardly: they manage to look good when anachronistically observed; they excel at different times for different reasons. They manifest a cyclical pattern: X appears beautiful under its SOC, C, then loses its good looks when observed under conditions D of another generation, and then again, at a later time, now seen under conditions E, it appears beautiful again in a different way. Under D it looked old and tired, but under E it appears romantic, mysterious, quaint, and provocative. It is "rediscovered" by later generations not because they bother to revive C, but because under the new conditions E the work happens to look beautiful again. Seen under conditions E, X seems to have TP that make it beautiful. Thus, John Donne is praised by modern critics for reasons different from those given by his contemporaries. The original makers of African art could not have liked it for those of its features that appealed to French cubists. Primitive art seems beautiful to us because we see it *as primitive,* that is, in a way that its creators could not see it in. We see it under our modern observation conditions; to be sure, these conditions are not standard, but that is not reason enough to forswear the beauty so generated.

4.3. TP and the Modern Artist

At no previous time in the history of art did artists make such extensive, *serious* use of TP as in our age. The hallmark of modern art, its essential feature, is the place of honor it gives to aesthetic properties that, in previous generations, were confined to objects of modest aesthetic importance and value. Those who do not realize that what they should look for in contemporary art is its TP can see no value in it; they do not understand the art form of this century.

Arthur Danto, who uses the puzzles of contemporary art as a key to reveal the nature of art,[4] stresses that in different settings the same object may be different works of art and have different aesthetic values. That which out of the museum is a urinal, a can opener, a bed, a piece of red cloth, or a box of laundry detergent is metamorphosed, when exhibited by an artist, into an artwork of considerable value. However, Danto gives no explanation of that phenomenon; his reference to an "artworld" that converts a thing into an artwork, albeit suggestive and indeed on the right track, does not explain how the transfiguration of the commonplace can occur. The notion of TP, I believe, does a better job, providing a general theory on the origin of the said phenomenon. The value of Danto's work is in highlighting the fact that never before have artworks derived so much of their aesthetic value from the relations they have to elements in their context. Danto calls that context "artworld," but I think it is simply the place of the work in its milieu.

Danto distinguishes between a commercial Brillo box, which is just a thing, and the entirely similar object made by Andy Warhol, which is an artwork. The difference, Danto says, is that only the latter box is interpreted, and that is an ontological difference between them. But why does interpretation change the ontological status of an object? And why is the first box uninterpreted? Let us suppose that the company's PR man says: "These Brillo boxes mean that we are dedicated to Clean America"; does that make all Brillo boxes into artworks? Against the philistines, Danto rightly claims that the supermarket's box is not an artwork, while Warhol's is, yet why that is so remains a mystery. The lacuna has been filled, in an utterly unacceptable way, by Dickie, who makes art a performative: X is art if you say it is.[5] It also utterly unacceptable to limit the difference between the boxes to the microscopic physical differences between them, which may in the future be detectable by unaided sight and found aesthetically significant.[6] Warhol could have created an artwork had he done what Duchamp did, that is, buy the box in a supermarket and take it to the museum.

4. Arthur C. Danto, *The Transfiguration of the Commonplace* (Cambridge: Harvard University Press, 1981); idem, *The Philosophical Disenfranchisement of Art* (New York: Columbia University Press, 1986).

5. See, by George Dickie, *Aesthetics: An Introduction* (New York: Pegasus, 1971), *Art and the Aesthetic: An Institutional Analysis* (Ithaca: Cornell University Press, 1974), *The Art Circle: A Theory of Art* (New York: Haven Publications, 1984), *Evaluating Art* (Philadelphia: Temple University Press, 1988).

6. Nelson Goodman, *Languages of Art* (Indianapolis: Bobbs-Merrill, 1968), 99–123.

The difference between an object X and the artwork X* that comprises X alone is not in their NTP. Therefore, their NTP identity does not imply identity of aesthetic properties. X and X* are different in that X blends into its environment, while the new positioning of X* highlights its relations to a certain privileged group of items, artworks, as an assumed background. X* contrasts with, and brings together, those select items, and thus it has TP that X does not have. X*'s position gives it TP that are, in fact, aesthetically significant. Warhol's work is valuable because it has valuable TP: out of its temporal background, that is, its place in the history of art, Warhol's work is worthless. Warhol is an important artist because he saw that he could generate significant TP by positioning his work between two traditions, industry and art, illuminating both in an interesting way. He saw that at this moment in history and the history of art, against the backdrop of our economic-cultural environment, a handmade Brillo box would have valuable TP, and he generated those TP by adroitly placing his work. The art critic must therefore agree with the philistine who grumbles, "My two-year-old can draw/play/write better than that!" Indeed, it is not hard to make things that have the same NTP as some works exhibited in museums today. The hard part is to see that, at our temporal location, such and such items, whose NTP are quite trivial, will have valuable TP. A dunghill that serves as an installation and a moment of silence that serves as a work of music (by John Cage) have thoroughly uninteresting NTP. Their value is in their TP, and only an artist who has an acute sense of beauty could have given them those TP.

4.4. The Keats Principles

Let us call a principle that makes aesthetic value an epistemic desideratum a 'Keats Principle,' for it is reminiscent of the lines from Keats's "Ode on a Grecian Urn," " 'Beauty is truth, truth beauty'—that is all / Ye know on earth, and all ye need to know." All scientists use two such principles: that a theory should be (1) internally and (2) externally beautiful. The *internal* aesthetic value of a theory is based on the degree to which that theory is simple, rich, and elegant, that is, its manifesting a high degree of unity in variety. The *external* aesthetic value of a theory is based on the degree to which that theory harmoniously and gracefully integrates with our other theories. The methodological desiderata of intuitiveness and conservatism are merits of external beauty: they require a theory not only to be internally unified but also nicely to interlock with others. A far-fetched theory conflicts with entrenched intuitions; a radical theory conflicts with entrenched beliefs. A good theory, contributing to a worldview, is compatible with basic intuitions and beliefs and nicely incorporates them into its model.

Consider Parmenides' view that the world is a uniform ball with no movement or change. His theory has great internal simplicity, and so the appeal of stark beauty. A theory that has such aesthetic virtue may be worthy of adoption, so the first Keats Principle moves us to consider Parmenides' view rather favorably. We have, however, *other* beliefs too; some of our beliefs are grounded in appearances: we seem to see differences and change in the world. With these beliefs Parmenides' theory integrates very poorly. Its way of coming to grips with them is by ignoring them altogether: all phenomena are declared illusory and unworthy of attention. Parmenides' theory therefore lacks external unity. Furthermore, it is low in richness and dramatic power (prediction), for it deprives us of perceptually based information. A theory that offers such meager explanations is ugly, hence unworthy of either acceptance or credence. On the opposite end, consider "phenomenological" theories, specific to one domain and subject to no universal laws. These theories are rich and dramatic, providing many precise predictions, but they lack unity. They lack *internal* unity, for their laws have no internal structure, and they lack *external* unity too, for they fail to connect with other phenomenological theories that we accept. They leave us with no world-picture, a serious aesthetic blemish.

These two Keats Principles apply to theories only, not to the objects discussed by those theories. A theory about manure can be no less beautiful than a theory about flowers, though flowers are more beautiful than manure. A theory about aesthetic value differs, however (for reasons soon to be made clear), from other theories: one of its desiderata is that the aesthetic value of the objects considered be maximized by the theory. SOC for molecules are fixed by a pretty theory about molecules (the first two Keats Principles) and not by the theory that presents molecules as pretty (the third Keats Principle). But a theory about the aesthetic aspect of things (e.g., literary criticism) is judged not only by the first two Keats Principles, but also by the third, mandating that aesthetically contemplated things should be viewed under those conditions that maximize their aesthetic value. That is, in deciding whether to adopt C as SOC for aesthetically considered objects K, it is valid to consider that K, when observed with C as their SOC, are more beautiful than they are with other conditions as their SOC.

Is the third Keats Principle valid? It seems to have serious problems. Suppose that from some temporal perspective X appears brave and bold (A+), whereas from other temporal points it appears banal and boring (A–). Why should the charitable perspective serve as SOC for X? Why say that the favorable point of view does justice to the object, while the unfavorable one distorts it? Why not adopt the opposite strategy, say that the unfavorable perspective presents it realistically, while the favorable one unduly flatters it? One may try the following answer: it is natural for us to prefer those conditions under which X appears beautiful. Surely it would be perverse to take as standard those conditions in which X appears ugly. We enjoy beauty, and we want to increase our pleasure, not decrease it. It is therefore rational to choose as an object's SOC those conditions under which the object displays maximum beauty.

That argument does not save the third Keats Principle from trouble. Consider the statement "X appears beautiful to you, but in fact it is not beautiful." That statement makes sense, and it is often used in literary and art criticism. A critic may say to a sentimental reader: "I do not doubt that this novel moves you, but you are wrong to think that it really is good. It is bad, and my duty as an art critic is to show you that." Yet the third Keats Principle says that X *is* as it appears from the perspective that presents it at its best. Thus, if the choice is between observation conditions C and C*, and if X looks best under C, then C (not C*) is the standard for observing X's aesthetic properties; X really is as it appears under C. That makes it self-contradictory to say that X is really uglier than it looks; X cannot seem more beautiful than it is. Surely that is wrong. We neither speak nor think this way. Why, then, do I advocate the third Keats Principle, according to which a theory that presents its object as more beautiful has a stronger claim to have presented it as it is?

The following are obvious a priori constraints on the choice of SOC: (1) All predicates of the same family must have the same SOC. Suppose, for instance, that 'red' has C and 'green' has C* as their SOC. Further suppose that X appears red under C and green under C*. Since SOC are those conditions under which an object is seen as it is, it follows that X is both red and green; hence it is red and not red: a contradiction. Therefore, there must be one SOC for each set of mutually exclusive predicates. (2) SOC for determining whether X is F must be the same for all objects of X's kind. It is impossible for each thing to have its own SOC, for that would make it impossible to learn from experience. A past encounter with a lion, for example, would teach us nothing about other lions, for their SOC might differ. Furthermore, we could examine two identical objects under the same conditions, obtain the same results, and yet validly reach the conclusion that one is red and the other green. If observable objects are to obey general laws, objects of a kind must have identical SOC. (3) To research objects K, SOC for K must be specified independently of how K appear under them. With regard to a tomato's color the SOC are twenty-twenty eyesight, daylight, and proximity to the tomato; they are not "those conditions under which tomatoes appear red." Otherwise the outcome of inquiry is given in advance, and observation is redundant.

Now, let us return to the example above: a sentimental reader engrossed in a second-rate, tear-jerking novel and finding it marvelously beautiful. Why should we not take the observation conditions of that reader as SOC for the said novel if under these conditions it appears highly beautiful? Because, if we accept these conditions as SOC, we shall profit as far as that novel and others like it are concerned, but this gain is offset by a great net loss. Constraint 2 above demands that the same SOC apply to all novels; yet if we apply these SOC to all novels, our losses outweigh our gain by far. The conditions that would make one see the said tearjerker as the epitome of beauty are, for example, no sense of humor, insensitivity to subtler use of language, psychological naivete, no sophistication in literary techniques, high tolerance for banality, ignorance of the heritage of literature, etc. If these conditions are to become SOC for literature, so that works that appear good under them *are* good and those that appear bad under them are bad, we shall have to say that all those literary artworks hitherto considered masterpieces are not at all aesthetically good. To see the masterpieces as beautiful we need those conditions we have just branded 'nonstandard.' Great works of art represent the highest achievement attained through the concerted effort of the most talented people throughout history; their loss is the loss of a civilization and a great aesthetic disaster. Hence the third Keats Principle is violated by adopting the state of mind of a sentimental reader as SOC. If we are intent on keeping all that beauty, SOC for literature must include sensitivity to language and style, ability to detect nuances and follow suggestions, life experience, musical ear, psychological sophistication, attention to plot and manner of narration, sensitivity to recurring motifs, broad liberal education, familiarity with the history of the culture, acquaintance with other works of the artist and the period, information about events known to educated people in that society, etc.

Under these conditions the said cheap novel appears not beautiful but crude, silly, clumsy, and boring. We say to the reader who weeps over its pages: "The novel seems to you perfect because you do not see it as it is.

Your observation conditions are nonstandard, so you are a victim to illusion. That illusion seems beneficial now, but it impedes your access to much greater beauty. Thus your belief that the novel is beautiful is wrong; if you observe it under the SOC for the aesthetic properties of novels you will see for yourself that this is so."

The third Keats Principle mandates that a theory increase the sum of available beauty. The first constraint above dictates that the true beauty of an object X of kind K appears (not under those conditions in which X looks most beautiful, but) under those conditions in which objects of kind K manifest the greatest beauty. Substituting Judy Bloom for Shakespeare as a general standard of literary taste will not, therefore, meet the third Keats Principle.

The taxonomy of kinds, that is, what objects are of the same kind K as a given X, should be somewhat vague, to allow flexibility in applying the second constraint. It is possible and desirable that different critics assign artworks to somewhat different kinds and thus have slightly different SOC for them. Cross-classification of an artwork by rival critics, schools, and movements is fruitful, for it generates many construals of that work. These construals need not be mutually compatible; I later show that allowing incompatible interpretations does not contradict the realistic tenet that an artwork has certain aesthetic properties and not others.

The third Keats Principle can be formulated thus: Let C and C* be conditions for observing aesthetic properties in objects of kind K. If these objects manifest an overall higher aesthetic value when observed under C than when observed under C*, then C are SOC for the aesthetic observation of objects of kind K. Even if some K object looks better when observed under C*, its SOC are still C. The SOC for observing Ks from the aesthetic point of view are, then, those conditions under which the aesthetic value of Ks is on the whole higher than it was had other conditions been SOC. That principle is iterable: it is possible that, if taken to be SOC, C increase the value of Ks, but on the whole decrease the value of a more inclusive kind K*. Aesthetic kinds come in inclusion sets (fiction, novels, realistic novels, French realistic novels, etc.), and therefore their SOC have that form too. SOC for novels are also SOC for realistic novels, so we should not adopt as SOC for novels conditions that increase the value of realistic novels yet decrease the total value of novels in general. The third Keats Principle is, then, an aesthetic categorical imperative: Thou shalt make beauty.

The Keats Principles check and balance each other. For example, a beautiful performance of a work cannot become more beautiful by taking too many liberties with the performed work. The third Keats Principle prompts us to make the performance as beautiful as we can, but since a performance is not only a thing but also a theory about another thing (the performed work), we must reckon with the second principle. A performance that does not sit well with the performed work is not a beautiful theory: if it leaves out recalcitrant features of the performed work, cutting off loose ends, it is too weak; if it twists the performed work, trying to force it into its mold, it lacks simplicity. On the other hand, a faithful performance with no originality is fainthearted and boring, sinning against the third Keats Principle. Thus principles 1 and 2 restrain the third, and principle 3 balances the other two.

4.5. The Dangers of Time Travel

To show the Keats Principles at work, consider the issue of anachronistic interpretations. Positioned against the background of the fifteenth century, many mediocre contemporary poems will seem to have highly positive TP: they look astounding, daring, and revolutionary. A carefully chosen anachronistic background may make any wretched poem appear a paragon of beauty. Borges explores the possibility of perceiving a work of art anachronistically in his story "Paul Menard, the Author of *Don Quixote*": Menard, a modern symbolist poet, composes Cervantes' *Don Quixote*.[7] Menard's work is better than Cervantes', Borges muses, because phrases and ideas that look flat and merely rhetorical in the context of seventeenth-century Spain make bold political statements when they appear as a cynical riposte to Nietzsche or as alluding to American pragmatism. Unlike Cervantes, Menard writes in a foreign language, and his style is alienated, deliberately archaic, menacing, even alarming, against the foil of the nineteenth century's fin de siècle. Anachronistic interpretation may, then, make a tired work appear in a new, surprising light, richly adorned with great TP. Has Borges found a philosophers' stone that turns poor art into aesthetic gold?

So, why not take Borges seriously and establish chairs at universities for an anachronistic study of literature? We may do even better than that: *invent* a virtual history, a background especially made up to highlight and

---

7. Jorge Luis Borges, "Pierre Menard, Autor del 'Quijote,'" in *Ficciones* (Buenos Aires: Sur, 1945).

dramatize a given work and thus immensely enhance its value.[8] If an artwork really is F if it appears F when it looks its best, does it not obligate us to adopt Borges's proposal and even go further and fit each artwork with tailor-made virtual or anachronistic "background data," since under such conditions it would appear most beautiful? Should we invent SOC for all works of art and jettison art history as an obstacle to the appreciation of art? My theory shows why we must reject this (ridiculous) proposal: it violates all three Keats Principles. Violating the second constraint, it has SOC for a single object, instead of having SOC for kinds of objects. However, it is *logically impossible* consistently to violate the second principle, because the strategy of taking the anachronistic conditions under which X looks best to be its SOC is self-destructive when universalized. That is similar to Kant's point about lying: lying can be profitable only if telling the truth is the norm. If the norm is to tell lies, lying is pointless; it becomes a way of telling the truth. Similarly, you can derive aesthetic benefits from locating a work elsewhere than in its actual place in history only if it alone is moved, that is, provided that all *other* works are kept in their places. Suppose that X profits from being shifted from its historical place to another temporal location, say, five hundred years earlier, where work Y is currently located. Against the foil of Y, X looks its best. Now, Y does not look best when X is placed next to it: it loses the good TP it had before X moved to its vicinity. If we put Leonardo before Giotto we enhance the value of Leonardo but destroy the stature of Giotto. To save Y, that is, Giotto's work, we need to move it to a location where it appears more beautiful than in other places. Yet once Y is removed from its historical location there is no reason to keep X there, for the background against which X appeared so radiant has now been changed; we must move X again to a new, more flattering location. The game of musical chairs continues in the new place too, and so on ad infinitum. No SOC for X can be made to stick. The virtual history game is, therefore, self-defeating.

It is not logically impossible that there is a nonhistorical way to maximize value. Perhaps there is a way to move all artworks around in time until a new order, different from the actual one, is found, whose total aesthetic value is greater than if actual history is taken as SOC. But finding such order is a task that far exceeds the abilities of the human mind. Furthermore,

8. I thank George Bailey for giving me entertaining and stunning examples of fictitious "histories" of a given painting that have palpably enhanced its aesthetic appeal. Cf. Bailey's "Pierre Menard's *Don Quixote*," *Iyyun* 39 (1990): 339–57.

it is unlikely that such order is possible. Artists are rational agents who endeavor as best they can to create things that look beautiful from their own perspective, from where they stand in time. The probability that all art can look better from some other, unintended perspective is nugatory. It takes reverse entropy for greater order to emerge by chance, without a concerted effort of rational agents intending to achieve that order. The second law of thermodynamics rules that possibility out.

4.6. The Third Keats Principle Justified

The three principles merge in evaluating art interpretation. As I show in Chapter 6, an interpretation of a work of art is a theoretical model of it. Like all models it is a theory *about* its interpretandum, showing how to understand it and what is essential in it. Now, an interpretation may be a *concrete model*, which is itself an instance of the work whose model it is. Gould's interpretation of a Chopin sonata is a theory about that sonata, advocating a certain understanding of it, yet at the same time the performance is an instance of the sonata; having heard Gould you heard the Chopin sonata (I discuss that point in Chapter 5). The same is true of theatrical interpretations, say, Jacobi interpreting *Hamlet*. A literary critic does not rewrite the poem he interprets, so his work is not an instance of the poem, but he, too, suggests how the poem should be read, so his theory *about* the poem specifies a particular *instance of* that poem that readers can enact or perform in their minds.

Outside art there are few concrete theoretical models. In Brussels there stands a huge model of the atom; it is a theory that says (by showing) what it takes the structure of the atom to be. That model is a concrete object, but it is not an atom, so unlike a performance of a Chopin sonata, which *is* that sonata, it is not an instance of its own object. But a restoration of an old building is a concrete theoretical model. The restoration is an archeological theory about that building: using theoretical reasons it interprets data that other archaeologists may interpret differently. But that concrete model, unlike the model of the atom in Brussels, is itself a building, the very same building about which it theorizes. Having visited it, we may say that we saw the famous building itself, not only that we learned a theory about it.

In Chapter 6, I show that a concrete model (an interpretation) is a token whose type is its subject matter (the interpreted work). This is also true for interpretations that present an interpretandum in a new medium (e.g., performances) and for interpretations that only suggest a new way of seeing the interpreted work. A model presents, concretely or only theoretically, what it claims the interpreted item to be. When Raffaello Sanzio (among other artists) let his pupils complete his sketches, they interpreted Raffaello's work. The pupil's work is a concrete object, a painting, but it is also an interpretation of the master's work, not simply a supplement to it. It is a concrete model: an embodiment of a type that is the work. Another pupil would have made another model, another interpretation, and it, too, would have been that very work of Raffaello. The pupil has to make a beautiful thing, a work of art, but he cannot do so unless his picture is also good as a theory. It is a good theory only if it interprets the master's sketch well, filling it out in a simple, elegant, powerful, and coherent way. Otherwise, the paining is not beautiful: the fillings do not fit the sketch. The data, that is, the sketch, is violated, forced into a discordant whole. Therefore, in a concrete model, a beautiful interpretation makes the interpretandum beautiful. That justifies the third Keats Principle: that X is most beautiful when seen under interpretation Y is a reason for believing that Y is a good (hence, correct) interpretation of X.

Methodology orders that a theory be coherent and rich; since that is the classical definition of Beauty (unity in variety), the Keats Principles are criteria for correctness of interpretation. Principles 1 and 2 say that an interpretation that is beautiful as a theory—that is, a pretty, powerful, parsimonious model of the data that nicely coalesces with other theories— is probably true. Now, since the theory instantiates the object it interprets, the third Keats Principle emerges naturally. A theory of the atom can be beautiful even if the atom is ugly, since the theory itself is not an atom. But if the interpretation itself is an instance of its subject matter, a requirement that it be beautiful is at the same time a requirement that its interpretandum be beautiful. If the theory is correct, it is about a beautiful object.[9]

---

9. Saul Smilansky asked me how I treat sociological explanations of aesthetic taste. For example, former centuries' preference for plump, untanned women is explained by the fact that a slim, tanned body would then divulge the farmer's dearth and hard work out in the sun, while a whitish pudgy body attested to a leisurely life spent in a castle. The twentieth century's preference runs in the opposite direction, sociologists say, because we associate an untanned heavy body with the poor life of factory hands and seamstresses, while the vacationing leisure class is tan and slim. Does that not prove the relativist's point?

Not at all; realists embrace sociological explanations. A background of opulence, comfort, and the good life may enhance the beauty of items integrated with it, while a sordid context may

A theory about a literary work has to be reasonable (satisfy the first Keats Principle) and informative (satisfy the second), but the criterion ranking the many reasonable and informative theories about a given work is the degree of aesthetic worth that the theory bestows on the interpreted work (the third principle). Some scientists (e.g., Kepler) took principle 3 very seriously, but usually it is regarded as illegitimate or meaningless; only principles 1 and 2 are now considered valid. However, in evaluating rival interpretations of artworks it is quite clear how to satisfy the third principle. We can say not only which interpretation is a better theory, being more beautiful than the other, but also that the work as exhibited by one interpretation is a better work than it is as exhibited by the other interpretation.

A concrete model claims to instantiate the thing it models. Thus, the beauty of the model as a theory is inseparable from its beauty as a reconstructed object. A beautiful theory may deal with hackneyed objects and a dismal theory may deal with beautiful ones, but if the theory is itself an instance of its object, no separation between their beauties is possible. Thus, an interpretation that presents its interpretandum must comply with the theoretical constraints (principles 1 and 2) as well as with principle 3, that is, maximize the aesthetic value of its object.

---

tarnish the looks of items associated with it. Similarly, in a picture, a tan spot may be beautiful against an apt (say, yellow) foil, and be ugly if set in a scarlet field.

5

THE ONTOLOGY OF AESTHETIC PROPERTIES

5.1. Two Theses

In this chapter I advocate two ontological theses that seem at odds with each other. The first is that aesthetic properties supervene on nonaesthetic properties because we observe the former by observing the latter through a special medium: Desire. Jones sees X as having an aesthetic property A if and only if X has a certain nonaesthetic phenomenal ("secondary") property N and Jones perceives the impact of X's being N on a desire of his. We see things aesthetically because we see things as effecting the satisfaction of our wants.

The above thesis has an irrealistic flavor. It seems to imply that aesthetic properties are twice removed from reality: the look of reality is twisted, first, by the thick glass of our senses (which phenomenal properties we perceive depends on our biology), and then it is twisted further by the thick glass of our desires (which desires we have depends on our psychology). So, a tertiary property—a property that a thing seems to have when we look at it through these *two* sets of distorting lenses—cannot be the way things really are. Am I saying, then, that aesthetic properties, being tertiary, are only the way we, human observers, react to reality, and that therefore they do not exist? Not at all. I say (as I said all along) that aesthetic properties *are* real. My second thesis is that, despite all the above, aesthetic properties are features of things as they are in themselves. Can these two theses be reconciled? But first: why should we subscribe to either of them?

5.2. Aesthetic and Nonaesthetic Properties

Philosophers say that aesthetic properties are related to nonaesthetic properties by (1) supervenience, (2) necessary laws, (3) induction, (4) causal laws, (5) identity. I now argue that of these, the first three do, and the latter two do not, obtain.

We have a strong intuition that aesthetic properties supervene on nonaesthetic properties: we cannot conceive of two things, X and Y, differing in aesthetic properties *only* and in no other way. If X and Y are aesthetically different, there must be some nonaesthetic difference between them that accounts for that aesthetic difference. Thus, two worlds, W_1 and W_2, cannot be exactly alike in every way except one: in W_1 X is coarse and in W_2 it is fine. If X is coarse, then coarseness is expressed in certain nonaesthetic features of X; some of X's nonaesthetic properties are responsible for X's being coarse. It is absurd to hold that the same nonaesthetic features that are responsible for X's being coarse in W_1 are those that in W_2 (which differs from W_1 in no other way) make it tender. There is type-type supervenience of each aesthetic property on some loose collection of phenomenal nonaesthetic properties, and also token-token supervenience of each aesthetic property of X on some loose collection of phenomenal nonaesthetic properties of X.

The supervenience of the aesthetic on the nonaesthetic is not disproved by Pierre Menard cases[1] (discussed in the previous chapter). Some contemporary aestheticians have suggested thought experiments in which exactly similar objects make up distinct works of art that have different aesthetic properties (e.g., Danto's *Red Square* and Walton's *Guernica*).[2] Pierre Menard cases are compatible with the aesthetic supervening on the nonaesthetic, because the nonaesthetic properties, on which the aesthetic properties of the object X supervene, need not be intrinsic to X. Observing X in isolation is not a good way to appraise its aesthetic properties, for, as the previous chapter shows, X's most significant aesthetic properties may be

---

1. In Jorge Luis Borges's story, "Pierre Menard, Autor del 'Quijote,' " in *Ficciones* (Buenos Aires: Sur, 1945). I believe I was the first who used that story in a philosophy article ("A Stitch in Time," *Journal of Value Inquiry* 1 [1967–68]: 223–41) to study the identity of an artwork.

2. Arthur C. Danto, *The Transfiguration of the Commonplace* (Cambridge: Harvard University Press, 1981), 1–2, formerly in idem, "The Artworld," *Journal of Philosophy* 61 (1964): 571–84. Kendall Walton, "Categories of Art," *Philosophical Review* 79 (1970): 334–67.

TP, in which case the nonaesthetic properties on which they supervene are relational.

Danto says that there is more to art than meets the eye; I think what he means is that there is more to art than meets an eye fixed on the artwork. For example, the etiology of X, which may be important to its aesthetic character, *can* "meet the eye"; that is, it can be observed, but not if one looks at X exclusively. X and Y may therefore be similar in every *intrinsic* nonaesthetic feature (e.g., consist of the same arrangement of words, sounds, or colors) and yet have distinct aesthetic features. That can happen if X and Y have different nonaesthetic *relational* properties: they are located in different contexts or different periods, have distinct titles, or are created by members of different art movements. If the SOC of X specify that we should view X against a background other than that against which we should view Y, then X and Y are distinct works of art. That difference between the relational properties of look-alike or sound-alike artworks (a difference in their cultural or physical environment, a difference in provenance, a difference in their manner of production, etc.) is a difference in nonaesthetic properties. It therefore remains true that if X is aesthetically different from Y, then they are nonaesthetically different too.

Why does the aesthetic supervene on the nonaesthetic? The simplest explanation of supervenience is by identity. If every aesthetic property is reducible to an arrangement of nonaesthetic properties, then every difference in aesthetic properties is a difference in nonaesthetic properties. An aesthetic property cannot change without change in nonaesthetic properties, because each aesthetic property is *identical with* some nonaesthetic properties. Yet the identity explanation notoriously fails, for substituting any nonaesthetic terms for an aesthetic predicate inevitably compromises the meaning and the implicational force of statements from which the aesthetic predicate is excised.

A predicate like 'coarse,' for instance, denotes a property that no nonaesthetic predicate can denote; therefore, no nonaesthetic sentence can express the statement that X is coarse. If the aesthetic strongly supervenes on the nonaesthetic, there may very well be nonaesthetic necessary and sufficient conditions for being coarse, so Smith, who knows that X has the nonaesthetic properties sufficient for X to be coarse, knows that X is coarse. Yet if Smith is aesthetically insensitive, she fails to see X as coarse and is not acquainted with that property. She may know that "X is coarse" is true but not what it means. Knowing sufficient nonaesthetic conditions for (1) being coarse, (2) being tender, and (3) being in contrast, she may calculate that the sentence

"X contrasts with Y" is true, without understanding it. She knows it in the way that a child can know that $E = MC^2$: the child truly and justifiably (daddy said so) believes that the sentence "$E = MC^2$" is true, but does not understand the proposition expressed by it.

One may understand every nonaesthetic statement that implies, and is implied by, an aesthetic statement, yet not understand that aesthetic statement. Smith, who does not understand what the terms 'coarse,' 'tender,' and 'visual clash' mean, cannot know *why* being coarse makes X clash with the tender Y. The reason is apparent to the aesthetically sensitive—they *see* the clash—but not to Smith. The relation of the nonaesthetic truth-makers of 'coarse' and 'tender' to the nonaesthetic truth-maker of 'clashes with' seems to her arbitrary. She will therefore regard the fact that "X is coarse" and "Y is tender" imply "X clashes with Y" as contingent. Those acquainted only with the nonaesthetic truth-makers of aesthetic properties will find it miraculous that an aesthetically sensitive person who has no idea what the nonaesthetic necessary and sufficient conditions are for being coarse and for being tender can tell, just by looking at X and Y, that they clash.[3]

Relations weaker than identity, such as inductive support and extensional equivalence, may obtain between aesthetic and nonaesthetic properties. Elsewhere I have argued that there are both empirical and conceptual connections between aesthetic and nonaesthetic statements.[4] Given a nonaesthetic description of X, we can very often infer what aesthetic properties it has. Inductive inference from past conjunction between certain aesthetic and nonaesthetic properties is common: if your previous novels were superb, that is a good reason to believe that your new novel will be good too. Empirically discovered relations obtain between many aesthetic properties and nonaesthetic ones. Stronger relations also exist: a score is a (mostly) nonaesthetic description of a piece of music, yet it gives a good idea on the aesthetic traits of the work. Reverse inference is also common: if X is tender,

<hr />

3. The irreducibility of the aesthetic to the nonaesthetic was advocated by Arnold Isenberg (*Aesthetics and the Theory of Criticism*, ed. William Calleghan et al. (Chicago: University of Chicago Press, 1973) and Frank N. Sibley ("Aesthetics and the Look of Things," *Journal of Philosophy* 56 [1959]: 905–15; "Aesthetic Concepts," *Philosophical Review* 68 [1959]: 421–50; "Aesthetic Concepts: A Rejoinder," *Philosophical Review* 72 [1963]: 79–83; "Aesthetic and Nonaesthetic," *Philosophical Review* 74 [1965]: 135–59; "About Taste," *British Journal of Aesthetics* 6 [1966]: 68–69; "Objectivity and Aesthetics," *Proceedings of the Aristotelian Society*, supp. vol. 42 [1968]: 31–54).

4. Eddy Zemach, "Aesthetic Properties, Aesthetic Laws, and Aesthetic Principles," *Journal of Aesthetics and Art Criticism* 45 (1987): 67–73.

then many nonaesthetic descriptions of it, say, 'not made of concrete,' are likely to be true.

Frank Sibley holds that aesthetic predicates are essentially not rule governed. According to Sibley, there are (1) nonaesthetic necessary conditions for applying an aesthetic predicate to an object and (2) nonaesthetic sufficient conditions for *not* applying an aesthetic predicate to an object, but there are no nonaesthetic sufficient conditions for applying an aesthetic predicate to an object. Moreover, no nonaesthetic conditions can increase the prima facie, defeasible, prior probability that a certain aesthetic predicate is true of an object. Hungerland, Isenberg, Hampshire, McDonald, and Mothersill agree with Sibley, but I do not. Sibley maintains that, ontologically, X has such and such aesthetic properties *because of* the nonaesthetic properties it has; so why not justify the belief that X is A by citing the nonaesthetic properties that cause it to be A?

Nonaesthetic descriptions often inform us about aesthetic qualities of the things described. A nonaesthetic description of a waterfall can give you an idea whether it is cute or frightful, pretty or plain. You may be wrong; to infer aesthetic properties from nonaesthetic descriptions is fallible, and you may have to revise your opinion after seeing the waterfall. Yet fallibility is common to all empirical beliefs; empirical reasoning may be defeated. Defeasibility, however, does not bar a nonaesthetic description of X from increasing or decreasing the probability that an aesthetic predicate A applies to X. A detailed nonaesthetic description of a Chinese vase can give a reason not only against thinking that it is crude but also for believing it is elegant.

Sibley asks: Will a snob who pretends to have aesthetic taste but has none be caught? His answer is yes. I am not so sure. A person who has no taste cannot see a line as coarse or as delicate; but can he not use nonaesthetic cues to distinguish coarse objects from delicate ones? Relying on nonaesthetic cues will not bring him one step closer to acquaintance with aesthetic properties, but inability to see things *as* delicate or *as* coarse is not inability to tell whether a thing is coarse or delicate. A parvenu may lack the former ability but have the latter. He may know what makes things delicate or coarse, though he never sees anything as delicate or coarse (and cannot understand how others can directly see that a given thing is delicate or coarse). A blind physicist, who cannot know what Red is, can be infallible in identifying red things; the aesthetically blind may never get caught either.

Not all valid inferences from nonaesthetic to aesthetic descriptions are inductive. Earlier I gave the example of a score, a description that uses (almost) no aesthetic terms, yet tells us what aesthetic features the work has.

Visual art can be described in that way too; with a standard color-numbering system and a coordinate system, we can describe a painting by number triads (the first two identify a place and the third gives the color). Surely one can learn something of aesthetic significance from such descriptions. Even if the description is partial, omitting various details, do these omissions completely annul its ability to tell us about the aesthetic properties of the work? Of course not. A partial nonaesthetic description is all that we usually get, yet we can, and do, make an educated (though fallible) guess about the aesthetic character of the work (say, a movie) so described. The less nonaesthetic information we get, the less we know about the aesthetic properties of the object described, but with a reasonable amount of background information we can (defeasibly) aesthetically evaluate that object. One may object that, given that nonaesthetic information, we visualize the work, or bring it to mind in other ways, and then read its aesthetic properties directly off of it. I doubt that this is what we do, but even if it is so, what of it? *How* we infer an aesthetic evaluation from a nonaesthetic description is immaterial; the important thing is that, most aestheticians to the contrary, we can do it, and we do do it every day.

The irreducibility of aesthetic to nonaesthetic properties despite the lawlike generalizations that connect them is typical to all phenomenal properties: supervenience is not reduction. We may identify (after long, cruel experiments) and name all the sonar-phenomenal states of bats, know how they interrelate and their relations to brain-states and external stimuli. We can then tell that a bat is in a phenomenal state X and correctly predict when it will be in it again. Yet, lacking the bat's sonar sense, we cannot know what the phenomenal quale we call 'X' is. We can learn to use predicates denoting sonar-phenomenal states, but cannot learn what they mean. One understands no sentence in which these terms occur even if one knows all the statements of biology that they imply and are implied by them, for to understand a predicate denoting a phenomenal property one needs to be acquainted with that property.

Aesthetic properties are irreducible for the same reason: what is said by using aesthetic predicates is different from what can be said by using nonaesthetic predicates. Albeit entailed by nonaesthetic sentences, an aesthetic sentence imparts information that no nonaesthetic sentence can carry, because these sentences have completely different meanings. Only those can understand the aesthetic predicate 'A' who are acquainted with the property A that 'A' denotes. Sensitivity to A, ability to see or hear something *as* A, is a necessary condition for understanding the sentence "X is A."

5.3. The Aesthetic Supervenes

The relation of aesthetic to nonaesthetic properties is not a mere Humean constant conjunction: the aesthetic property A and the nonaesthetic property N do not just happen to coincide in this world. We do talk as if an instance of N caused an instance of A; for example, we say that this red spot *makes* the painting unbalanced or that it *gives* it its dramatic character. Does that mean that aesthetic properties are only contingently related to the nonaesthetic properties on which they supervene? Is it just a matter of brute fact that having the nonaesthetic property N makes X have the aesthetic property A? No, for then N could make X not-A instead of A. I think this is conceptually impossible. Under the given conditions, X's being N conceptually entails its being A. Suppose that a certain sound of the cello gives a quartet its disturbing, unsettling, character. Can you imagine that very sound making that quartet sweet, gentle, and soothing when all other relevant (biological, psychological, etc.) factors stay the same? Surely not. Therefore, aesthetic properties *strongly* supervene on nonaesthetic ones. Not only (1) every aesthetic property supervenes in each world on some nonaesthetic property, but also (2) if some aesthetic property supervenes on some nonaesthetic property in some world, then it supervenes on it in all relevantly similar worlds.

That relation is stronger than the one presumed by dualists to obtain between physical and phenomenal properties. Dualists agree that phenomenal properties causally depend on the physical properties of brains, but that relation seems contingent. In fact the mental state M does not occur without the physical state P occurring. That much we know. But we do not know of any conceptual connection between M and P. Nothing we know precludes the existence of a world, similar in all relevant respects to ours, where the neuronic state P, which in fact causes us to see blue, makes us see red. On the other hand, I cannot imagine a world, similar in all relevant respects to ours, where X's tenderness is due to those phenomenal nonaesthetic traits that in our reality make X coarse. I cannot conceive of a world that is like ours in every relevant detail except that the phenomenal nonaesthetic properties we cite as evidence that X is tender serve there as evidence that X is coarse.

Thus, nonaesthetic and aesthetic properties are not only inductively related. The relation of phenomenal properties to physical ones may be contingent; we have no clue why nerve spiking N makes us sense a coffee aroma and not a timpani sound. No scientific theory deduces phenomenal properties from physical properties. We have evidence that phenomenal properties are caused by physical ones, but there is no indication that this causation is not

Humean. By contrast, art theory conceptually relates aesthetic to nonaesthetic properties; aesthetic traits cannot be imagined independently of some nonaesthetic ones.

Gaudiness, for example, stands in logical relation to the nonaesthetic property of showing pure, bright colors. Being dramatic is logically related to radically significant changes in one's circumstances of life. Being tragic, as Aristotle taught, is logically related to events that involve the fall of the great and make us feel fear and pity. Harmony is logically related to symmetry, that is, invariance under certain (e.g., topological) permutations. Being graceful is logically related to not having sharp angles and abrupt transitions. The relation between these (and scores of other aesthetic properties) and the nonaesthetic properties on which they supervene is not contingent. Knowing that X has the nonaesthetic property N, we conclude right off that it probably is A, without checking whether, in the past, being A has occurred together with being N: linguistic competence mandates that such conjunction cannot but be the rule. When you support an attribution of daintiness to X by citing nonaesthetic properties of it, you need not rely on statistically significant correlations between being dainty and being N; you know of no research that found such correlations. Rather, you refer to the *meaning* of 'dainty.' Thus, when we say 'N *makes* X dainty,' that causality cannot be Humean. Further, a Humean causal relation requires a temporal succession that is here absent: for instance, saying "What makes Sue piquant is her high cheekbones and snub nose," you do not imply that Sue had high cheekbones and a snub nose first, and then, later, she became piquant.

The causal idiom in aesthetics expresses supervenience based on a conceptual connection: stronger than causality, weaker than identity. "X is A because it is N" says that, necessarily, if X is N, it is also A. It is a meaning-rule that "X is N" implies "X is A." Such rules are the basis of art criticism: critics cite nonaesthetic descriptions of X and derive, by these rules, statements about the aesthetic features of X. They do not cite statistical data on the coinstantiation frequency of A and N. Given that X is N, they conclude that X is A. But what do these rules rely on? N and A are different properties, and 'A' is not synonymous with 'N' (or any other nonaesthetic predicate), so what justifies the inference of "X is A" from "X is N"? The answer, I said, is supervenience: aesthetic properties strongly supervene on nonaesthetic ones. But how do we know that? Since the answer must be conceptual, not statistical, one asks: Why are these properties so related? Why do the aesthetic properties supervene on the nonaesthetic ones if they are entirely distinct?

5.4. Aesthetic Objects = Phenomena + Desire

Let me define three kinds of property: *primary properties* are properties of noumena (real things); *secondary properties* are properties of phenomena (appearances of real things to minds); *tertiary properties* are properties of significant phenomena (phenomena mediated by interest). The five properties Locke called 'primary' (Number, Solidity, Motion, Shape, Size) are certainly not primary properties: none of them is invariant across frameworks (they vary according to an arbitrary decision regarding which events are considered simultaneous). We should classify them as secondary properties, together with the phenomenal properties Locke called 'secondary': colors, sounds, smells, tastes, etc. Now, many philosophers called aesthetic properties 'tertiary,' and so do I, but for a reason that differs from theirs. By my definition, a tertiary property is a way a phenomenon appears to an interested party, a person whose way of seeing it is affected by its impact on his or her interests. The Romantic tradition associates the aesthetic with the disinterested. I, on the other hand, hold that aesthetic properties are tertiary because they are tinged by desire.

A mind that has no interests can discern nonaesthetic phenomenal properties, say, see X as blue, but it cannot see things aesthetically, that is, as having aesthetic properties. Aesthetic properties appear only to those whose seeing is modulated by desire. To prove this thesis, grade aesthetic predicates by their generality, from specific predicates to the most general ones. The most general aesthetic predicates are 'beautiful' and 'ugly'; they inform us of the total aesthetic value of a thing without saying how, in what way, that thing has that value. Low in generality are 'gaudy,' 'vulgar,' 'dainty,' 'coarse,' 'tragic,' 'graceful,' 'dramatic,' etc.; they too are value-laden predicates, but give a more detailed view of the object that has them.

When a real thing X impacts on a perceptual system, the latter presents X's primary properties as modulated and modified by the system's specific nature. The result is a phenomenal object having secondary properties: X's properties as rendered by the system. A tertiary property results when yet another mental system further modulates a secondary property. That additional system is, I say, desire. Aesthetic properties perceptibly present the desirability of things as ingrained in those things themselves. We perceive X as having an aesthetic property A only if we perceive it, so to speak, conatively. An aesthetic object is, then, a desire-mediated phenomenon. Let us start with some examples of the less general aesthetic properties.

X is lovely only if we love it and desire to have X (in some way). X is ominous only if it forebodes eminent danger to us. It is tragic only if it frustrates our noble desires. It is funny only if it fulfills our just desire that someone else's desire be frustrated. It is lyrical only if it expresses our pure and noble desires. It is vulgar only if it constitutes a contemptible way of satisfying our desires. It is brutal only if it satisfies our desire by frustrating the desires of others. It is cheap only if it is a satisfaction of desire in a dishonest or unworthy way. It is ostentatious or gaudy only if it satisfies a desire for self-assertion and self-aggrandizement. Sublime and awesome things are only those that are mightier than we are, things that may harm us and that we cannot force to comply with our desires. Tender things are those that are at our mercy, things whose desires (were they to have any) we could easily frustrate. Cute things are those that appeal to our parental or protective instincts and sentiments and give us an easy way of gratifying their desires. A thing is dainty only if it is tender, lovely, and cute. These aesthetic properties and their ilk are observed only if desire perceptually interprets nature.

All these aesthetic properties reflect the bearing their object has on our actual desires. Consider Cuteness: my cat looks cute to me, but if I were to shrink in size (say, as in Disney's *Honey, I Shrunk the Kids*), it would look menacing, terrible, sinister, even evil. Godzilla and King Kong look horrendous, since they could have a devastating impact on our desires, but they are also a bit ludicrous because we are subtly assured that, being dumb, we can control them (the latter aspect is avoided in a tragedy). Their aesthetic attraction is also due to our (shameful) desire to see others destroyed while we remain safe and secure (satisfaction of *Schadenfreude*).

When one's desires go unsatisfied without one's being aware of it, we have irony and comedy; when one's desires go unsatisfied and one pretends otherwise, we have the ridiculous and the burlesque. Nobility is registered when one sacrifices satisfaction of desire for other values (thus what we see as noble is, relative to another system of values, silly and pompous). A funeral looks gloomy because it embodies our fear of dying. The happy end of a Victorian novel cannot look happy to feminists for whom marriage, far from desirable, is house arrest with forced labor; to get their lofty tone, Wagner's *Flying Dutchman* and Verdi's *Rigoletto* rely on the alleged desire of women to sacrifice; in the absence of is such desire, their aesthetic quality is horror and debasement, not the intended exaltation.

Some aesthetic properties, the expressive ones, require that we see the things that have them as manifesting an attitude to a satisfaction or frustration of desire. Inanimate objects are somber, or gay, or dismal, or happy, or melancholy, or hesitant, or serene, or bright, or reckless, or tentative, or rash, or sad, etc. only if they seem to behave as we do when we are in these psychological states. We see things as having certain aesthetic features when we see them as having those desires that we would be having had we looked, or behaved, as they do. Looking for the aesthetical aspect of things, we regard their natural properties as if they were ways of displaying or satisfying desires. Things that remind us of moderate people, who are restrained in pursuing their desires, are graceful; their beauty is controlled and self-collected. An object looks dramatic only if it looks like a person possessed by great desire: disheveled and excited, precariously balanced, willing to risk all.

Specific aesthetic properties are then phenomenal properties of desire-constituted aesthetic objects, things seen as if they were living beings whose physiognomy is akin to ours. All arts use our ability to see inanimate things anthropomorphically, as if they had the human build and desires. Were we to look at things as Kant's aesthetics says we should, that is, to bracket our desire and observe things as covered by Rawls's veil of ignorance, abstracting from what they mean to us, we could discern no aesthetic properties in nature, and art would be impossible.

Even abstract art is thoroughly anthropomorphic: a visual or melodic line is seen as striving, ascending, climbing, gaining in power, becoming carefree, frolicking, then carefully maintaining a tense, precarious balance, eventually losing control, falling down, crushed, vanquished, disintegrating, dying out, and then emerging, miraculously coming back to life, triumphing over its adversaries, reasserting itself gloriously, making peace and restoring harmony. These and other anthropomorphic ways of perceiving form are essential to art. We interpret formal traits empathically, as manifestations of desire; that way of seeing gives art, nonfigurative art and pure design (e.g., arabesques) included, its significance, hence its aesthetic value.

Beauty and its opposite, Ugliness, are on the other end of the generality scale. Other general aesthetic properties are Unity, Coherence, Balance, Harmony, Power, Significance, Tension, and their opposites. These properties reflect one desire. The medium through which nonaesthetic phenomenal properties are sifted to become the general aesthetic properties is a *cognitive* desire. The general aesthetic merit of a thing depends on the degree to which it satisfies our desire to organize the world, perceptually and conceptually, making it comprehensible to our cognitive faculties. Here Kant's aesthetics is right on the mark: the general aesthetic properties echo the satisfaction of our cognitive desire. Aesthetic merit qua good design is a condition for being an object, as Kant says, *überhaupt*.

An object is ugly if it generates too much information for our data-processing capacity. What is too rich for us to digest, what has more items than we can possibly integrate, is noisy and chaotic. Also ugly is an item that has too much order and too little innovation, generating information that is too meager relative to the capacity of our cognitive system; it is boring. Repetitive, or too well known, items are trivial, tedious, trite, and dull; in a word, they are ugly.[5] Thomas Aquinas can be interpreted in that way too: Beauty is that which makes an object good to observe (*id quod visum placet*). Quine is surely right that every assortment of items (say, the Taj Mahal plus a certain shriek in the night) can be regarded as a single object, but (as Quine is the first to admit) such anarchic objects are epistemologically parasitic on more coherent ones we can readily reify, such as mama or water. An extremely disunited, hence ugly, object is not even observable: we do not see it as one thing. In beautiful objects the ratio of richness to order is optimal for us to grasp. The beautiful object perfectly (for us) balances richness (what is rich for us: that is, *significant* richness) and unity. If it is too easy (too unified) or too difficult (too rich) for us to process, it is ugly. Paraphrasing Aquinas, beauty is the glow of well-formed things that richly satisfy our cognitive desire.

That explains why the aesthetic strongly supervenes on the nonaesthetic: an aesthetic property—a degree of unified significance—is a nonaesthetic property when viewed through the medium of desire. Significance is its impact on desire, which it may satisfy or frustrate. The desire that gives things their significance is ours, but it need not be perceived as ours: we may impute our desires to inanimate things. To say of X that it is gaudy, tender, pretty, or hideous is to describe it under categories that sort objects by their impact on desire, whether it is ours or a desire we imaginatively impute to them. Aesthetic sensitivity requires an ability to see things as having interest-determined properties, to listen to the desires of things. An aesthetically sensitive person sees whether things fit or clash, enhance each other or are incompatible with each other, whether their combination is gaudy or graceful. (Note that to have bad taste is to see the *wrong* things as having these properties; to have no taste is to see nothing as having these properties.) We say that poets feel which words "like each other," "feel right together," and which combination is cacophonous, jarring, and discordant.

5. See D. E. Berlyne, *Studies in the New Experimental Aesthetics* (New York: John Wiley, 1974).

To summarize: We see things via desire. Specific aesthetic properties are modifications of phenomenal properties by any manner of desire; the general ones are perceived when things are *seen as* suited to cognitive desires only. The latter are ways of sorting things by fitness to our cognitive apparatus, that is, by their degree of perceived cognitive goodness.

So far, the discussion seems to imply antirealistic conclusions. It seems to say that aesthetic properties *ontologically* depend on human (or other sentient and conative) beings and cannot exist without them; they emerge only when we perceive things via interest-filtered sensitivity, when desire perceptually and directly informs us about ambient things. Therefore it seems that noumena, things whose existence is not perceiver-dependent, cannot have aesthetic properties. If aesthetic properties reflect the value that *we* put on things, then no aesthetic (tertiary) properties can be primary properties too. That conclusion, I now argue, is mistaken.

5.5. Noumena and Phenomenal Properties

Before getting to the aesthetic properties of reality, let me ask another question first. Suppose that reality has all and only those properties attributed to it by mature science. For the argument's sake, let us also suppose that today science is that fully adequate, mature science whose description of reality, and it alone, we are justified in believing. Does this imply that no secondary property is true of reality and that nothing in reality has the properties we sense?

Suppose that it is so: no phenomenal properties are primary; reality as such has no sensible properties. I now ask what seems a silly question: how do the properties that science *does* ascribe to reality differ from each other? One may answer that distinct properties may get different numerical values; that is true, but what are the properties to which these values are assigned? For instance, how do Spin and Charge differ? Usually we do not find the existence of different physical properties puzzling, because we understand how a body can have distinct phenomenal properties. A body in motion is not at all similar to increased illumination; we can, visually, tell them apart; so we understand the distinction between a 15 percent increase in acceleration and a 15 percent increase in radiation. Yet how can we make sense of that difference with no phenomenal properties to illustrate it? They are supposed to be distinct in and of themselves, regardless of their impact on us, so it is not their phenomenal appearance to sentient beings that distinguishes them. What does? We immediately understand the term 'light,' for we know how light looks, we are acquainted with the way it appears. But how can we understand the meaning of 'light' if our acquaintance with phenomena is not to be relied on? Without recourse to phenomena, physics is uninterpreted.

Distinct physical properties differ not only by magnitude, but by their content as well. A difference in content must be manifest in some way. Thus, although physical properties need not be perceptible to us, they must, having a content, be perceptible. Those who perceive these properties perceive phenomenal *primary* properties. If physical entities do not have, in and of themselves, some qualitative distinction observable by humans or others, then those entities are different from each other only numerically, by magnitude. But that is wrong: the same numbers may apply to acceleration and to radiation. The difference is qualitative; hence, it is, in principle, observable, phenomenal.

Conjoin all the theorems of physics and substitute bound variables for all semantically interpreted constants ('charge,' 'spin,' etc.). The ensuing Ramsey sentence includes logical and arithmetical symbols but no semantically meaningful predicates. That sentence is equivalent to physics, hence true of reality, but it is also true of numerous other worlds that are isomorphic with, but very different from, ours. It says next to nothing about our world because isomorphism is so cheap; all infinite magnitudes can be mapped on each other. Failing to distinguish between entirely different worlds, the said Ramsey sentence is nearly hollow. The difference between meaningful physics and the hollow Ramsey sentence is due to the meanings of the constants of physics, yet these meanings differ in phenomenal properties only, so they are inexpressible by physics as we know it.

Take, for instance, time. A physics text does not tell you what 'time' refers to; you ought to know that from experience. Many things can have the formal properties time has and play the same role in the equations of physics. What makes it true that time, and no other item with the same mathematical properties, is referred to? Only the phenomenal properties associated with time, time as experienced. We know what time is and how it is different from, say, light, because we *feel* time. We have a sense of time; that is, we directly perceive temporal intervals. You can tell by direct observation whether a given event, A, comes before or after another event, B, and whether a given temporal interval, D_1, is longer or shorter than another felt interval, D_2. Time feels different from light: we need not measure them to distinguish between

THE ONTOLOGY OF AESTHETIC PROPERTIES

them. Its phenomenal properties distinguish time from other magnitudes: an experienced temporal stretch feels different from a rise in temperature. Sheared of phenomenal properties, time is but a set of numbers.

Some philosophers toyed with the Pythagorean idea that reality is a pure mathematical structure with no material properties at all. But we saw that at least some real things, persons, have real, yet irreducibly phenomenal properties: beliefs. Even if the world is contentless, beliefs about it are not. Having such and such beliefs is a phenomenal property that differs in content in isomorphic worlds. It is caused by something in reality, so reality can cause modifications of content in persons, a property numbers lack. Thus, reality is not a formal structure; it has some *primary phenomenal* properties as well.

5.6. The Aesthetic Properties of Reality

Above (Chapter 3) I already gave several arguments that some tertiary properties are also primary. I now summarize one of those arguments and then go on to advance additional evidence that aesthetic predicates are true of reality.

Acceptability of a theory, I said, depends on its aesthetic merits. To be worthy of acceptance a theory needs to cohere with other maintained beliefs, explain them and be explained by them. Unity, simplicity, scope, elegance, dramatic power (prediction), all of them aesthetic virtues, make a theory beliefworthy. Now, if a theory's beauty is what justifies believing it is true, then some aesthetic propositions need to be true in order for us to be justified in believing any other proposition is true. A theory claiming that aesthetic properties are not real undermines itself and attests to its own falsity. If no aesthetic properties exist, then all attributions of beauty are false, and thus the theory that denies the reality of aesthetic properties is not beautiful. But a nonbeautiful theory is unworthy of acceptance.

I further argued that aesthetic properties are irreducible. Let T be the theory that aesthetic properties are reducible. T is acceptable only if a sentence using the unreduced predicates ('simple,' 'dramatic,' 'parsimonious,' 'elegant,' 'rich,' etc.) is true of T. Thus, any reason for accepting T presupposes its falsity. It is the *truth* of *unreduced* aesthetic statements on which acceptability hangs. So, if it is justified to believe that some nonaesthetic property is primary, it is a fortiori justified to believe that some aesthetic properties are primary.

Let me now continue the argument. I shall not raise the question why the world is aesthetically perfect. Saint Augustine explains that by saying that a perfect Being made it; there are other explanations too. However, the question, Why is reality beautiful? is not at issue here; my claim is only that reality *is* beautiful. What reason is there to hold that aesthetic excellence is truth-tropic except that the truth is aesthetically excellent? It would be irrational to use Beauty as a guide to reality unless we believed that reality is beautiful. You track F-ness to get to X only if you believe that X is F. Thus, science has no rational justification unless we hold that aesthetic excellence is a property the world *really has*.

Elsewhere I have argued that the miracle argument used by scientific realists to prove the literal truth of science (to wit: only the *truth* of science explains its enormous success; otherwise, the success of science would be a miracle) is invalid.[6] Pierre Duhem showed that our science is but one of infinitely many theories that account for the same data; every body of data can be derived from infinitely many distinct theories.[7] The predictive power of our science does not show it is true, because each of those infinitely many other theories would have had the same rate of success had *it*, instead of our science, been used to make the prediction. That our science was in fact used to predict, while those other theories were not, goes nowhere toward proving that it is true and they are not.

The original miracle argument is invalid; yet let me suggest a variation that may work. The uncountable Duhemian alternative sciences may be no less *successful* than our science, but they are not as pretty. Duhem does show that, pragmatism to the contrary, our science is not the one that works best, but I think it is unquestionably the fairest of those that work. Now, were the requirement of beauty irrelevant to truth, it would be a severe handicap to a theory. The success of such a handicapped theory would be a great miracle. It is much more reasonable to assume that beauty, far from being irrelevant to truth, is truth-tropic.

I repeat: Science is constrained by aesthetic criteria. It is undeniable (even by irrealists) that science progresses toward empirical adequacy. That progress is truly miraculous if science is encumbered by totally irrelevant aesthetic demands. The effectiveness of science is better explained if these demands are not irrelevant, that is, if they are an asset and not just a hurdle,

6. Eddy Zemach, "Truth and Beauty," *Philosophical Forum* 18 (1986): 21–39.
7. Pierre Duhem, *The Aim and Structure of Physical Theory* (New York: Atheneum, 1954).

not just extra baggage. If cleaving to beauty, rather than, say, to scripture, is a good guide to empirical adequacy, then perhaps beauty is an objective feature of reality. That would explain why, as long as we cleave to beauty, science manages to be empirically adequate. Against that modified miracle argument the Duhem—Van Fraasen arguments cannot be used. Although there are infinitely many empirically adequate alternative sciences, it is not true (nor do irrealists claim it) that any of them is *beautiful*; on the contrary, we have very good reasons to believe that these "sciences," being ad hoc theories, are exceedingly ugly. In its beauty our science is unique. Thus, even if the empirical adequacy of science needs no explanation, the empirical adequacy of a beautiful science does.

So, we may resuscitate a miracle argument in a new form. If the success of a theory that adheres, say, to a principle of mass/energy conservation is best explained by the world's really being such that mass/energy is conserved in it, then perhaps the success of our practice of following aesthetic constraints is best explained by the world's really being beautiful.

5.7. Aesthetics in Action

Here is a fantasy: when elementary particles are discovered, we are astonished to find that they gyrate in ballet motions. Hydrogen results from around-the-clock performance of *Swan Lake;* oxygen is elementary particles dancing *Romeo and Juliet;* and so on for all elements. Elementary particles unerringly obey the rules of classical ballet, move only in ways allowed by it, and execute these figures with supreme grace and ease.

Had that been a fact, we would all agree that aesthetic properties are real, moreover, are basic constituents of reality, so that an adequate explanation of nature must employ aesthetic concepts. Now, our fairy tale is closer to fact than to fantasy. The role of aesthetic properties is even more central in truth than it is in the above fairy tale. Mathematicians play a game related to experienced reality much less than football, chess, or *Swan Lake;* the abstract structures of mathematics are creatures of pure imagination, constrained by aesthetic considerations only. Along come elementary-particle physicists and find that these mathematical artworks (e.g., group theory) describe reality— that is, reality obeys these anthropocentric aesthetic considerations to a tee. We go along with the game even when no interpretation for it seems possible; we trust that eventually an interpretation will emerge, and it does. Predictions based on lovely equations whose justification is merely aesthetic, consisting of tenuous, even merely notational analogy with classical laws, turn out to be accurate to ten orders of magnitude, a degree of precision never reached before.[8] The empirical adequacy of mathematics, a game built on aesthetic considerations, is astonishing. John von Neumann (and other great mathematicians) stress the aesthetic nature of mathematical constraints by insisting that the criteria used by mathematical theory "are clearly those of any creative art."[9]

In "The Application of Mathematics to Natural Science" Mark Steiner (who holds that mathematical, hence aesthetic, concepts are natural kinds) illustrates how formal analogy guided modern science even when the analogy seemed physically irrelevant or meaningless. Let me quote:

> My thesis, then, is: the use of formal mathematical analogies—not between events, but between their descriptions—has been indispensable in recent physical discovery. But such formal analogies appear to be irrelevant analogies—and irrelevant analogies should not work at all. One would be quite surprised, for example, if one could make even one substantial physical discovery based upon the statistical distribution of the letters of the Roman alphabet in Newton's *Principia* . . . (I shall suggest, for example, that even the geometrical properties of the mathematical notation used in physics have played a role in physical discovery!)

> Schroedinger relied on a formal, second-order mathematical analogy. The procedure worked. The equation yielded known results as solutions, and previously unknown solutions were found in nature.

> Schroedinger multiplied the probability density function by the electric charge e . . . [a]nd his equation was derived by substituting in the relativistic energy-momentum equation for an electron in an electromagnetic field, rather than in that of the free particle. What justified these substitutions? In Schroedinger's own words, nothing but a "purely formal analogy"!

8. Cf. Eugene Wigner, "The Unreasonable Effectiveness of Mathematics in the Natural Sciences," in his *Symmetries and Reflections* (Bloomington: Indiana University Press, 1967).

9. Quoted in Mark Steiner, "The Application of Mathematics to Natural Science," *Journal of Philosophy* 86 (1989): 455.

In 1932, Heisenberg conjectured that the proton and the neutron are two states of the same particle, "spinning" in opposite directions in a totally fictitious three-dimensional "space" with the same mathematical properties as ordinary space. The space has to be fictitious, since (unlike the situation with the "up-down" electronic states) one cannot turn a neutron into a proton by standing on one's head. Heisenberg reasoned that the nucleus of the atom is invariant under abstract "rotations" in this fictitious space, and that there had to be, therefore, a new conserved quantity, mathematically analogous to spin. This quantity is today called isospin, and its discovery launched nuclear physics.

But what Gell-Mann did, in effect, was to generalize the concept of a "rotation" to include transformations of complex space, and then generalize the complex two-dimensional "rotations" to three dimensions! The crucial point is that, unlike the case of two dimensions, three-dimensional complex "rotations" no longer correspond to rotations of any real space of any dimension.[10]

There are many other examples of the same phenomenon: scientific discovery due to regarding an ever increasing dosage of aesthetic constraints as reasons for accepting a theory.

Naturally, naturalist aestheticians find that unacceptable. They cannot believe that it is dovetailing *aesthetic* properties that decides theory acceptance and is responsible for science's uncanny success. Alan Goldman, in discussing my view as expressed in a previous article, says: "I have proposed a different defense of inference to the best explanation (as it generates scientific realism) elsewhere, one that does not rely on the defense of aesthetic criteria for truth. According to this view . . . it is likely that our brains have evolved in part for such truth-preserving, inferential capacities . . . If these grounds are wired into our brains by evolution then it should not be surprising that analogues of them constitute some (but by no means all) of the reasons why certain objects appeal to us aesthetically."[11] This is playing fast and loose

10. Ibid., 454. 458, 470, 461, 463. See also his "Autonomy of Mathematics," *Iyyun* 39 (1990): 101–14, and James W. McAllister, "Truth and Beauty in Scientific Reason," *Synthese* 78 (1989): 25–51.

11. Alan H. Goldman, "Realism About Aesthetic Properties," *Journal of Aesthetics and Art Criticism* 51 (1993): 35–36. Cf. his *Empirical Knowledge* (Berkeley and Los Angeles: University of California Press, 1988), chap. 13.

with history. Our species evolved under harsh conditions that put no survival value on preference for symmetry, harmony, and elegance. Mathematical beauty had very little to do with our growing knowledge of nature; its role grew considerably in the seventeenth and the eighteenth centuries, but only in the twentieth century did it become the paramount tool of scientific discovery. Thus, the very opposite of Goldman's thesis is true: notoriously, aesthetic considerations of symmetry and harmony (e.g., the *Timaeus*) were impediments to immature science, the scourge of natural philosophy that empiricists replaced by unassuming observation. To serve physics, mathematics had to be radically curbed.[12] There is no mathematical significance to the number of leaves on a branch or the number of teeth in a mouth, so as long as the objects of science are all molar, it has no use for mathematical beauty. Numerological considerations thrived in mystical theories, but in science they were worse than worthless. That the Keats constraints are no longer regarded by scientists as crackpot is a phenomenon so new that anthropic explanations of it are grossly anachronistic.

In explaining why a work of art X has feature F we often use aesthetic statements: we say that were X to lack that property, it would have been uglier: that is the third Keats Principle. A good study of a given painting would, for example, explain the presence of a yellow spot in the lower corner of the painting by its balancing a blue spot in the upper corner. What we see now is that such aesthetic explanations reveal basic laws of nature. Perhaps in order to understand how the world is (say, how wave functions develop), we need to use aesthetic reasoning. Some may even say that the beauty of the mathematical structures (say, group theory) that lie at the core of reality is its raison d'être. I shall not express an opinion on these speculations; I merely say that they may to some extent be corroborated, and if they are, we have another reason to believe that some primary properties of the world are aesthetic.

---

12. "In the seventeenth century, it seems, natural philosophy emancipated itself from the tyranny of mathematics—and was, therefore, capable of *using* much more mathematics . . . [P]hysics now turned to mathematics with concrete problems to be solved for *a* formula or figure—not necessarily the simplest or even a perfect one in mathematical terms. If circles do not describe celestial orbits, then the ellipse, a less perfect but more general figure, does. Again, the physicist of the seventeenth century employs mathematics rather as a language than as an inventory of real entities" (Amos Funkenstein, *Theology and the Scientific Imagination from the Middle Ages to the Seventeenth Century* [Princeton: Princeton University Press, 1986], 314).

6

CRITERIA OF
INTERPRETATION

6.1. Paradigms of Interpretation

To interpret X is to say what X means, that is, to assign X a meaning. What is a meaning? I maintain that meanings are things.[1] If X *refers us to* Y, then X means Y—that is, Y is the meaning of X. A sign is a thing that refers us to, makes us focus on, another thing, and a meaning is a thing to which a sign, in its role as a sign, calls our attention. Note that X may *refer us to* Y yet not *refer to* Y. If X refers to Y, then X means Y, but not vice versa: X may refer *us* to Y, hence mean Y, but not refer to Y.[2]

How can one thing refer us to another thing? Here are two ways in which a thing can acquire a meaning, that is, become a sign. In the first way, X refers us to Y in virtue of some well-known connections between them. We look up and say, "That cloud means rain"; we examine a dog's carcass next to our camp and say: "This means that we are in bear territory." The cloud

---

1. For details and explanations of this view and the following rough sketch of my theory of meaning, see my *Reality of Meaning and the Meaning of "Reality"* (Providence, R.I.: Brown University Press, 1992).

2. I assimilate meaning to reference: the meaning of a sign, what it means, is what it refers us to. That move is not, however, a complete break with the Fregean tradition, since I treat semantic reference (X refers to Y) as based on a more elementary notion: *directing attention to something* (X calls our attention to Y). Both Frege (who held that the *Sinn* of a term directs us to its *Bedeutung*) and Wittgenstein (*Tractatus* 3.144) capitalized on the etymology of 'sense,' i.e., direction, in their theories of meaning. My ploy is similar: "X refers to Y," I say, entails "X refers us to Y," but not vice versa.

acquired its meaning through the well-known connections between it and rain[3]—similarly for the dead dog and the local presence of bears. These things are linked, so the first (cloud, dead dog) refers us to the second (rain, bear). That is also how words acquire a meaning. How did the French word *'cheval'* come to mean Horse? Roughly, because for generations *'cheval'* interacted with horses in a variety of language games that together realized the various linguistic functions. These games were played by French people, so *'cheval'* became their sign for horses; they perceive it as calling their attention to, that is, referring them to, horses.

The other way in which something becomes a sign, referring us to its meaning, involves no previous connections; we go ahead to establish a connection on the spot. With X present to us, we *bring in* Y and engage in a game that links X and Y, hoping that our student (who has a native ability to intend) gets the idea of X being a sign for Y. For example, to teach the word 'horse' to a baby you start playing a language game: if you are lucky enough to have horses around, you initiate various kinds of activity that involve both horse and 'horse'; if not, you use a connection already in place between horse pictures and horses, and engage the baby in a language game that involves, *inter alia*, the word 'horse' and that picture.

These two ways of introducing meanings parallel two ways of interpreting. A literary critic does not *produce* the meanings he attributes to the interpreted text; rather, he *refers* his readers to these meanings by using words of his own. The readers know what his words mean, so they focus on these meanings and thus get to know what, in the critic's opinion, is the meaning of the interpreted text. In music and in the theater, on the other hand, the interpreter cannot assume such competence on the part of the audience. Therefore, he goes ahead to *produce*, there and then, (what he thinks is) the meaning of the interpreted work. To perform an artwork is to bring into existence, that is, to produce, its (alleged) meaning. The performed artwork is, thus, regarded as a sign, and the object that the performer brings into existence is claimed to be its meaning. A pianist interprets a piano sonata by producing the thing he wishes to refer us to, a thing that, according to him, is the meaning of the work he interprets. To interpret X is, then, to use some

---

3. One may think that the past interactions were not between *that* cloud and rain, so the singular term is misplaced. I discuss and defend my use of the singular in the next chapter. One may also feel uncomfortable with my use of the term 'thing,' which I apply to Rain in general, and even to the situation that there are bears around here. Again, that use is deliberate, and its justification is spelled out in the next chapter.

relation that X has to Y (which may or may not exist prior to interpreting), so that we see X as referring us to Y.

The notion of interpretation is problematic because it has two constraints, indirectly related to the above two strategies: an interpretation is required to be correct, and it is required to be exciting. That generates two paradigms of interpretation: heuristic and creative. On the heuristic paradigm interpretation is carried out by substituting an expression that you understand for another that you do not understand. Both expressions already *have* a meaning, the same meaning, but you can gather that meaning from the first expression only. On that paradigm interpretation should be right and satisfy a need: it is good iff it is correct and helpful, bad iff it is incorrect or unhelpful. An interpretation is correct if it preserves the meaning of the interpretandum, and it is helpful if it gets you to a meaning that you could not reach without it. That value is purely heuristic: you need X to be interpreted if you cannot get its meaning otherwise. Once interpreted, however, you understand X, and the interpretation has no further value to you.

That paradigm conflicts with our belief that interpretation in art has intrinsic value. First, we hold that an artwork may have several good yet incompatible interpretations; but if a good interpretation is a correct one, that seems impossible: identical readings cannot be incompatible. Second, interpretations do not become redundant when understood; they, too, are works of art, and interpreters (performers) are artists in their own right. The heuristic paradigm (interpretation as translation) cannot account for that. Third, on the heuristic paradigm interpreters decipher the meaning of the work, helping those who cannot figure out its meaning by themselves. It leaves no place for creativity. On that paradigm, creative interpretation is absurd.

Realism in aesthetics seems to favor the heuristic paradigm, since on it the question whether X has an aesthetic property A is strictly factual; you empirically investigate the artwork X to verify whether X is A. If you cannot conduct that investigation, someone else may do it for you, for there is nothing personal in that question. Realists say that critics describe the aesthetic properties of objects; so coming up with conflicting reports is a failure, an embarrassment to avoid! Surely, that is not what we think. The heuristic paradigm fails to explain the creativity and the possible disagreement of *good* interpretations.

I now turn to the creative paradigm. If interpretation is meaning assignment, it can be creative; you can assign meanings creatively. On that view a word is a mark that does not inherently stand for anything; we may assign it any meaning we please. Is it true, however, that interpreters arbitrarily assign semantic values to the interpreted work, as we arbitrarily assign the meaning *stop* to octagonal red signs?[4] Are meanings assigned by the author of the work?

If to interpret is to assign a meaning and yet there are proper and improper interpretations, you cannot find the proper interpretation of X by investigating X, for no scrutiny given to X can tell what item was assigned to it. Rather, an investigation into the meaning of X should start by finding who assigned X its meaning, that is, who is the author of X, and then finding what meaning the author wished to assign to X. The author decides what semantic value his sign is to have, for it is his sign, a sign he produces for the express purpose of giving it that semantic value. Further, the author's intention exclusively decides the meaning of the work, for there is nothing more to assigning Y to the sign X than intending to do so. The question, What does X mean? is therefore equivalent to the question, What semantic value did the author wish to assign to X? However, we all know that searching for such biographical information is *not* the only thing literary critics do. Second, that paradigm, too, cannot make sense of our benign acceptance of conflicting interpretations; if the author assigned Y to X, those who accept other interpretations are guilty of epistemic turpitude.

We reach an interesting result: it appears that advocates of the author's intention criterion of interpretation agree with those usually considered their arch-rivals, the relativists, according to whom a text has no correct interpretation. What is common to them is the tacit assumption that we assign meaning to something meaningless. That Tractarian view is assumed by both intentionalists and relativists.[5] They differ only in defining 'work of art.' For the intentionalist an artwork is an interpreted text, an object cum meaning assignment, which has one meaning assigner, its author, and hence only one meaning. For the relativist, texts have no inherent meaning, so you may assign any meaning you please to the text, possibly more than one meaning per text. Radical relativism makes interpretation a masquerade: if an author can decide what X means, so can I, and I will have X mean something else. The latter view is popular with the deconstructionists. It does provide a solution to our puzzle, explaining why we need interpretation (to assign meaning to signs) and why interpretations conflict (readers may assign the same signs many meanings). What that solution does not do, of

---

4. I.e., the situation P-required, where P is the situation your-stopping-here.

5. An explicit follower of it is Arthur Danto; see the last two chapters of *The Transfiguration of the Commonplace* (Cambridge: Harvard University Press, 1981).

course, is explain our intuition that interpretation is not arbitrary, that there is an objective correlative that makes some interpretations right and others wrong, some correct and others incorrect. Taken to the extreme, the creative paradigm reduces the interpreted work to the bare meaningless ink-spotted pages of the text. Such a raw object, however, has no value, and it puts no constraints on interpretation; its author deserves no credit, for any other object could take its place and be assigned the same meaning. That, I think, is a *reductio ad absurdum* of relativism about interpretation.

The interpreted work, say, a novel, can be translated; what is invariant between different-language editions of the same work is its meaning. That meaning is also common to all its distinct interpretations. So, the work as it is, uninterpreted, has a meaning of its own. The argument applies to distinct editions of the same work executed in distinct fonts, scripts, or media; abridged editions of the work, censured and expurgated editions, corrected and modernized editions of it are all editions *of it*, the same work. What decides the identity of the work from edition to edition is its meaning. That makes it implausible that an artwork is a meaningless, passive receptacle awaiting meaning assignment by its various interpreters. In the present chapter I do not challenge the above paradigms of interpretation; I do that in the next chapter, where I explain my own view of interpretation. Here I examine only their derivatives: the criteria of interpretation that stem from those paradigms; I ask whether these paradigms provide a criterion of interpretation acceptability that accounts for our basic intuitions about art.

6.2. The Causal Account

Deconstructionist theorists and relativist philosophers tell us now that interpretation is unconstrained by truth and falsity. However, the best argument for that view was given, many years ago, by Charles Stevenson, whose seminal work in aesthetics is unjustly neglected. Like today's literary theorists, and for very similar reasons, Stevenson holds what he calls a "normative" approach to art interpretation. On that view no interpretation of a literary text is true or false. A method of interpretation can be criticized internally, but externally, 'right' and 'wrong' do not apply to interpretations.[6] Stevenson

6. See Charles L. Stevenson, "Interpretation and Evaluation in Aesthetics," in *Philosophical Analysis,* ed. M. Block (Ithaca: Cornell University Press, 1950), 341–82 (henceforth

formulates the idea currently advocated by irrealists (Nelson Goodman, Simon Blackburn, Crispin Wright, Richard Rorty, Arthur Fine, Joseph Margolis, and others),[7] that 'right' and 'wrong' are relative to discourse; there are many culturally conditioned criteria of rightness for a critic to choose from. A discourse, Stevenson holds (like the relativists), is limited in scope. In a discourse a criterion can be incorrectly applied, but the adoption of a criterion for interpretation can be neither correct nor incorrect; it sets up a discourse and therefore is not cognitively constrained. Criteria specify various "correct" strategies for reading a text and posit an "ideal reader" for each criterion. "A text is correctly understood iff it is understood as its author meant it" is one such criterion; "a text is correctly understood iff understood as a political tool" is another. Criteria for interpretation are chosen by readers and critics, not by philosophers. Stevenson says that the "normative approach carefully avoids" deciding between criteria. "It leaves it to the critic to decide, as he sees fit."[8]

To answer those who wonder how the critic decides which of the many criteria to adopt, Stevenson offers a postmodernist defense of the relativistic contention that reasons are relative to systems; therefore that decision cannot be justified at all. The relation "x is a good reason for y" is discourse-relative, he says. There can be no transhistorical, generally valid reasons for choosing a criterion. The critic's decision is determined by psychological, sociological, etc. *causes,* and science may discover which they are, but that is all. Are critics not guided by what they know, or believe, to be true? Yes, says Stevenson, but only in the sense that what one believes *causes* one to do certain things:

> In just what sense can such knowledge "guide" a decision? We must not suppose that a logical relation is involved. For a decision is a *process,* in which certain ways of responding to a work of art are accepted and others are rejected. It is not, then, the assertion of a proposition . . . And only if it involved a proposition could it meaningfully be said to stand in a logical relation to knowledge.

"Interpretation"), and his "On the Reasons That Can Be Given for the Interpretation of a Poem," in *Philosophy Looks at the Arts,* ed. Joseph Margolis (New York: Scribner's Sons, 1962), 121–39 (henceforth "Reasons").

7. See, e.g., Huw Price, *Facts and the Function of Truth* (Oxford: Basil Blackwell, 1988), and his "Metaphysical Pluralism," *Journal of Philosophy* 89 (1992): 387–409.

8. "Reasons," 131.

> Rather, the guiding relation is a *causal* one . . . Like any psycho-
> logical process, the critic's decision has a great many causes; and
> among these causes we must include the critic's beliefs which
> will . . . influence him both conatively and affectively.[9]

First, is it true that decision is a process? Stevenson knew of Ryle's distinction between performance verbs and achievement verbs, and undoubtedly 'decide' is an achievement verb. 'Think' (cf. 'travel') is a performance verb denoting a process, but 'decide' (like 'arrive') is not. A decision may be the result of a lengthy process of deliberation, but the decision itself is not one. Second, Stevenson is right in saying that if decision is an act, it is not a proposition; yet this does not imply that it cannot have logical relations to propositions. Since certain propositions are true, a decision that ignores them, does not take them into account, is irrational, unjustified, and silly. These predicates apply to acts such as accepting or rejecting a criterion, not to propositions. Furthermore, causal statements do lend support to a choice of a criterion of interpretation, making it reasonable or not, under the described conditions ("At the time, he was taking optimism-inducing drugs"). Stevenson's refusal to accord truth and falsity to interpretations is, thus, wrong. (Annette Barnes makes a similar point, her reason for ascribing truth to interpretations being ordinary usage.[10] Barnes needs to show, however, that usage is not based on error and must be accepted by aestheticians.)

Let the critic's decision to interpret X as meaning *that p* be caused by an Oedipus complex. The critic may know this (his analyst tells him so), but that cause cannot justify a choice of a criterion of interpretation. "X should be read thus and so because I have an Oedipus complex" is no justification. The cause of my choosing a Marxist criterion may be my being a Marxist, but then I would justify my choice, not by the fact that I am a Marxist, but by arguing that Marxism is true. Postmodernist theorists do not claim their views to be true, but they do say that they are justified in holding them, so being caused to adopt such and such interpretative strategies is not the end of the matter. Beliefs, as Davidson says, are causes; but so are headaches. Now, postmodernist critics indeed do not attempt to justify their beliefs, yet they cite their beliefs and not their headaches to justify their choice of a criterion.

---

9. "Interpretation," 359.
10. Annette Barnes, *On Interpretation* (Oxford: Basil Blackwell, 1988), 52ff.

That shows that beliefs have a special role in justification. A belief may cause one to adopt a criterion of interpretation, but even a relativist would demand that it should logically support the purported criterion; otherwise, it is irrelevant.

The grain of truth in Stevenson's position is that a chain of reasons and justifications must come to an end; like a tired parent, a critic may answer the persistent questioner by the proverbial 'because.' But that indicates that we gave an explanation, that the explanation consisted of reasons, and that those reasons were good enough. The very fact that we reach an end point is a mark of a chain of reasons; a causal chain can go back as far as one cares to go, without the question, Why? ever becoming otiose, nonsensical, or inappropriate. A Derridian may reject the entire reason-giving game and decline to take part in it, but that does not show that one cannot justify a choice of an interpretative strategy, only that one may decline to justify it.

Stevenson admits that some interpretations should be ruled out, some strategies it is unreasonable to accept.[11] What rules these strategies out, however, except absolute criteria that are *not* discourse-relative? The term 'unreasonable' is used here in an absolute sense (since in *some* discourses— the Mad Hatter kind of discourse, perhaps—an interpretation that we rule out would be right at home). This implies, by *modus tollens,* that criteria that *do not* imply outrageous interpretations *do* have some objective epistemic advantage over their rivals.

A contemporary deconstructionist may be more radical and insist that Stevenson need not have conceded that point, that *no* criterion of interpretation is open to external criticism: a choice of a criterion of interpretation is sovereign. Such radical relativism, however, is vulnerable to a new version of the old refutation of relativism: Interpret the radical relativist as having just said that Stevenson is right and some outrageous interpretations *are* absolutely wrong. Will the relativist not protest that your interpretation of his words is wrong, absolutely wrong? The relativist may try again: "You may," he might say, "interpret me as saying that some interpretations are wrong, but that is not how I understand myself. I choose to interpret myself as rejecting all allegations of wrongness in interpretation; they are symptoms of power-hungry hegemonism." This confession of the relativist again requires interpretation. Suppose that you interpret it as saying that the relativist understands his own position as making an absolute, metahistorical

11. "Interpretation," 365.

value judgment. Surely a relativist will say that you are twisting his words, that your interpretation of his *own* way of conceiving of his position is *not true.*

A relativist may make his own interpretation criterion C explicit and insist that we interpret his words by C only. Yet C can be interpreted as enjoining views that the postmodernist spurns. It is futile for him to demand that we use C to interpret C; a detractor may accept that demand too, but, since the detractor interprets C not as the relativist does, use C to interpret him as endorsing absolutism in interpretation. Furthermore, a truly radical relativist may have excellent pragmatic reasons to interpret the postmodernist as endorsing absolute values. For example, it amuses us to interpret him in that way. Radical relativists Barry Barnes and David Bloor proclaim: "For the relativist there is no sense attached to the idea that some standards or beliefs are really rational as distinct from locally accepted as such. Because he thinks that there are no context-free or super-cultural norms of rationality, he does not see rationally and irrationally held beliefs as two distinct and qualitatively different classes of things . . . Hence the relativist conclusion that they are to be explained in the same way."[12] The self-destructiveness of this position becomes apparent when we apply it to relativism itself. Irrational people cannot function in purposive ways and need a special protective environment. Had Barnes and Bloor believed that their standards and beliefs were not "really rational" they would have sought not a publisher but medical help.

Barnes and Bloor believe that their views are "locally accepted," so they need not care about their rationality. Is it true that their views are locally accepted? Is it rational or irrational to hold that belief? If it is irrational, we need not pay attention to it. If they cannot tell whether it is rational, their situation is worse; those who doubt the rationality of their own beliefs (mental patients often do) and yet publish them are, for sure, irrational. Can they justify their behavior (they publish material whose rationality they doubt) by arguing that their wretched condition is universal? No, for those who cannot tell whether their beliefs are rational cannot presume to *know* that everyone suffers from the same predicament! We are left with one conclusion: Barnes and Bloor maintain that the belief that their views are

12. Barry Barnes and David Bloor, "Relativism, Rationalism, and the Sociology of Knowledge," in *Rationality and Relativism,* ed. Marin Hollis and Steven Lukes (Cambridge: MIT Press, 1982), 28.

locally accepted *is* rational, and thus we *should* accept it. This last statement, however, is not only flagrantly antirelativistic. It is also false. Had Barnes and Bloor polled their respective neighborhoods on whether there is no difference between rational and irrational arguments, there is no doubt at all what the results would have been.

One cannot claim to have established that one's beliefs are "locally accepted" if one rejects the objective validity of the methods used to establish this and similar claims. The iterative move, that the method of establishing whether a belief is locally accepted need be only locally accepted, is useless, for we must know whether it is locally accepted that the said method need only be locally accepted. There is no way to get around the implied claim of the rationality, if not the truth, of one's own beliefs.

Suppose that the Barnes-Bloor view *is* locally accepted (and, as I said, that is patently false; otherwise, there would be no need for Barnes and Bloor to convert us to it!). What makes a belief of their locality worthy of my acceptance? Why is it better than a belief accepted in another locality? People can and often do reject "locally accepted" views. Is it wrong to do so? Why? A causal account, how one acquired a belief, is not a good reason for one's continuing to adhere to that belief. Furthermore, believing that causal account (how I acquired my belief) depends on its cogency, that is, on its being rational, not just a locally accepted story. Finally, if the content of Bloor's beliefs depends on the locally accepted interpretation strategy,[13] I can change Bloor's views by changing the local custom. Suppose that in exchange for a large sum of money the locals change their custom[14]; is that tantamount to Bloor's changing his mind? Still better, why not be broad-minded and use on Bloor an interpretation strategy other than the one practiced by the locals? People who live in England can still enjoy, say, Thai cuisine; one need not stick to the local fare. If foreign food is fine, why not use a foreign interpretation strategy rather than a humdrum local one? Why not a new, piquant interpretation custom every week? We do it with food, so why not with interpretation? The bottom line is that relativism is self-destructive. The very identification of the normative-causal view of interpretation as having a definite content presupposes the existence of a *correct* interpretation of it, and thus it mandates its own rejection.

13. See David Bloor, *Wittgenstein: A Social Theory of Knowledge* (New York: Macmillan, 1983). Would Bloor justify his radical Skinnerization of Wittgenstein by citing the fame and other reinforcements that his interpretation brought him? I doubt that very much.
14. The rights for this idea belong to Friedrich Dürrenmatt's play *Besuch der alten Dame*.

6.3. Linguistic Norms

The linguistic criterion of interpretation is that if X is in language L, its interpretation depends on the linguistic norms internalized by competent L speakers, that is, the way most native speakers of L would understand X. That criterion is unhelpful, however, when X is an artwork, because the meaning of many highly valued artworks is notoriously opaque to most native speakers of the language. We do not accept the authority of most competent speakers of a natural language in interpreting literary works of art in their language. The critic's interpretation is innovative and surprising to average readers; were it not so, professional *explications de texte* in literary criticism would be redundant. The role of literary critics is to offer interpretations that average readers cannot get by themselves. Experts interpret texts (literary, legal, historical, and sacred) that leave untutored readers puzzled. Academic explications have acquired a new prominence with modern literature that leaves average readers completely lost, but surely the profession is not new; it has been around, interpreting hollowed texts, gnomic sayings, etc., from the earliest days of human civilization.

The suggested criterion can be altered: can the correct interpretation of artworks be decided not by average speakers but by expert linguists, those who are fully conversant with the entire historical vocabulary of the language in question? Perhaps the right interpretation of X is adjudged by professional grammarians? No, that criterion is subject to objections similar to those that derailed its predecessor. Writers may use an idiosyncratic vocabulary and a personal grammar. The degree of grammaticality of sentences in modern poetry is very low: an artist has poetic license in the use of language. Descriptive linguists do not have enough data to handle new poetic diction, and normative linguists will dismiss it as incorrect (think of normative grammarians given a free hand editing Joyce!). A good linguist need not be a good critic. It takes more that being versed in the intricacies of the language to match the performance of literary critics. We need much more than linguistic expertise. Even if linguists can plot all the interpretations that a given expression may sustain, they need not know which of these interpretations is the right one, or which are the right ones. Linguists codify entrenched uses of language, but poets cannot be restricted to well-established uses of standard speakers. A linguist may therefore be even less suited than others to interpret a creative poet.

Another argument against the said criterion runs as follows: We have turned to native speakers of L and to the experts on the norms of L to interpret X, because we assume that X is written in L. This assumption is already an interpretation of X, namely, that X should be interpreted as if it were in that language, L. Appeal to L linguists cannot ground that interpretation; it presupposes it. You can say that X is written in L only after having interpreted it; you cannot assume so a priori. Perhaps X is written in an idiolect that is outwardly similar to standard English but whose words, although homonymic with English words, have a completely different sense. The assumption that X is in the language spoken by inhabitants of the place where it is composed at the time of composition is *another* interpretative criterion, and it, too, needs to be justified. Suppose that a text X has a different meaning in different dialects of English; each philologist specializing in a dialect of English will interpret X according to its norms, so the number of distinct interpretations given to X will equal the number of philologists to which X is submitted for interpretation. If only one philologist (or set of linguistic norms) is chosen, X's interpretation is fixed by that choice. What criterion may ground that choice?

The case described above is not fictional; *every* text that has a meaning in one dialect can also be interpreted in another. Every English poem can also be interpreted in Hungarian: the sorry but correct verdict of the Hungarian linguist will be that it is gibberish. That verdict does not disqualify the interpreter: surely not all interpretations according to which a given text is nonsensical are wrong. Lewis Carroll's poem "Jabberwocky" is nonsense; that is one reason we love it. Surely we do not have to find a system of interpretation on which every nonsense poem comes out meaningful? I therefore conclude that the linguistic criterion fails; it cannot be the one we use. We must go back to the original question: what is the criterion for accepting an interpretation?

6.4. Critics and Aesthetes

In arguing against the previous proposal I said that we usually approach a literary critic, not a linguist, in order to get an interpretation of a literary artwork. Can it be, then, that the correct interpretation of X is that which a good literary critic would assign it after careful examination? No, that begs the question. We say that Smith is a good critic, or a better critic than Jones, *because* Smith has a good record (she usually has the right interpretation) or a record better than Jones's. That is why we rely on her judgment when it comes to a new artwork, X. The notion of a *good interpreter* can be significantly used only after the notion of *a good interpretation* is consistently applied. It is conceptually impossible to use the former to elucidate the latter, for if the latter is unclear, then so, *mutatis mutandis*, is the former. You need not check the critic's reliability with each new work; we have a good inductive reason to believe that, having proved reliable in the past, she is likely to be right again. But to prove a critic right, we must first establish that the critic's interpretations are right. The proposed criterion therefore begs the question: it assumes that we know which interpretations are right, so we can tell which critics are reliable, and thus find out which interpretations are right by asking a reliable critic.

Performativism (e.g., Dickie's) points a way out of the vicious circle: the critic's status is not earned, but conferred by the artworld. The artworld's reasons for conferring that status on a given individual are social: a group of influential people (artists, critics, curators, conspicuous art consumers, and other "beautiful people") anoint *arbiters* of taste, and whatever they say goes. This theory has some attraction, but I think it is demonstrably false. If you believe that the critic's source of authority is an arbitrary designation by a cabal of socialites, you have no reason to *believe* the critic. People who want to be *in*, to say and do whatever it takes to be socially accepted, have some reason to emulate (though not to believe!) that critic. Art lovers, on the other hand, do not believe that a critic's say so *makes* X aesthetically good. They hold that an artwork may be aesthetically good even when no critic calls it 'good.' Performativism implies that love of art is an offshoot of a desire to follow the social tone setters. Art lovers would vehemently deny that. One may answer that art lovers are wrong about themselves and are deluded by vanity, but such an answer is hardly credible. Those who *see* what the critic talks about, *see* that X is aesthetically excellent, may have been hypnotized or brainwashed, but such perceptual illusions are rare. It is precisely our knowledge of such pathological cases that tells against the performativist, for the degree of manipulation needed to bring these illusions about is much more massive than the subtle pressure art lovers are exposed to. Most people enjoy art; to construe all their experiences of beauty as illusions induced by their desire to conform is exceedingly implausible.

If the status of being an artwork or an artist is conferred by fiat, performatively, then a critic who says he has discovered a new artist or artwork is a hypocrite. A jury does not *discover* that the defendant is guilty, nor does the priest *discover* the name of the baby he baptizes. Critics should behave like them: instead of pretending to discover, they should just *order* that X *be* a work of art, and Jones an artist. Unfortunately, a critic who issues such a decree will be laughed out of the profession. Thus, critics hide the true nature of their activity; we find no trace of their conspiracy because they are incredibly devious and cunning. Can anybody believe that preposterous theory?

There is another way to avoid the vicious circle (acceptable interpretations are those chosen by one whose interpretations are acceptable): let the best interpreter be the one who most enhances the aesthetic value of the interpretandum. To increase aesthetic value is to give us more pleasure, so we have a reason to accept the beauty-making interpretation. The criterion of acceptance is, then, aesthetic value. We decide between interpretations A and B of X by checking which one of them generates more beauty. If the aesthetic value of X is greater according to A than it is according to B, then A is the correct interpretation of X. Of course, A and B must do more than just *pronounce* X to have a great aesthetic value. We must read X according to A and B; if X *looks* aesthetically better when read as suggested by A than when read as suggested by B, then A is right and B is wrong.

Ultimately I endorse a revised version of this maxim, which seems sanctioned by the third Keats Principle, but as it stands now, it is false. A beauty-making interpretation need not be right. Bad fiction and ugly poetry are surely *possible*. A good critic should not cover up for failed works but interpret them so as to expose their weaknesses until they become evident to all. X may be much uglier when construed according to interpretation A than when construed according to interpretation B, yet A, not B, is correct. The following argument, I think, is conclusive: Suppose that, under honest interpretation A, X seems ugly. To rectify that, take any great work of art and interpret X as expressing the content of that great work; that is interpretation B. If correctness of interpretation varies with the degree of aesthetic value it confers on its interpretandum, the correct interpretation of X is B. You can interpret any text so that what it means is the content of some well-known great work of art; so every text is a masterpiece. Yet interpretation B is incorrect; it is ridiculously incorrect; therefore, the aesthete fails to solve our problem.

6.5. The Author's Intention

A widely accepted criterion of interpretation is this: X means what its author intends it to mean. In section 6.1, I have shown that, on either paradigm of interpretation, this criterion is almost self-evident. As a mere set of marks,

X has no meaning, but artworks are not meaningless. To be meaningful those marks must be assigned a meaning, something they stand for; and what meaning can X have except the one assigned it by its author, that is, what the author intended it to mean? If you do not like what the author has intended, you can assign other meanings to those marks, but then you create a new work; it is not the author's work X that you interpret.

What is wrong with this criterion is its conception of meaning assignment as constrained by the author's intention only. Let me start with William Wimsatt and Monroe Beardsley's well-known argument against taking the author's intention as determining a work's correct interpretation.[15] I think the argument is basically sound; its later discrediting by intentionalists is due to superficial flaws. The argument is that an author can intend X to mean *that p*, but fail; despite his intention to make X mean *that p*, it does not. Like anyone else, an author may sometimes fail to carry out his intentions; who is immune to failure? As noted in section 6.1, that argument was rebutted thus: one cannot fail to make X mean *that p*, for there is nothing more to X's meaning *that p* than one's intending by X to mean *that p*, and in that one cannot fail. Semantic value depends on speakers' reference, and the latter is purely a matter of intention. In fact, "X means *that p*" is short for "By X, its author, S, means to express *that p*."

Here Wittgenstein comes to the rescue. The thrust of his private-language argument is that it is not a private mental affair to intend X to mean *that p*. An internal ostensive definition cannot give 'X' a meaning without an extant language game where X has a well-established role. You can use X to mean, say, *a rabbit* only if you have a battery of relevant concepts; for instance, you need the notion of an enduring individual, the notion of an animal, and the notion of a name. These notions are interwoven in a network of language-game moves, which come into play in intending 'rabbit' to name rabbits; they are needed for assigning *that* meaning to 'rabbit.' Unless you conceive of rabbits in terms of some such interrelated system of concepts, you cannot intend to refer to them. Pointing to the rabbit while uttering "rabbit" will not do, for even if I have the notion of a name, I may have named (to echo Quine) rabbit stuff, or a temporal slice of a rabbit, or an animal that eats rabbits, or what rabbits eat, or my having a toothache, or anything at all.

15. William K. Wimsatt and Monroe Beardsley, "The Intentional Fallacy," *Sewanee Review* 54 (1946). Reprinted in Wimsatt's *Verbal Icon: Studies in the Meaning of Poetry* (Lexington: University of Kentucky Press, 1954).

Meaning is possible only within the framework of language games.[16] The middle Wittgenstein tells us that he was wrong to regard (in the *Tractatus*) naming as a primordial, inexplicable act. Rather, X means Y if they interact in certain ways in some language games. To have the concept of a rabbit one needs to play a language game where that concept is used, and (the late Wittgenstein adds) *see* Y *as* playing that role, that is, as a rabbit. To use X to name a rabbit one needs to take part in a public game of naming in which reidentifiable rabbits feature as such, and X and Y are seen *as* having these roles in the game. Unless the intention to use X to name a rabbit occurs in such a game (if it is a private ostensive definition), it makes no sense:

> 70. Would it be conceivable that someone who knows rabbits but not ducks should say: "I can see the drawing as a rabbit and also in another way, although I have no word for the second aspect?" Later he gets to know ducks and says: "That's what I saw the drawing as that time!"—Why is that not possible?
> 71. Or suppose someone said: This rabbit has a complacent expression.—If someone knew nothing about a complacent expression—might *something strike* him here, and he later on, having learnt to recognize complacency, say that that was the expression that struck him then?
> 72. The *appropriate* word. How do we find it? . . .
> 73. I see that the word is appropriate even before I know, and even when I never know, *why* it is appropriate.
> 74. I should not *understand* someone who said that he had seen the picture as that of a rabbit, but had not been able to say so, because at that time he had not been aware of the existence of such a creature.[17]

16. Since the term 'language game' is often grotesquely misused, let me define it. A language game is a structured segment of life (like the bits of behavior described in *Philosophical Investigations,* pt. 1, nos. 2, 8, 15, 19, etc.) in the course of which a connection is established between words and other objects with which the words interact. The players *directly see* various elements of the game *as* having the roles they have in that game; that is the *primary* way of identifying these objects. The players *see* a word as right for uses sanctioned in the game and wrong for others; seeing it in that way guides their use of the word in referring to objects, that is, what they can mean by it. For further details and textual support , see chap. 2 of my *Reality of Meaning and the Meaning of "Reality"* and "Meaning, the Experience of Meaning, and the Meaning-Blind in Wittgenstein's Late Philosophy," *Monist* 78 (1995): 480–95.

17. Ludwig Wittgenstein, *Remarks on the Philosophy of Psychology* (Oxford: Basil Blackwell, 1980), vol. 1, 70–74.

That is the entire private-language argument in a nutshell, and an outline of an alternative theory of meaning. To see Y as a rabbit one must have the concept *rabbit*, that is, know what a rabbit is, what it can and cannot do, what its anatomy is, how it lives, etc. Those who do not have that concept cannot see *that* as a rabbit, hence cannot introduce the term 'rabbit' to name rabbits. An ostensive definition outside the game does nothing to constrain the use of 'rabbit.' Outside the game one cannot distinguish features that are essential to rabbits from those that *this* rabbit has at the moment. One cannot see the ears of the rabbit as ears rather than, say, as tails, or its tail as a tail and not, say, as a horrible tumor. If the Y you intend to name 'rabbit' is not seen against the background of a game where it has a role, Y has no specificity; in fact, without such a role, there is no Y you can name. I cannot see the rabbit's posture as hesitant if I do not have the concept *rabbit*, "for how could I see that this posture was hesitant before I knew that it was a posture and not the anatomy of the animal?"[18]

An author can neither invent a concept (say, *rabbit*) nor attach it by fiat to a word ('rabbit'), for the concept *rabbit* is the role that the word 'rabbit' plays in language games, and to understand the word 'rabbit' is to see it *as* playing that role. Only then does it make sense to say that 'rabbit' refers to rabbits (or, as I say in the next chapter, the meaning of 'rabbit' is the thing, Rabbit). Writers use language; they do not invent it. They use words that already have a use, a role in a language game, that is, a concept, a way of conceptualizing the world. Writers cannot assign concepts to words, because concepts are never separated from words; the concept *rabbit* is the role of 'rabbit' in our life, *as we see it*. The writer is a matchmaker, but he does not marry words to meanings; in this sense words are already married when they come to him. The writer arranges word-word dates, eases them into relationships, and watches over their progeny, the fruit of their union. Linguistic expressions are officers of sorts: a word is meaningful when seen in the office it holds in a language game. Because words already have meaning, artists can use them in new ways to create new aesthetically valuable wholes.

The word 'rabbit' I have now written down has a meaning. How? That token-word is new and has never participated in any language games. Texts are made of brand new token-words minted for the occasion. (We do

18. Ludwig Wittgenstein, *Philosophical Investigations* (New York: Macmillan, 1953), pt. 2, xi, 112 (209b). See also idem, *Last Writings* (Oxford: Basil Blackwell, 1985), vol. 1, 736, 741, 776.

not use "old" tokens, chips that were already used in language games and consequently were laid to rest on this page.) It is not this token, this blotch of black ink you see on the paper, that had a long history of participating in many language games; it could not have played games before it was made! Rather, this token-word 'rabbit' that I just created has a meaning because we see it as a token of a type, *other* tokens of which have indeed previously been used in language games. We *see* this *as* a token of the type-word 'rabbit,' and older tokens of that type-word did play a role in language games. We see the newborn token as a veteran officer of our language games.[19] Interpretation, then, involves seeing objects as instances of certain types. The same is true of items that are not words: we see a certain patch in a painting as a human face, and a certain block of marble in a sculpture as an instance of the type leg.[20] Wittgenstein puts succinctly and accurately: it is, he says, "precisely *a meaning* that I see."[21]

It is therefore not true that texts mean what their authors intend them to mean; rather, given meaningful words, words that have a meaning in virtue of their extended public role, an author can breed new meanings by carefully matching them. The intention an artist harbors is not to attach roles to words; words are already seen as having certain roles. Is it possible that, being unable to express *that p* in public language, you intend X in your poem to mean *that p*? No, for to intend this, you need to express *that p* in public language after all.

Wimsatt and Beardsley are right because artists intend to achieve goals that they may or may not achieve. Artists intend to express an idea, an emotion, an atmosphere, and these projects are not fail-safe. A project intended in broad terms may be entirely beyond one's capabilities when one tries to carry it out; one may be at a loss on how to go on, or may take the wrong way. An intention to express passion or irony may fail, just as one may fail to be passionate or sarcastic. It takes skill to do things with words; a mere intention to do so-and-so is not enough.

Intention to express *that p* by X is, then, insufficient for X to mean *that p*. I think it is not necessary either. One may express a statement unintentionally: the statement *that p* may be expressed by one who has no

---

19. "The glance which a word in a certain context casts at us. Of course, the way in which it looks at us depends on the surroundings in which it is located" (Wittgenstein, *Last Writings,* vol. 1, 366).

20. Cf., e.g., Wittgenstein, *Remarks on the Philosophy of Psychology,* vol. 1, 874, 880, etc.

21. Ibid., 869.

intention to express it. For a long time I thought that was impossible and that therefore an authorial intention to say *that p* was a necessary condition for a text to mean *that p*. In an article written many years ago I formulated what I thought was a convincing proof of that thesis.[22] That proof is best presented through an example.

Recall the story of a million monkeys who strike a million typewriters at random until a batch of pages emerges that is letter for letter identical with a standard copy of *Hamlet*. Do these pages mean what *Hamlet* means? If you think these monkey-produced pages do express the content of *Hamlet*, the example can be carried a step further: use only one monkey and the first thousand pages it produces. English can be written in code; our orthography is only one way of representing English words. So, there is a spelling system according to which these thousand pages are, word for word, the text of *Hamlet*. That the code is complicated is immaterial: a complicated system of spelling can express a meaning as well as a simple one. The argument can be made even more dramatic if we leave typing out and instead interpret the usual actions of one monkey in its natural habitat as symbols that spell out the text of *Hamlet*. Hanging from a branch, eating a banana, jumping, grunting, etc. can be interpreted as signs for the words of *Hamlet*. Of course, that interpretation of the monkey's behavior is ludicrous, but why? Is it not because the monkey did not intend its jumps and grunts as signs? To say that, however, is to admit that one's intention to express *that p* is a necessary condition for one's words to mean *that p*.

I now think that a text of *Hamlet* was produced in the first case, but not in the latter two. Above I endorsed Wittgenstein's view that a meaningful sign is seen as *right* or *wrong* in certain uses—that is, we see it as normatively embodying the role it plays in our language game.[23] The first document (which looks like a standard English text of *Hamlet*) passes that test, for we will see it as meaningful, while the second and third nonstandard "texts" in my example fail that test: to us, they do not look meaningful. My earlier argument was an attempt to show, by a *reductio ad absurdum*, that a text is not *Hamlet* unless it is intended to mean what *Hamlet* means. The *reductio* does not work, however, because there is a great difference between the first

22. Eddy Zemach, "Intention, Attention, and the Nature of Fiction," *Hebrew University Studies in Literature* 5 (1977): 135–54.

23. See *Philosophical Investigations*, pt. 2 , xi, p. 215, and many other places, e.g., *Last Writings*, vol. 2, 281–82: "The atmosphere of the word is its use. Or: we represent to ourselves its use as an atmosphere. The 'atmosphere' of the word is a picture of its use."

text and the two others. The latter two cases are not seen as meaningful; they do not seem to enjoin a way of using them, so, prima facie, we have no reason to believe they have any meaning. We may believe that they are signs only if we can overrule the presumption by relevant evidence. That can be done by a proof of authorial intention. On the other hand, in the first case no intention is needed, for the meaning stares us in the face: we make a presumption of meaningfulness that later is justified by satisfying the Keats Principles. Thus, there is no slippery slope, and the proof fails.

Suppose that we have infallible information about the author's intentions at all times. If the intention criterion is to be of any use, we need to match intentions with texts to know which intention is relevant to the interpretation of which text. Yet such a criterion of relevance presupposes that we understand the text prior to, and independently of, the writer's intentions. Otherwise, how can we tell which intention is relevant to a given text? We cannot, unless a text means whatever it means regardless of the author's intention.

A rock cracks in a pattern that by accident looks like English words that make up a new, truly beautiful poem. Shall we, knowing that no intention was involved, deny that it is a poem? Shall we refuse to enjoy it? Shall we reproduce it, not in anthologies of verse, but in geology books only? No, given our use of English words, we see something that looks meaningful to us, although it was not intended to be seen that way, against the background of *our* language games. We see its meaning and enjoy it too. It is a new poem, an aesthetically valuable thing, and we are happy for the serendipitous event that gave it to us. It is not what any author intended, but what we get out of it is beautiful, and that is what counts.

No one doubts that *Hamlet* describes events in the life of a Danish prince whose uncle assassinated his father. But how do we know that? If intention is necessary for interpretation, *Hamlet* means that only if Shakespeare intended it. Did he, or did he not, intend it? We raise Shakespeare's ghost and ask him about his intentions; suppose that he is willing to help, and answers every question fully and candidly. So he talks to us, using so many words to describe his intentions. Does it help? Does this settle the problem of what *Hamlet* means? Not at all. How can we know what the words of Shakespeare mean? To know that, we must, by hypothesis, know what are his intentions in uttering these words, but that we do not know. Nor can Shakespeare tell us what his intentions are, for the question will be raised about the meaning of these new words, and so on ad infinitum. Thus, if we cannot tell what plain English-looking sentences mean without knowing what the author intended to express by them, we can know the meaning of no sentence. If what a text means depends on its authors' intentions, we cannot be told what those intentions are, for all that the author can say is just words, words, words. Nothing can be understood; there is no literature, no criticism, and no philosophical discussion of it either.

Texts have meaning because we see some things as meaningful. Authors manipulate meaningful signs by combining them in various ways against the foil of a language game, using the impact of one sign on another to create new complex meanings. The writer does not have to intend the outcome any more than a painter who puts colors on canvas needs to intend the final effect of the picture: the writer may be as surprised as anyone to see what emerges. The basic elements that writers work on are already meaningful; what they mean when put together is also out of the writer's hand. Art takes care of itself.

Practice confirms that an intention of the writer to express by X *that p* is not a necessary condition for X's expressing *that p*. Critics often say that X expresses *that p,* though the writer did not intend that. No one believes that Shakespeare, great genius as he was, intended even the ten best-known readings of *Hamlet,* those that we all accept as legitimate. Yet that does not deter scholars from adding each year scores of new interpretations of *Hamlet.* It would be disingenuous to pretend that all this immense body of scholarship was unconsciously entertained by the bard. Had authorial intention been necessary for adequate interpretation, we would have ceased reinterpreting the classics long ago. Since that is not happening nor is likely to happen, evidently in practice we do not accept a criterion according to which all that work is a sheer waste of time.

Why, then, if intention to express *that p* is not required in order for a text to mean *that p,* do we not interpret some random text as expressing great literary works? Given any text X, there is a code according to which X means *that p* for any p. Why not interpret my laundry list as notes for a great symphony? I answer: because that is not how it looks to us. A critic may interpret X as a symphony, but such unobvious interpretation must be justified. One would be hard put to explain how a person who can barely follow a score could write one. The said reading has implications that fail to satisfy the Keats Principles. For example, the interpretation that X is a laundry list can predict and illuminatingly interpret other texts produced by the author of X, while the interpretation that X is a musical score will fail even to predict which items are likely to appear further down on X. Thus the second interpretation is inferior to the first. Since X is not seen *as* a score, and since the theory that interprets it as a score is poor, the said interpretation should be rejected. Try to interpret the line "5 shirts, 2 pants" on the list as meaning "To be, or not to be—that is the question." If "to be" is symbolized by '5,' you must explain how '5' is the negation of '2,' and give a full grammar of that odd language. That can be done, but doing it makes it obvious that the hypothesis according to which X is a laundry list is simpler, more elegant, and more coherent.

What if a deviant code deviates only slightly from the common one? Suppose that a text contains a sentence X that in English means *that p*, but the author says that it means *that q*. The author admits that this is not what X means in English, but claims that the text is not in English. He says he intended to use an idiolect almost identical with English except for X, which in that idiolect means *that q*. Does that avowal of authorial intention settle the question in favor of X meaning *that q*? I think not. That X has a meaning in the said idiolect does not cancel the fact that it also has a meaning in English, and there is no reason for us not to avail ourselves of it. If, read as English, X is valuable, we cherish it. The author can disavow that object, but he cannot deny us the thing of beauty that he has inadvertently created.

Here is another example: I owe you a hundred dollars. To pay my debt I give you a check, but on it mistakenly write '$1,000' instead of what I intend to write, '$100.' A court of law may find for me, acknowledging that I made a genuine error and should pay you only a hundred, not a thousand, dollars. Yet the court will not rule that what I have written, that is, '$1,000,' denotes not one thousand but one hundred dollars, because that is what I intended to write! To us, what I wrote has an apparent sense; a judge can order my bank to disregard that sense because it was unintentionally made, but he cannot decree that '$1,000' does not have that sense in the first place. I may escape paying for my silly mistake, but I cannot be said not to have made that mistake at all, for the sign '$1,000' in my idiolect of the moment denoted not a thousand but a hundred dollars! The conclusion is clear: compliance with authorial intention is neither a necessary nor a sufficient condition for admissibility of interpretation.

6.6. Contemporaries and Anachronism

I have argued that we should regard a text X as meaning *that p* even without authorial intention to mean by X *that p,* if, given our language game, that is how X appears and that interpretation of X is aesthetically rewarding. But who, it may be asked, are "we"? Observers are many, and they perceive art in a great many ways. Surely some of these ways (a London skinhead watching a Noh play, a nineteenth-century Papuan listening to Wagner) are biased, inadequate, and inappropriate. Leonard Meyer remarks that even a single sound may have different meanings when heard against different backgrounds:

> [S]ince the listener is part of a culture that he takes for granted, a single isolated sound stimulus will tend to be interpreted as part of the prevalent style system of the culture, i.e., as a sound term. Thus a dominant seventh-chord, for example, even though not incorporated into a specific context, is for the Western listener still a sound term, since the sound stimulus is heard within the prevalent style of Western music . . . [T]he same sound stimulus often has different meanings, it is a different sound term, in different musical cultures and styles and that seeming similarities are often very deceptive . . . a piece of Indian music which sounds to Western ears as though it were in C major actually has quite a different "tonic" and, consequently, quite a different group of tendencies and probability relationships for the knowledgeable Hindu listener.[24]

Therefore, there must be an audience, whose way of perceiving is SOC, determining what the work really means. This motivates some philosophers (e.g., Anthony Savile)[25] to adopt a criterion according to which the meaning of a work of art is what its contemporaries, those who immediately follow them, or some select group of them took or would have taken it to mean.

That criterion has many problems. What makes contemporaries infallible? Why should they be constituted as the standard against which future understanding must be measured? Following Hume, Savile acknowledges the shortcomings of contemporaries and the ways in which later generations can better understand an artwork, being less biased and having a more balanced perspective on it. There are visionary artists whose contemporaries did not

24. L. B. Meyer, *Emotion and Meaning in Music* (Chicago: University of Chicago Press, 1956), 46.
25. Anthony Savile, *The Test of Time: An Essay on Philosophical Aesthetics* (Oxford: Clarendon Press, 1982).

and indeed could not understand. Those we consider the greatest of all, Shakespeare and Bach, were truly appreciated only several generations after their deaths.

Advocates of the historical criterion have one good argument for it: it outlaws anachronistic interpretations. Shakespeare teachers tell their students to look for the Elizabethan meaning of a word and not to attribute to it the meaning it has in modern English. That practice suggests that the historical criterion is our standard, thus barring barbaric (mis)interpretations of old texts from gaining equal status with historically correct interpretations. Thus, historicists argue, it is a necessary condition for adequacy of interpretation that we use the linguistic rules, conventions, and vocabulary of the author's contemporaries or a select group of them (say, the educated).

The motives for suggesting the historical criterion are laudable, yet it is wrong. Anachronistic interpretation, though objectionable, should not be banned by a meaning postulate; its falsity is not a matter of logic. Suppose that we find in Rome an ancient scroll X that as all physical evidence indicates was written in the first century b.c., yet it naturally reads not as Latin but as English. It is a diary telling, in plain English, of various events in the life of its author, a well-known Roman senator. Surely we may read it as English. That interpretation is anachronistic, for X's contemporaries would not interpret it that way: they spoke no English. Yet the question, How could a Roman write English? is meaningful. We do not know how a Roman wrote English, but it is not logically impossible that he did.

Anachronistic interpretations should not be ruled out by definition. It is only a brute fact, not a logical truth, that a sign's meaning is accessible to its author's contemporaries. An English diary written in ancient Rome will make us revise many of our beliefs about time and human abilities, but not our notion of meaning. An anachronistic interpretation *can* be justified: X may contain verifiable historical information; will we refuse to avail ourselves of it? We reject anachronistic readings, but the reason is not that 'what X means' is synonymous with 'what X means to its contemporaries.' It is an *empirical*, not a logical, truth that texts are usually understood by their contemporaries. Our very perplexity shows that we read the manuscript X in English. Had it been a conceptual truth that a text can only mean what its contemporaries would take it to mean, there would be no problem there: we would have simply thrown X away as a piece of nonsense. Yet that is the last thing we would do. That locals are well placed to interpret a text is an important fact, but not an analysis of 'interpretation.'

In the previous section I denied that the writer's intention is either sufficient or necessary to decide a text's meaning. I did not deny, however, that intentions can help one interpret a text. Intention is a relevant consideration because a theory about the meaning of a text, like all theories, needs to cohere with other accepted theories. Psychology says what people can and cannot do; therefore, an interpretation that construes a text as expressing only what, according to accepted psychology, its author was capable of expressing and likely to express in that manner has a big advantage over one that conflicts with accepted psychological theories. We want our theories to converge; that is a general desideratum of science. So, theories about people, including writers and their contemporaries, should not contradict our interpretative theories. This consideration mandates that in interpreting a text we consider the writer's intention, as well as the use of language among contemporaries and coculturalists, for we know that people usually say what they intend to say and that one's environment does influence what one says and one's manner of saying it. Anachronistic interpretation usually fails to satisfy the second Keats Principle, so we exclude it. 'A historically accurate reading,' however, is not an analysans of 'interpretation,' and therefore it is neither a necessary nor a sufficient condition for the admissibility of interpretations.

7

ONTOLOGY AND ART

7.1. Who Needs Universals?

To get clear about interpretation one needs to know what the ontological status of artworks is and to know that one needs to be clear about ontology in general, that is, know what the world, so to speak, is made of. Therefore, I start this chapter with an outline of what I think is an adequate ontology. That account will not take us far from aesthetics, because my ontology is born of aesthetics. For centuries, the ontology of art took a back seat to metaphysics and had to use retreads from the warehouse of metaphysical systems whose paradigms never came from the arts. From Plato to Quine, metaphysicians recognized two ontological categories: (1) nonrecurring particulars and (2) recurring universals. Platonists accepted the reality of both; nominalists, only the former. The aesthetician faced a Hobson's choice: artworks had to belong either in the first or in the second ontological category, yet both categories failed to fit artworks. Beethoven's Fifth Symphony is not (1) a nonrecurring particular, for it can occur in Rome, in Tokyo, and in Jerusalem simultaneously. You can hear it now, and tomorrow hear *it*, the same symphony, *again*; it is the same work in all its recurrences. Yet that symphony is not (2) a recurring universal either. The Fifth Symphony is about thirty minutes long; it was created in 1807 by a human being, Ludwig van Beethoven; and it is perceived by the senses. None of this can be true of a universal, which is an abstract entity, a set of properties. Elsewhere I have shown that clever attempts of Platonists to reconcile features of artworks with those of universals inevitably fail.[1]

I am a nominalist, one who recognizes only particulars and no universals in the world. The notion of universals, that is, properties as beings in their own right that particular things exemplify, is riddled with difficulties, self-contradictions, and paradoxes, so it is better left alone. Here are a four ([1] is from Aristotle, [2] is from Bradley, and [3] and [4] are mine):[2] (1) The third-man argument: What binds properties to things? Exemplification, Platonists say. So what binds exemplification to properties and things? Call it 'Superexemplification.' It, too, needs to be bound to the entities *it* binds, and so on ad infinitum. (2) For *a* to exemplify *F*, the pair {*a,F*}, Platonists say, must exemplify the property *Exemplification;* to exemplify that property the set {{*a,F*},*Exemp*} must exemplify either *Exemplification* itself, which raises Russell's paradox, or else *Superexemplification,* a new property, which yields an infinite regress. (3) May a universal exemplify itself? If it may, *Does Not Exemplify Itself* generates Russell's paradox (if it exemplifies itself, it does not, and if it does not, it does). If it may not, *Is a Property* is not a property, so if X exemplifies a property, it does not exemplify a property. (4) According to Platonists, what makes X red is the property *Red* it exemplifies. So *Red* has the property *MER* (Makes Its Exemplifier Red). *MER* is distinct from *Red* (proof: whatever exemplifies *Red* is red; *Red* exemplifies *MER; Red* is not red). Without *MER, Red* is irrelevant to X's being red. So it is not *Red* that makes X red; it is *MER*. So, *Red* does not exemplify *MER*. We have a contradiction. That argument can be repeated against *MER* (unless it exemplifies *MEER* [Makes Its Exemplifier's Exemplifier Red], it is irrelevant to X's being red; therefore, it does not exemplify *MEER*) and any set, finite or infinite, of properties. Properties are, therefore, irrelevant to predication. I conclude that these dubious beings, the universals, have no place in ontology.

I call my nominalistic theory 'Substance Logic.'[3] The logic has only proper names and identity—no predicates, hence no predication. The sentence "Plato is white" contains, I think, two names: 'Plato' and 'White.' 'Plato' is a name of one thing, a substance that we recognize and reidentify at many indexes. Its occurrences vary in appearance from index to index:

1. Eddy Zemach, "No Identification Without Evaluation," *British Journal of Aesthetics* 26 (1986): 239–51. For a Platonist gambit, see, e.g., Nicholas Wolterstorff, in *Works and Worlds of Art* (New York: Oxford University Press, 1980).

2. See my "Some Horse Sense," *Pacific Philosophical Quarterly* 63 (1982): 69–74.

3. See chaps. 1–3 of my *Types: Essays in Metaphysics* (London: Brill, 1992).

Plato at one time is hirsute; Plato at a later time is bald; yet it is the same thing, Plato, at both these indexes. 'White' also names a thing that we recognize and reidentify at various indexes. Its occurrences, too, vary in appearance from index to index: White at this place is a man; White at that place is a shirt. The general form of propositions is "$X =_Y Z$." A proposition states that, at some index (indexes are things) Y, two things, X and Z, are identical. These two things, X and Z, which are identical at Y, may be distinct at another index, W. The proposition "Plato is White" says of two things, Plato and White, that they are identical at Plato's:

$$1.\ P =_P W.$$

At another location, say, in Greece, there are White things that are not Plato, so it is false that, in Greece, whatever is (an occurrence of) Plato is (an occurrence of) White. That is,

$$2.\ P =_G W$$

is false. At yet another location, at Socrates', Socrates is identical with White (i.e., Socrates is white):

$$3.\ S =_S W$$

is true. Yet (1) and (3) do not imply that Socrates is identical with Plato, for these identities hold at different indexes. Had

$$4.\ S =_W W$$

been true (i.e., White and Plato were identical throughout White), and had White and Socrates been identical in the same domain, that is,

$$5.\ P =_W W,$$

then it follows that Socrates would have been Plato. That is as it should be, for if (as [4] says) Socrates is the only white thing and (as [5] says) Plato is the only white thing, then Socrates is Plato.

Substance Logic needs no quantifiers. The sentence "All Greeks are white" says that two things (The Greek and The White) are identical at The Greek. The Greek (a thing you reidentify whenever you call something 'Greek') and The White (a thing you reidentify whenever you call something 'white') are identical at The Greek:

$$6.\ G =_G W.$$

Identity is contingent, for two things may be identical at one index and not identical at another. In Socrates' House (H), whatever we call by the name 'Socrates' we also call by the name 'Philosopher,' so, Socrates and

Philosopher are identical in Socrates' house (S =$_H$ P). In Greece, however, there are other philosophers beside Socrates, so it is not true that, in Greece, whatever you call 'Philosopher' you also call 'Socrates.' At the index Greece, Socrates and The Philosopher are not identical; "S =$_G$ P" is false.

My extensive use of the term 'property' in this essay does not commit me to the existence of properties. In saying "X has the property F" I do not say, of a universal, that X exemplifies it. Rather, I say of two particular things, X and F, that they are identical at X. I regard the *Principia* sentence "F(*a*)" as an abbreviation of "A =$_A$ F."

7.2. Things

Charles Pierce distinguished tokens from types in order unequivocally to answer questions like, How many letters are there in the word 'tomorrow'? The answer, he said, depends on what we mean by 'letter.' 'Tomorrow' contains (1) five type-letters (three occur once, one occurs twice, and one occurs thrice) and (2) eight token-letters. Rudolf Carnap, Willard Quine, and following them almost all modern philosophers have held that (2) is ontologically fundamental, parsing (1) as saying that some of the eight letters in 'tomorrow' are equiform. I strongly disagree. You can tell that there are eight token-letters in the word 'tomorrow' only if you have the concept *letter* and can recognize objects that fall under it. What you do is this: you identify the thing, Letter, and distinguish distinct occurrences of it. You see that the said thing (type), Letter, recurs eight times in 'tomorrow.'

You cannot identify tokens except in relation to some type that they are tokens of. Thus, the Carnap-Quine preference for token-letters is mistaken; token-letters can be counted only after we identify and reidentify *occurrences* of a type-letter. In the example above, (1) is, therefore, ontologically basic, and (2) is derived from it. The basic entities we identify are types that occur, that is, have distinct occurrences at various indexes. Things are types, not tokens: they recur. We can count women, soldiers, dogs, and books because we can reidentify the types Woman, Soldier, Dog, and Book wherever they occur. An occurrence O of the thing X is a thing such that O =$_O$ X but not O =$_X$ X. For instance, both Socrates and Man are types; Man occurs wherever Socrates occurs, but not vice versa.

Types are *not* universals. Universals cannot be friends, but Dog is Man's best friend. The types Man and Dog are particulars, not universals. Universals have no color, but The Red Flag is red and The Polar Bear is white.

Universals are not edible, but Carrot is. Universals are not mortal, but Man is. The types Dog, Man, Carrot, Polar Bear, Red Flag, are therefore not abstract entities but material things. Quine suggested that types are scattered objects:[4] 'the dog' names the canine part of the world; 'water' names the aqueous part of the world; 'blue' names the blue part of the world; etc. That is surely wrong: the scattered object that is the mereological whole made up of all dogs has millions of heads; moreover, the number of heads of this scattered object changes every time a dog is born or dies. But Dog has only one head. Thus, Dog is not a mereological whole but a recurrent thing; wherever *it* is, *it* has one head.

Particulars are types. I met David at school today, and I shall meet *him* in town tomorrow. David is one and the same thing in both occurrences, at school and in town, although these two occurrences of him are not identical with each other. David is identical with his occurrence O *at* that occurrence, that is, at O (David $=_O$ O), and with his occurrence I at I (David $=_I$ I), but these two occurrences are nowhere identical (O $\neq$ I). David is a recurring type, one thing that occurs on two separate occasions, in two different places. He, David, is wholly present at all those indexes: At school I met David, not a part of him.

Like David, Beethoven's Fifth Symphony is a type; you listen to it at *t* in New York, so at *t* it occurs in New York. I listen to *it* (therefore it occurs) at *t* in Jerusalem. Paintings are types too. *The Last Supper* is in Milan and in Paris simultaneously. Its Milan occurrence has features somewhat different from those of its Paris occurrence: one is made of oil paint on canvas, the other of a paper photograph in an art book. The same goes for Joyce's *Ulysses*, whose presence in your home does not preclude its occurring, at the same time, in mine. My instance of *Ulysses* differs from yours in many details, yet both are occurrences of the same thing (type). The Fifth Symphony, *The Last Supper*, and *Ulysses* are types, yet they are all particulars, material things.

Dog (the type) is present in its entirety wherever a dog is present. Dog is now sleeping on my carpet just when, at another place, *it* is chasing a rabbit. Quine would say that Dog is a mere abstraction: one dog is sleeping on my carpet, and another dog is chasing a rabbit. But if recurrent entities such as the type Dog do not exist, then my dog, Max, does not exist either, for Max, too, is a recurrent. Max is sleeping now, but this morning he was

4. Willard Quine, "Identity, Ostension, and Hypostasis," in *From a Logical Point of View* (New York: Harper, 1961), 65–79.

digging up the garden. These descriptions (sleeping, digging up the garden) are incompatible; so, Quine ought to say that Max does not exist, that he is a mere abstraction. Only Max stages exist: one Max stage is sleeping and another Max stage digs up the garden. Yet the regress does not stop here: a Max stage *could* be different from what it is, so it recurs in many possible worlds. Its occurrences in different worlds differ from each other and thus *it* does not exist. We see that the reason against the existence of types counts against the existence of everything. I conclude that recurrent particulars exist. Dog (the type) is a material thing that exists in its entirety at many indexes; dogs are occurrences of the type Dog.

The *Mona Lisa* is completely present at different times at the same place (e.g., the original canvas at various times) and in different places at the same time (reproductions of *Mona Lisa*). These occurrences of *Mona Lisa* differ from each other: for instance, the original now is much darker than the original in 1510. These two occurrences do not look alike, they are chemically different, and aesthetically they differ too—the present occurrence is inferior to the earlier one. Similarly, not all those who attempt to *reproduce* the *Mona Lisa* (copying it by hand or by photographic means) succeed to the same degree. Again, the distinct occurrences (reproductions) of the *Mona Lisa* do not look exactly alike, they are chemically different, and their aesthetic value widely differs too. Yet it is possible to *reproduce* the *Mona Lisa itself*. If a given occurrence has enough essential features of the *Mona Lisa*, it is a (good or poor) occurrence of the *Mona Lisa*. Further, the *Mona Lisa* could be other than it is; that is to say that this painting, the *Mona Lisa*, also occurs in other possible worlds, where it differs in various ways from its occurrences in reality. These occurrences of the *Mona Lisa* in time, space, and possibility-space are occurrences of one thing. The *Mona Lisa* is identical *at* each of its occurrences with that occurrence, but these occurrences are nowhere identical with each other. Identity is transitive only in the same domain.

Is there a systematic relation between traits of occurrences of a given type and traits of the type itself? John Bacon has argued that there is no true formula of the form "The type A is F iff its tokens are G."[5] He shows that Twardowski's formula, "The A is F iff all A's are F," fails to meet ordinary

---

5. "Do Generic Descriptions Denote?" *Mind* 82 (1973): 331–47; "The Untenability of Genera," *Logique et Analyse* 17 (1974): 197–208; "The Semantics of the Generic *The*," *Journal of Philosophical Logic* 2 (1973): 323–39.

intuitions; "The lion has a tail" is true, but "All lions have tails" is false. "The A is F iff normal A's are F" will not do either: "The squill appears at the beginning of autumn" is true, but "Normal squills appear at the beginning of autumn" is false. Another attempt, "The A is F iff most A's are F" fails too: "Man has reached the moon" is true, but "Most men have reached the moon" is false. Worse: "The Lion is a type" is true, but "All lions are types" is false. In each of these examples the problem is different, and no formula fits them all. Bacon takes this as a proof that types do not exist.

The conclusion does not follow: failure of reduction does not prove inexistence. There is no single function to features of things from features of their temporal occurrences either; does that prove that no enduring things exist? David is human iff *all* his occurrences are human, but not *all* the occurrences of a killer engage in killing. Surely that disparity does not imply that there are no killers or that David does not exist. Why should there be a mechanical way to export predicates from tokens to their types and vice versa? Twardowski's formula is correct, but it applies to *essential* properties, properties that things (types) have *as such*. X as such is F iff all its occurrences have it, that is, iff it is F everywhere. However, when we say that X is F, we allege, not that X as such is F, only that at some understood index it is F. "John is ill" does not mean that John is always ill; "John is tall" does not mean that John is necessarily tall. "The Lion has a tail" means not that The Lion as such has a tail (that is false: a lion that loses its tail is a lion); it means that normally, The Lion has a tail; and indeed all occurrences of The Normal Lion have a tail. "Man reached the moon" says that some actual occurrence of Man reached the moon, and that is true: it is true of all occurrences of Man that some occurrence of Man (the type to which they all belong) reached the moon. The same applies to "David is a killer," etc.

Thus, to say that Beethoven's *Grosse Fuge* starts in B-flat is not to say that all its performances (tokens) start this way; the *Grosse Fuge* has deviant performances that start with another note. Since starting in B-flat is not essential to it, there are tokens of the *Grosse Fuge* that start otherwise. It is only true that The *Correct Grosse Fuge* starts in B-flat, and indeed all occurrences of *that* type do start thus. To say that The *Grosse Fuge* was composed in 1826 is not to say that all its tokens were produced in 1826, which is false, but that its first real-world occurrence was made in 1826. To say that I heard the *Grosse Fuge* is certainly not to say that I heard all its occurrences, but that I heard some of them. The *Grosse Fuge* is a type, and so are all its occurrences; each of them ($O_1 \ldots O_n$) is identical with the *Grosse Fuge* at some index.

7.3. Identity Conditions

I agree with the metaphysical realists that things are what they are no matter how we think of them. *Independence of Thought*, however, is often misconstrued. The point is this: to change X is not to destroy it; but whether a given item is X-as-changed or is not X anymore but another thing, Y, that X became is a matter of our concept X. Observation cannot give us an answer. Thus, my desk cannot be fully described by physics, for its identity conditions, which decide when it is changed and when it is destroyed, cannot be expressed by physics. My desk undergoes changes: *it* is stained, scratched, moved closer to the door, while staying the same desk. But if it burns, the ashes are not the desk; the desk has gone out of existence. The heap of atoms that my desk consists of now has other identity conditions: it may survive burning but not scratching. Having distinct identity conditions, these two things, my desk and this heap of atoms, are different things that are *identical at* this spatiotemporal index in the real world. The atoms in my desk may be gradually replaced, and yet it will be the same desk; but if you replace the atoms in this heap of atoms, you destroy it. This heap of atoms may at some future time make up a cat and still be the same heap of atoms, but my desk cannot turn into a cat and still be the same desk.

The distinction between (1) a change *in* the object and (2) the object's going out of existence and replacement by another is relative to our concepts: it depends on a *choice* of a system of substance concepts. We cannot distinguish case 1 from case 2 by observing the object; what makes them different is not anything that a perceptive observer who is unaware of our system of substance concepts can discover. Yet the distinction between change and annihilation is very important to us; all things we identify and talk about have identity conditions; that is, we endow some of their properties with a privileged status.

The identity conditions of X are those features of X that are *essential* to X, that is, features that are necessary for it to be X. These are the features X has wherever and whenever it occurs. Without a distinction between essential and inessential features, that is, between features that may vary between occurrences of the same thing and features that may not, no thing could recur at various indexes (e.g., space, time, and possible worlds). An occurrence at one index is obviously unlike (even if for that reason alone, that it is at *this* index) any occurrence that is at another index. Thus, to have an ontology of things that occur in more than one index, a world of recurring things, is to conceive of things as having identity conditions.

Most types (things) we recognize cannot be reduced to other types, nor can sentences about them (e.g., sentences about Plato or about London) be rephrased as logical constructs of sentences about more elementary types. To analyze the name 'X' of the type X we need to know, for every property, whether it is essential for being X, inessential for but compatible with being X, or incompatible with being X. For ontological, and not only epistemological, reasons, such a list cannot be compiled. Even an omniscient being cannot have it, for the question whether some feature that we shall never conceive of would have been regarded by us as essential or inessential to X, had we conceived of it, has no truth conditions.

Types are open-textured, since, given a type X, it is not determinate for every possible condition whether the condition is or is not essential for (or incompatible with) being X. What feature is essential for being a desk is an interest-relative issue, and interest may change as a result of finding the knowledge needed to raise the question whether some hitherto unthought-of feature should or should not be considered essential to being a desk. It is impossible to consider *all* properties in advance and define 'desk' by an exhaustive list of all the conditions under which a thing is to be called 'a desk.' Terms used by finite beings are necessarily open-textured.

7.4. More Identity Conditions

Many aestheticians think that there ought to be value-free identity conditions for artworks; we just have to look hard to find them.[6] Goodman has two such conditions and distinguishes two kinds of artworks: autographic, whose identity is fixed by physical criteria, and allographic, whose identity is fixed by notational criteria. These conditions are said to be necessary and sufficient for being the artwork X: if X is autographic, the criterion is identity with a physical thing, the original of X; and if X is allographic, the criterion is compliance with the notation for X. A painting (an autographic art) not identical with the original canvas of X, and a bit of music (an allographic art) that deviates from the score of Y, are not instances of X and of Y, respectively. A performer who makes one sound not authorized by Y's score, a restorer

6. See, e.g., Jerrold Levinson, "What a Musical Work Is," *Journal of Philosophy* 77 (1980): 5–28.

replacing X's rotting original canvas, each creates entirely new works of art. The new work is inspired by the original work, but it is not it.

I cannot agree: compliance with a score need not produce X. First, the frequency of what counts as, say, the oboe's A note (regulating the orchestra) changed through the ages; a sound that was once A is now another note. If that is allowed, then by Goodman's favorite argument from the transitivity of identity every sound sequence is the work X. Second, the condition is not sufficient: if the right notes are sounded but are too loud or too soft for us to hear, too fast or too slow for us to follow, the outcome is not X. If years pass between consecutive notes, X is not produced (or else it is always produced, for these sounds, in that order, can be found in nature somewhere, sometime). Third, the condition is not necessary: an artist may modify or rescore his or her work; since for Goodman that is impossible, his account is inadequate.

These counterintuitive results show the basic flaw of Goodman's approach: identity conditions are not value-free, for self-identity of a thing is preservation of its essence, and what is essential is a matter of evaluation. The identity criteria of things of kind K depend on our reason for identifying Ks. Thus, if X's heart is transplanted into Y's body, Y survives and X dies, but if X's brain is transplanted into Y's body, X survives and Y dies. Why? Because we appreciate persons for their minds, not for their hearts, and thus personal identity can forgo the heart and not the brain. What is valuable in an artwork X is, then, what is essential to it. An artwork is appreciated for its aesthetic value, so whether Y is an instance of the artwork X depends on whether Y has what is aesthetically valued in X, and what makes X valuable is a matter of evaluative criteria.

Suppose that changes in our biology make us stone-deaf but that we become sensitive to a magnetic field isomorphic to the field of sounds. Can we rescore the classical works for magnets? If in the future the piano sounds childish and naive, should we use it to play Beethoven? The answers are neither trivial nor automatic; they involve appreciation of what is gained and what is lost by such changes. A blanket ruling that compliance with the score is all that matters for identity—never mind all of X's other features—is arbitrary. What we need to detect identity is the sensitivity of a critic, not the arrogance of a philosopher. Goodman's is a typical administrative decision: simple, arbitrary, and crude.

Alleged "autographic" works have many instances too. From the minute the last brush stroke is applied to the canvas, the painting relentlessly changes: chemically, in color, in form, and in its relation to the world around it. Every painting is in flux: a smooth green surface becomes a blue cracked mound, and a red surface becomes purple. What is so sacrosanct about the original canvas if what is on it now is so different from what the artist originally put there? Why is uncontrolled deterioration less detrimental to the painting's identity than intentional change? Even if artworks did not physically change with time (which is impossible), we might need to reproduce them differently to salvage their meaning. Even if X meant *that p* to its contemporaries, we (diligent scholars included) might be unable to see it as meaning *that p*.[7] Sometimes, the best we can do is to recast it in a new idiom to preserve meaning. That again is a delicate decision, a matter of aesthetic gain and loss, which cannot be decided for all possible cases in advance, by fiat.

The original canvas is a poor guardian of painting identity, for it may still exist when the painting has disappeared, and it may be destroyed when the painting survives. If the original canvas of the painting X is gradually replaced, thread by thread, when the painting goes through periodic restorations, I think that X still exists. Goodman, however, will reject it as a forgery, not X itself. What, then, if in the natural course of events all atoms in the canvas are gradually replaced? Do we have only forgeries, then?

Color identity is a poor identity criterion too: both too liberal and too strict. It is too liberal because (as Danto has it) there is more to a painting than meets the eye: time and means of production may be essential for some paintings. It is too strict because color changes occur in all paintings without the painting going out of existence. Plastic art may be notated, but notation is parasitic, for we have to decide what to notate, and I contend that this is decided by value considerations. Each artwork has its own source of value, its own kind of beauty. Preserving the identity of an artwork is preserving the aesthetic contribution of *that* work.

What, then, are the identity conditions of a work of art? The question is moot; answering it is counterproductive. Long ago, philosophers came to realize that definitions of empirical concepts have counterexamples. Because we are not omniscient, our concepts are open-textured, not predetermined for all possible circumstances. A concept may be perfectly useful, yet we may be unable to say whether it does or does not apply in outlandish, undreamt-of circumstances. Arcane questions about the identity conditions of artworks

---

7. As rightly required, and wrongly assumed to solve the problem of the artwork's changing with time, by Anthony Savile, in *The Test of Time* (New York: Oxford University Press, 1982).

resemble questions of personal identity: the philosopher concocts science-fiction circumstances, radically changing the conditions under which we can apply the notion *same person*, and then asks, as if this were a factual matter: is X the same person as Y? Wittgenstein would have told them that under such conditions the question has no sense; intuition cannot be infinitely stretched. You cannot derive a taxonomy of flowers by extrapolating from ornithological classification! The conviction that X and Y must be occurrences either of the same work or else of different works, and that we can *discover* which is the case, is a superstition. It is a belief based on a confused version of the law of excluded middle. Only those who do not understand the nature of our concepts think that an embryo is either the same as the person it grows into (hence it is a person) or else distinct from the person it grows into(hence it is cell tissue). This "dilemma" makes a muddle look like a deep philosophical problem. The puzzle is genuine, but it has no straightforward answer, for it is a question of what we value in persons.

There can *be* no answer to all questions of identity, for we keep no list of necessary and sufficient conditions for empirical concepts. Can the *Eroica* be electronically produced and still be the same work? Could *it* be written at another time? Would it be the same work if composed by Schubert and not by Beethoven? There is no nonevaluative algorithm you can use to answer this: you cannot recruit our linguistic intuitions where we have none. Leibniz's law is useless here, for to find whether X is F iff Y is F for every property F, we must first know what X is and what Y is, thus know whether X and Y are identical or not. We know what to say in normal conditions; elsewhere, intuition runs dry. If an incredible event, such as two people composing exactly sound-alike works, happens, we shall need to tighten the artwork identity conditions just enough to take care of this case.[8] If one author antecedes the other, we may prefer to say that the author of the first occurrence authored the work, whereas the second created only a new occurrence of it. Jerrold Levinson and Gregory Currie,[9] who debate whether Beethoven and a doppelgänger in another world have both created the same *Eroica*, engage in such a futile debate. Levinson says no, taking artwork identity to involve the author. Currie says yes, taking works to be action types. What is their evidence? Levinson, who thinks there is a factual

8. For details, see my "Vague Objects," *Nous* 25 (1991): 323–40.
9. Jerrold Levinson, *Music, Art, and Metaphysics* (Ithaca: Cornell University Press, 1990); Gregory Currie, *An Ontology of Art* (New York: Macmillan, 1989).

answer, tries to show that the two authors create two works, not one, for these works differ in sources of influence. And what if not? The effort is futile anyway, for differences between occurrences do not exclude their being the same work. In a world where Schumann composes an *Eroica*-sounding work and Beethoven does not, that work has different properties from the *Eroica* in reality. For example, we listen to it in the context of Schumann's life and works, which may influence its aesthetic qualities. But that does not decide the issue of work identity: everything has different traits in different worlds. Some differences are mandated, not prohibited, by the logic of transworld identity. The only consideration that is meaningful for work identity is whether these differences are aesthetically essential or not. The only question we need to ask is whether a difference in authorship, time, language, ambient society, means of production, physical basis, etc. is aesthetically essential *for that work*. If it is, if it deeply matters and substantially changes the nature of the work, then these different occurrences are occurrences of distinct works; if not, they are different occurrences of the same work.

7.5. Nesting

A thing (Mozart or *The Magic Flute*) is identified by its essential features; whatever has those features is an occurrence of it. If some Z is an occurrence of X and an occurrence of Y, then X and Y overlap: they are identical *at* Z. Recall the case of the desk and the heap of atoms: having different identity conditions, they are distinct things, though identical *at some* of their occurrences.

Now, consider a thing, X, *all* of whose identity conditions are included in the identity conditions of another thing, Y. X and Y are identical at Y: every occurrence of Y is an occurrence of X, but not vice versa. That relation is *nesting*. I define: Y is *nested* in X (or X *nests* Y) iff every essential property of X is also an essential property of Y. Formally,

$$\text{Nest}(X,Y) \equiv (F)[\Box F(X) \rightarrow \Box F(Y)]$$

The essential properties of X are those that X has as such, that are its identity conditions, the properties it has at all times, places, and possible worlds where it occurs. F is essential for X iff, wherever X is, it is F: if X occurs at O, then X is F at O. Nesting can be perspicuously defined in Substance Logic:

$$\text{Nest}(X,Y) \equiv X =_Y Y$$

Thus every token of *Gould's Bach's Sinfonia no. 1* is also a token of *Bach's Sinfonia no. 1*, but not the other way around. Whatever is Mozart-the-child is Mozart, but not vice versa. If X nests Y then $X = Y$ at Y; it does not follow that $X = Y$ at X. *Gould's Bach's Sinfonia no. 1* is identical with *Bach's Sinfonia no. 1* only where the former is found, not where the latter is found. *Bach's Sinfonia no. 1* also occurs where *Landowska's Bach's Sinfonia no. 1* occurs, where it is not identical with *Gould's Bach's Sinfonia no. 1*. Mozart occurs at indexes where Mozart-the-child does not occur, but wherever Mozart-the-child occurs, Mozart occurs too. Mozart as such is not a child, that is, being a child is not essential to him. Therefore, not *all* his occurrences are occurrences of The Child, but some are.

Nesting is transitive: if X nests Y and Y nests Z, then X nests Z. It is a one-many/many-one relation: Suppose that X's essential properties are {F,G}, Y's are {H,I}, Z's are {F,G,H,I}, and V's are {F,G,J,K}. Then both X and Y nest Z, and X nests both Z and V. We can also say that Z is a model for both X and Y, and Z and V are distinct models for X.

Let "$(\exists X)[F(X)]$" abbreviate "Some occurrence of X is F'" and "$(\forall X)[F(X)]$" abbreviate "Every occurrence of X is F." Thus, if X nests Y, it can be that $(\exists X)[F(X)]$ and not $(\exists Y)[F(Y)]$, that $(\exists Y)[F(Y)]$ and not $(\forall X)[F(X)]$, but it cannot be that $(\exists Y)[F(Y)]$ and not $(\exists X)[F(X)]$, because Y is an occurrence of X. Being F may be essential to Y but inessential to X; then, if X nests Y, not all X's occurrences are F. If X nests several things, each one of them having all of X's essential features, these things are ontologically distinct models (e.g., performances) of X. These models are fully realized, that is, *concrete*, alternative interpretations of X.

Interpreting is a kind of nesting: Y is an interpretation of X iff X nests Y and Y explains X. Interpretations are explanatory models of their interpretanda. To be an interpretation of X is to have as essential all of X's essential properties and in addition some essential properties that X as such does not have. These additional properties of Y integrate X's properties and explain why X has them.

"$(\forall X)[F(X)]$" is synonymous with "X as such is F"; thus X as such may lack G, while some of its occurrences have it; for example, its interpretation Y may very well have it. If Y interprets X, then some aspects that are open in X as such are closed in Y. For instance, how loud sonata X is, is left open, but that does not mean that some sounds have no loudness or that the sonata is an abstract entity that has no sound. Rather, what it means is that different occurrences of X have different degrees of loudness. The interpretation Y of X closes that option and specifies n as the loudness degree essential for Y: all of Y's occurrences have loudness n. That degree of loudness is how Y accounts for X.

In music and the theater, performers *produce* a model of the work they interpret; in art and literature critics *specify*, describe, a model for it. Usually, the essential properties of things are weighted disjunctions. Thus an item Y, which has sufficiently many disjuncts of some disjunctive property F that is essential for X, is an occurrence of X.[10] Interpreters of X either produce (perform) or specify an entity, Y, which is an occurrence of X but in which the features of X are alleged to be interconnected, coherent, and follow from each other, as they do not in X as such. Every work X has plenty of interpretations, and the best interpretation is that which best fits X: its most beautiful occurrence.

Art critics tell us which properties of an artwork X are so essential that if X loses them, it ceases to exist, and if a reproducer fails to reproduce them, what he makes is not X. What if critics disagree? Let Jones hold that feature H is essential to X, while Smith disagrees. Their interpretations (J and S) of X accordingly differ. These interpretations are distinct models, things or blueprints for things, nested in X. J and S are both occurrences of the painting X, but they differ in their essential properties: J has the property H essentially, while S has H nonessentially.

For example, let X be a picture of Venus, painted in 1650, in Rome, by a pupil of Rubens. Jones's interpretation of X amounts to specifying a painting, J, that is identical with X at J, but has different identity conditions: the property H (say, Rubens's influence) is essential in J. J is an explanatory model for X that claims to illuminate X; by placing X in context of Rubens's works it aspires to make it intelligible and interesting. Smith, on the other hand, dismisses the painter's contact with Rubens as inconsequential. The artwork Smith specifies, S, is also a model for X, but H is unessential in it; some occurrences of S have it and others do not. Smith thinks that if you see X as S it will look better; Jones, naturally, suggests that seeing X as J is preferable.

A copier of X includes in his reproduction every feature that he considers essential to X. Nonpictorial properties one finds essential to X must

---

10. Let the interpretation I of *Hamlet* be that Hamlet is mad: M(I). Let *Hamlet* itself only have the property that Hamlet is mad or not mad: M-or-not-M(H). But 'M(I)' implies 'M-or-not-M (I).' Thus I has that essential property of *Hamlet* and can be nested in it.

be attributed to it only verbally. If the hue H is a feature that the repro-ducer, hence the interpreter, of X considers essential, he can realize it in his interpretation, but some features cannot be reproduced. For example, interpretation Y may take communism as essential to X: to see X as it is, you must see it as hailing communism. Y's communism is essential to it; allegedly, it makes all of Y's other features fall into place, thus making Y an integrated, beautiful instance of X. The interpreter cannot paint communism into his reproduction, so he has to specify his version Y of X verbally, trying to make you see X as Y.

The same is true of music: in his playing, a pianist can realize some features of his interpretation of X, but not all musical interpretation can be so realized. If a relation R to a social milieu or to a personal experience of the composer is considered essential to X, the critic cannot do what the pianist does, that is, produce an object where R is realized. Instead, the critic verbally specifies a model (interpretation) Y of X; Y reconfigures X and, allegedly, enhances it aesthetically. I repeat: to impute R to X is to specify a richer thing Y which is nested in X and in which R is essential. Seeing X as Y, the critic claims, gives X a value that, otherwise, it does not have.[11]

7.6. Being Reasonable

Relativists believe that there is no way for us to identify the interpretandum, the artwork X itself, through the veil of its interpretations. Being what we are, we are necessarily biased: we cannot see the work as uninterpreted, and each reader construes the interpretandum differently. In a word, interpretation is all there is; the interpretandum is a myth. Now, in one limited sense this is entirely true: the only way to examine the work X is via one of its interpretations, just as we cannot examine a thing except by examining a certain occurrence of it. You cannot meet Jack as such without meeting some temporal slice of Jack. So what? That we need to meet Jack at a certain age does not say that we cannot meet Jack; on the contrary, to meet a temporal

---

11. Richard Shusterman, who commented on an earlier version of this section at an ASA convention, asked how a critic can interpret a work (e.g., in biblical exegesis) as disunited and segmented between several sources. I answer that such segmentation increases the unity of the text by eliminating internal incongruities that would otherwise mar it. Another unity aspired to is coherence with our worldview; so, if prophecy is impossible, we increase, not decrease, the cogency of the biblical text by construing prophecies as after-the-fact interpolations.

slice of Jack *is* to meet Jack. To examine X is to examine some occurrence of X, and if X is an artwork, its occurrences are its interpretations. Interpreters *impute* (as Margolis says)[12] their interpretations to the interpretandum, and different interpreters impute different essential properties to the work, but that does not obliterate the work X as it is in itself. The properties X has as such are those shared by all its instances, so if you know X's occurrences, you know what X is as such.

Can we, then, identify occurrences of X and tell them apart from those that are not X? Yes, because we can apply the words of our language: to learn the word 'X' is to distinguish what is X from what is not (an occurrence of X). Normally, we can tell a chair from what is not a chair, so there is no reason to think we cannot tell what is *Fidelio* from what is not. Of course there are borderline cases, where according to one reasonable construal a given item is, but according to another reasonable construal it is not, *Fidelio*. There is no necessary and sufficient condition for being *Fidelio*, just as there are no such conditions for being a chair, so not all cases are decidable. Yet we generally know what traits a chair, or *Fidelio*, has, so we can tell whether an interpretation (even a bad one) is an interpretation *of Fidelio*. We, all of us, make such decisions daily, when we identify things that are far from perfect examples of their kind. Language users use words in new situations and apply them to items they never encountered before. How can I tell whether this term applies here? Wittgenstein answered: in virtue of the language game we play, we see things as instances of types.[13] Those who do not see what the right application of a term is will never learn to speak a language.

Given an interpretation Y, we can usually tell what features the interpreted X has as such. Let interpretation Y impute to X the properties {F,G,H} and interpretation Z impute to X the properties {F,G,K}. Do Y and Z have a common interpretandum? Both agree that the interpretandum has {F,G}. Whether that is sufficient for saying that Y and Z are interpretations of the same work X depends on what F and G are. To take a ridiculous example, if F is Fugue, and G is German, then that is much too poor a ground for saying that Y and Z are interpretations of one work of art. If some occurrences have only that in common, that they are all German fugues, we will not say

12. Joseph Margolis, *Art and Philosophy* (Atlantic Highlands, N.J.: Humanities Press, 1980), chap. 3.

13. See section 6.5 above.

that they are all performances of the same work; what they have in common is too meager to qualify as a work of art. But the common ground may be much richer. If more and more features are added to the two mentioned above, then, at a certain point, we shall say that these occurrences are all the same artwork, somewhat different interpretations of one work of art. How much more is required? How many features are needed for it to be the same work variously interpreted rather than a series of similar works, where the common basis is a theme or an idea or a style but not a work in its own right? The answer is "Just enough." It is not vacuous: it cannot be formalized, but we can apply it.

Here is an example: Mozart did not complete his *Requiem*. It is not that he fully completed some parts of it and Suessmayr the rest. Rather, Mozart completed various parts of the *Requiem* to various degrees: a scheme of the melodic line here, a few bars there, a key and tempo suggested at another place, a harmonic structure specified elsewhere. How much of the *Requiem* should have Mozart completed in order for us to say that he created a work of art and not merely suggested a general idea for one? There is no cutoff line, a point where we say: That is the minimum; nothing less than that qualifies as an artwork. Yet vagueness does not render meaningless the question whether Mozart left us a work of art or an idea for one. Similarly, whether Y is an interpretation of a work X or an independent work inspired by elements of another is a question of utmost importance. All critics ask, when they encounter a new item: Is it plagiarized? Is it a pastiche of other works? Or is it really a *new work*? Usually, they have good reasons for their answers.

The features a work has wherever it occurs are its essence. Interpreters who disagree on the properties of X do not take their disagreement so far that the intersection of the features of their interpretations is too poor to qualify as a work of art. Otherwise, we would not have said that these are interpretations of the same work, or that they conflict. To contend that a rival interpretation of X is wrong is to agree that it, too, is an interpretation of X. The features that various interpretations of X have in common must therefore be rich enough to make X an identifiable work of art in its own right. If there were not enough properties to identify X as such, X could not have been the subject of competing interpretations.[14]

---

14. In *Is There a Text in This Class?* (Cambridge: Harvard University Press, 1980), 345–47, Stanley Fish claims that "A Rose for Emily" can be given any reading at all; but by granting

Unlike scientific theories, art interpretations are not ontologically exclusive. If the scientific model Y is the best one, a scientific realist will reject all the other models of reality. On the other hand, an aesthetic realist who finds Y the best interpretation of a work X need not reject the other interpretations of it. We enjoy having a variety of rival interpretations in music, in literature, and in the visual arts. Great artworks inspire many interpretations that present them and complete them in different ways, thus making many aesthetically good objects. Multiple interpretation is desirable for the same reason that art is desirable: it is a creation of beauty. Those who think that, if one interpretation of X is right, all others are wrong cannot explain our enjoying a variety of interpretations of artworks we like.

How is that possible? Interpretations conflict, so do we accept both p and not-p? Of course not. Recurrence implies ontological incompleteness. That phenomenon is not peculiar to art: every explanatory model is nested in its explanandum. If X is F at I and not-F at J, then X as such is open with respect to being F; X as such is neither F nor not-F. It is completed, for example, by an interpretation Y that *says* that X *should* be understood as F—that is, the non-F occurrences of X (its other interpretations) are nonstandard. A non-F occurrence of X is like a tailless lion: it is a lion, but a maimed, nonstandard one. Y *says* that F *should* be interpreted as F in that all *its* (Y's) occurrences are F. Interpretation is a precisification and can be supervaluated:[15] X is F if all its precisifications are F. A singer takes a lied X that is open with respect to being F, and in his singing of the lied F is essential. The lied X as he sings it is a new thing, Y, which is nested in X, unifies X, and illuminates it. The singer produces Y, a splendid occurrence of X, and invites us to hear X as Y. But there may be other splendid occurrences of X that are incompatible with Y.

Let X be a novel. One interpretation of it says that the hero dies (p); another says that the hero survives ($\sim p$). These two interpretations are incompatible with each other, but both are compatible with X. If D is the set of worlds where the hero dies, S the worlds where the hero survives, and X* the worlds that satisfy X, then X* $=_D$ D and X* $=_S$ S. As Roman Ingarden saw, an interpretation closes some open options of its interpretandum.

---

that those are all readings of "A Rose for Emily," he grants the very thesis he challenges, that "A Rose for Emily" can be objectively identified and hence has some essential features of its own.

15. Cf. Bas van Fraasen, "Singular Terms, Truth-Value Gaps, and Free Logic," *Journal of Philosophy* 53 (1966): 481–85; Kit Fine, "Vagueness, Truth, and Logic," *Synthese* 30 (1975): 265–300.

The lied as performed by the singer is a thing, Y, in which other artworks can nest, just as Y is nested in the musical work X. Acting can interpret Y; thus Z, singing plus acting, is different from Y, which as such has only acoustic features and is ontologically open with respect to action. Z may be a part of an opera, where actors modify the meaning of the purely acoustic Y. The operatic role Z may, in turn, nest a ballet role V, where some bodily movements further amplify Z, and so forth and so on. The chain has no end: interpretation can expand any thing into a richer thing, which integrates the thing that nests it in ever widening, more encompassing artworks.

7.7. Art and Mere Things

Arthur Danto draws a distinction between a work of art and the mere thing of which it consists.[16] That the distinction is important is best shown by the case of ready-made artworks like Duchamp's *Fountain*, which consists of a plain urinal. I agree with Danto that *Fountain* has aesthetic properties that the urinal does not have, but how can we explain the difference between *Fountain* and the urinal of which it consists? Danto replies that the 'is' in sentences like "*Fountain* is a urinal" is not a copula but a connective he calls "The *is* of Artistic Identification," standing for a sui generis relation between artworks and physical things. That mysterious relation is characterized only as a "transfigurative kin to *magical* identification, as when one says a wooden doll is one's enemy,"[17] so Danto's account has no explanatory value whatever.

Margolis substitutes for that ad hoc relation another gnomic one: embodiment. "We must admit a logically distinctive use of 'is,' " Margolis says, "the 'is' of embodiment, which is not to be collapsed into the 'is' of identity."[18] By saying that embodiment is the relation that obtains between persons and their bodies and between cultural and physical objects,[19]

16. E.g., in *The Transfiguration of the Commonplace* (Cambridge: Harvard University Press, 1981) and *The Philosophical Disenfranchisement of Art* (New York: Columbia University Press, 1986).

17. Danto, *Transfiguration of the Commonplace*, 126.

18. Margolis, *Art and Philosophy*, 43–44.

19. Ibid., 40.

Margolis gives embodiment a wider use, but that is still unhelpful: it is an explanation of the murky by the mysterious. Since no logic of embodiment is given, it is mysterious how embodiment works, that is, how a particular can "instantiate another particular."[20] Margolis says that his 'is' of embodiment is like David Wiggins's 'is' of composition. That is to say, the relation of *Fountain* to the urinal is like the relation of a sweater to the wool of which it is made. But that wool is reshaped by knitting; the problem of a readymade is that the artist does not physically reshape it. Moreover, Wiggins, too, does not explain how particulars can instantiate each other.[21] We need an account of the logic at work, but none is given. I object to this misinterpretation of the good word 'is,' as if it were ambiguous between a multitude of murky connectives (none of which explains why an artwork is not identical with the material it consists of). Danto and Margolis masterfully present ingenious examples, but the theory that explains them is missing.

In Substance Logic the word 'is' has one and only one sense: identity in a domain. "A is B" says that at the understood index (most often a place, time, and possible world) A is identical with B. That sense of 'is' is also used in "*Fountain* is this urinal." *Fountain* and the urinal are distinct things, since they have different essences. Being a part of a certain artworld is essential to *Fountain*; out of that context *Fountain* cannot exist, for it would lack its essential aesthetic property, its contrast to traditional artworks, which makes it the artwork it is. Its significance is due to its appearance as an artwork at a specific historical and art-historical period. For the urinal, on the other hand, its relation to that artworld is inessential; it can survive without it. Therefore *Fountain* and the urinal are identical, but not necessarily, that is, not everywhere. *Fountain* is nested in the urinal: the two things are identical *at Fountain*. In each possible world or spatiotemporal index where the urinal does not stand in the required relation to an artworld, the urinal occurs and *Fountain* does not occur. On the other hand, wherever *Fountain* occurs, the urinal occurs too; there, *Fountain* (F) and the urinal (U) are identical: $F =_U U$.[22]

20. Ibid., 22.
21. See David Wiggins, *Sameness and Substance* (Oxford: Basil Blackwell, 1980), and idem, *Identity and Spatiotemporal Continuity* (Oxford: Basil Blackwell, 1964).
22. In subsequent years Duchamp made several copies of *Fountain* (that is, presented some other urinals as copies of *Fountain*). So now it is not true any more that *Fountain* nests in the original urinal. Rather, it is wherever each of its copies is.

Another puzzle case discussed by Danto, where one object (say, a monochromatic canvas) is the same physical object as several distinct artworks whose aesthetic properties differ,[23] is also negotiated by the present theory. These works of art have distinct transworld extensions, hence different essences. A change that does not compromise the identity of one artwork is lethal to another. The change need not be in the canvas; it may be in the cultural milieu, artworld, or production conditions of the work. The present ontology allows distinct artworks, A and B, to be identical in one index and diverge at other indexes: A occurs there, B does not. Danto's intuition is thus explained and vindicated without recourse to nonlogical pseudo–identity relations. Instead, we say that since A and B overlap in reality but are nonidentical at other indexes, they are distinct things, therefore distinct works of art. No special distinction between artworks and mere things is necessary.

Danto is fond of Menard examples, but the actual absence of such artworks is more instructive than their logical possibility. Works of art are created by intelligent people who strive to make them aesthetically excellent given *their own* cultural background. Thus, a historically faithful interpretation is likely to succeed. We saw that an interpretation Y tries to present a work X as an integral whole (first Keats Principle) that fits the world as we believe it is (second Keats Principle). That is no simple task; ahistorical interpretations are less likely to succeed in it.

7.8. The Mode of Being of Art

A work of art is a material thing. Many aestheticians (e.g., Danto, Wollheim, Levinson) demur: they think that literary and musical artworks are immaterial. Paintings and sculptures, they say, are not types but tokens, and each picture is a unique material object; in contrast, musical and verbal works are types: they exist in many copies, each of which exemplifies the abstract work. I think that is entirely wrong. All artworks are types; the tokens of a certain artwork are its occurrences, that is, that artwork as it is at some

---

23. *The Transfiguration of the Commonplace*, chap. 1. A square red canvas is said to be the distinct paintings *Crossing the Red Sea, Kierkegaard's Mood, Red Square* (as in Moscow), *Red Square* (the canvas), and *Untitled*.

indexes. There are many instances of Beethoven's Ninth Symphony and many copies of Donatello's *David* (two of which were made by Donatello himself; three copies of *Madonna* were made by Munk). Many aestheticians, idealists (Croce, Bosanquet, Collingwood), as well as realists (Ingarden, Alexander, Gilson, Vivas, Weiss, Dufrenne), attributed a nonmaterial ontological status to all artworks, postulating a special phenomenal thing, the aesthetic object, as the object of aesthetic appreciation. Paul Weiss says that an art object "exists whether it is known or not" but that an aesthetic object "exists only while we take an interest in it."[24] Étienne Gilson, too, says that "a painting has actual existence only during those moments that it is being actually experienced as a work of art"; "like musical pieces, paintings exist only while they actually are being perceived."[25] Richard Wollheim claims that while some artworks (e.g., paintings) are material things, "certain works of art are not physical *objects*"; "there are arts where it is impossible to find physical objects that are even candidates for being identified with works of art."[26]

These immaterial "aesthetic objects" that spring into being when you enter the museum take us to the world of Bishop Berkeley or to Alice's Wonderland; Paul Ziff rightly calls them "the ghost of aesthetics."[27] If the object of aesthetic judgment were abstract, a human being could not have made it, it could not contain red paint, nor could it be in this room. Only material things can have these properties. Sound can shatter a glass and scratch a magnetic tape; for that it needs to be a physical thing.

Music is sound, a configuration of a medium, usually air; it occurs wherever air in these configurations is found. Its spatial location need not be sharply defined unless a physical barrier (e.g., the walls of a concert hall) stop these air configurations from spreading out. You hear *Fidelio* in hall X at time Y, and that is where *Fidelio* is; in some other places and times it does

---

24. Paul Weiss, *The World of Art* (Carbondale: Southern Illinois University Press, 1961), 20.

25. Étienne Gilson, *Painting and Reality* (New York: Meridian Books, 1959), 35, 38.

26. Richard Wollheim, *Art and Its Objects* (New York: Harper & Row, 1968), 64, 29. Wollheim's argument is similar to Bacon's and should be rejected for the same reason. Wollheim is impressed by the fact that, where X is a work of art, 'F(X)' may be true, while 'F(my copy of X),' 'F(the original copy of X),' 'F(this performance of X),' etc. are false. That is his proof that X is not material. Yet all material things have that feature: "This house is dark" may be true and "This house is dark now" false; "Jones was a teacher" may be true and "Jones was a teacher at birth" false. Does this show that this house and Jones are abstract objects?

27. Paul Ziff, "Art and the 'Object of Art,'" in *Aesthetics and Language,* ed. W. Elton (Oxford: Oxford University Press, 1954), 186.

not occur. Not having a sharp boundary is common to all physical things: my desk's boundaries are too fuzzy for its length to be given in microns, so, like *Fidelio*, my desk has no precise borders. *Fidelio* is less precisely demarcated than my table, but not less than a mountain; if *Fidelio* is a nonphysical entity, so is a mountain. *Fidelio* occurs in space-time; the question, "Where is *Fidelio* tonight?" sounds a bit odd, but it can be reformulated as "Where can I see (hear) *Fidelio* tonight?" which is quite natural, and a reply to it answers the original question.

René Wellek and Austin Warren argue that "[i]f we should take seriously the view that a poem is an artifact . . . [t]here would be no *a priori* reason why copies in different editions should be copies of the same [poem]."[28] There is no such a priori reason! We *could* attach aesthetic significance to the number of lines on a page, the place of a word on the page, the font and the size of words, etc. Wellek and Warren note that typographical devices are used in poetry, but a novel, too, may use italics to indicate irony, boldface to indicate the presence of another "voice," etc. So editions that radically modify typographical features need be the same book no more than an edition that radically modifies the text. That the same novel exists in typographically distinct copies shows, not that a novel is not a material thing, but that most novels avoid such devices. It is not an a priori but an empirical fact that we seldom give typography an essential role crucial to the artwork's identity.

Gilson argues that, unlike painting, music is not in space:

> To the question, where is the "Kreutzer" Sonata? there is no answer. Its score is to be found in many places, because it is a thing; the sonata itself does not exist anywhere else than, ideally, in the minds of the music lovers . . . Strictly speaking, it is nowhere. On the contrary, we can say with precision where a painting is to be found, and its location is the only place where it can really be seen. Because it is a thing, *The Death of Procris* by Piero de Cosimo occupies a certain place, and only one. If we want to see it, we must go the National Gallery in London, for this is where it is and it can be seen nowhere else. But where is *Parsifal?* . . . *Parsifal* exists nowhere in particular.[29]

28. René Wellek and Austin Warren, *Theory of Literature* (New York: Harcourt, Brace & World, 1955), 130.

29. Gilson, *Painting and Reality*, 32–33.

This is false. All reproductions of *The Death of Procris* are occurrences of that painting. It recurs at many times, in many places, and in many possible worlds, and some of its occurrences are aesthetically better than others. Literature and music are not different from painting in that respect: the only copy of Aristotle's dialogues was in the great library of Alexandria, so those who wanted to read them had to go to Alexandria. The only way to hear some of Mozart's early works is to have been present where and when he played them, for that performance was the only one, ever. Scores facilitate the reproduction of music; cameras facilitate the reproduction of paintings; but the use of neither device is guaranteed to produce an occurrence of the work one intends to reproduce. Obviously, they do not guarantee that the new occurrence will have all the aesthetic merits of the original. Atrocious performances of music are no less prevalent than bad reproductions of paintings.

What about unrealized works? You compose a poem or a piece of music "in your head" and never commit it to paper. The work is never performed, yet it exists; you know it by heart. That, say Wellek and Warren, proves that artworks are not material things.[30] I answer that to write a poem "in the head" is to think of words and that to compose music is to think of sounds. To think of words or of sounds is to think of material things. Sounds are obviously physical, and words, too, are physical things classified by their role in language games and *seen as* having that role. Poets imagine material things: words.[31] To compose a text is, then, to imagine word combinations, and a new work comes into being when you imagine words combined in a new way.

"But a poem," one may say, "is not a series of words. It is the meaning these words stand for. A recipe for a cake is not a cake; it merely tells one how

---

30. Wellek and Warren, *Theory of Literature*, 143–45.

31. You train yourself to visualize cities that you saw in the past. You imagine them in sequences, for example, Paris-Rome-Venice or Miami-Cannes-Sarajevo-Delhi. Some of these series relax you, others amuse you, still others make you tense, etc. With time you forget the names of the individual cities; their identity is unimportant to you; you think of them as the grim, or the funny, series. You are so thoroughly trained in visualizing those series that, whenever you want one of them, it pops up in your mind.

The analogy is obvious: to think is to evoke series of sounds and sights. With training these series (sentences) spontaneously come to mind in the appropriate circumstances. We do not think of the components of the series, since we are only interested in the role that this combination of sounds plays. Each sound-combination is classified by the role it plays, and not according to the identity of the sights and sounds originally seen and heard.

to make a cake. Similarly, words tell us what meaning to countenance; that meaning, not the words, is the poem." If meanings were abstract entities, then this argument would indeed prove that some artworks are abstract entities. As previously explained, however, I subscribe to another view of meaning, based on Wittgenstein's ideas in his latest period. Wittgenstein held that to understand a sign is to *see* it *as* playing a certain role in a language game. Due to its past career, its association with certain things, we see it as having a character, a "face" of its own. To understand a symbol is to see it as an officeholder, as if its use were perceptibly written all over it, so that you could see it as *fitting, right for,* a certain use. What one sees a symbol as (e.g., as a duck or as a rabbit) perceptually guides its application (to ducks or else to rabbits). The meaning of a sentence, says Wittgenstein, is like the meaning of a phrase in a musical artwork: you get it if you hear it as a result of a certain development and as requiring a certain solution, that is, as having a role in that work. A language game (*Sprachspiel*), like a game of chess (*Schachspiel*), endows certain pieces with meaning: the role they play makes them meaningful.

The token words in a given text do not *themselves* have a long career behind them; texts do not contain "veteran" tokens. Rather, this token is meaningful because we see it as an occurrence of a type, other occurrences of which have played a specific role in a language game of ours. We regard a newly minted token as an occurrence of a type (a recurrent *particular*) that had previous occurrences. Words recur. When you see a new token-word you see it as an occurrence of its type; you see the present token as holding a role played in our life by other tokens of its type.

Consider this drawing: A. It is composed of three lines placed at certain angles to each other, but you do not see it in that way; you see it as the letter A, that is, as an officeholder in a language game. You see this token as a type having a certain function; as Wittgenstein says, you see a meaning. That drawing would not look to you as the letter A were you unfamiliar with the game we play. Again, consider ☺; it is a circle and some dots, but you see it as a human face. Strictly speaking, ☺ does not have much in common with a human face; it resembles * * much more. Yet we do not see ☺ as a complex design that is isomorphic with a human face; that is possible only for those unfamiliar with human faces. *We* perform a metaphorical act: we see ☺ as belonging to the type Human Face, therefore as having that meaning: human face. The thing, The Human Face, is its meaning. To see X as F is to see X as having the role that the type it is seen to instantiate has in a certain language game. A sign is not an occurrence of the type it represents (☺ is not a human face), but we see it as standing in an *internal relation* to it.[32] To understand X is, then, to see it as an occurrence of a type that means another type, in virtue of their past career in a language game.

---

32. The notion of *internal relations* was central in Wittgenstein's thought throughout his life. In the *Tractatus* he was interested in the internal relation of, e.g., "X is colored" to "X is blue." In his middle period he wondered about the internal relation between a belief-state and its truth-maker. Finally, he used internal relations to explain how we can follow a rule: perceived as a rabbit-sign, X stands in internal relation to rabbits, so we need no rule to sanction its application to rabbits.

8

REFERRING TO NONEXISTENTS

8.1. The Thesis

You sit back in your chair, take a novel, and start reading. If a philosopher asks you whether you understand what you read, you will be insulted. Of course you do, otherwise, why would you be reading it? Does the philosopher think you are a moron who cannot figure out what the novel says? Yet the philosopher has a genuine problem there. You can understand what the novel says only if it says something. According to standard theories of language, a sentence says something only if its subject refers to an entity that its predicate describes. In fiction, however, the subject often is a name of a nonexistent such as Hamlet or the Wizard of Oz. Does the 'Hamlet' refer to Hamlet? Contemporary philosophers do not think so. Hamlet and the Wizard of Oz do not exist, they say, therefore 'Hamlet' and 'the Wizard of Oz' do not refer. It would then seem that a novel cannot say anything, and, consequently, you cannot understand it, because there is nothing in it to understand. In the present chapter I argue that sentences in novels do express statements, for the terms 'Hamlet' and 'the Wizard of Oz' do refer, although the things to which they refer do not exist.

Britain is an island; Atlantis is an island too, but it, unlike Britain, does not exist. Charles is a real prince, Hamlet an unreal prince. The highest mountain is actual, the golden mountain is not. The apparent truth of these statements is my initial reason (Alvin Plantinga calls it "The Classical

Argument")[1] for holding that Existence is a basic, first-order property that some things (Britain, Charles, the highest mountain) have and other things (Atlantis, Hamlet, the golden mountain) do not have.[2] Existence, Reality, and Actuality are the same property.[3] Worlds are things, and thus they do, or do not, exist. Things that are not worlds occur in worlds: Prince Charles occurs in the real world and in other, possible but nonexistent worlds; his real-world occurrences exist, and his occurrences in nonexistent worlds are nonexistent. In one world, all the properties of a thing are mutually compatible[4] (nothing is both round and square in the same world), and all things are compatible with each other. Finally, each thing can exist (note: 'can exist' means 'occurs in some world' and not 'exists in some world').

A *world* is a thing whose parts interact. X and Y are in the same world if (not iff!) X interacts with Y. The is-in-the-same-world-with relation is transitive.[5] "X interacts with Y" does not imply "X and Y exist." If you call off the wedding, it does not exist, yet the description 'the wedding' is *true* of it, or else you would not have called it off! The real world (W_0) is the only world that exists, but we can describe other worlds just as well.

A world divides into world-bound *occurrences* of things. Things are transworld individuals: a thing that occurs in a world occurs in other worlds

---

1. Alvin Plantinga, *The Nature of Necessity* (Oxford: Oxford University Press, 1974), 133–77.

2. Nathan Salmon ("Existence," *Philosophical Perspectives* 1 [1987]: 49–108, esp. 63) thinks that Existence is a property, but like Russell he defines it as Identity-with-Some-Thing: $(\lambda x)(\exists y)(x = y)$. These variables range over existents; so what good is having Existence as a property if one cannot use it to define existents as *things that exist*? Second, Existence is a monadic property; Identity-with-an-Existent is dyadic. Third, a thing can go out of existence, but nothing can lose its self-identity, so these properties are distinct.

3. Peter van Inwagen ("Two Concepts of Possible Worlds," *Midwest Studies in Philosophy* 11 [1986]: 189) says that he knows of no one who holds "that actuality is just existence; that just as a nonactual horse is a nonexistent horse, a nonactual C[oncrete] world is a nonexistent C[oncrete] world." This exactly is my view. I deny that 'actual' is an indexical and reject the bloated ontology where all possible worlds exist. An author who comes close to my view is Richard Routley, in "The Semantical Structure of Fictional Discourse," *Poetics* 8 (1979): 3–30.

4. W. J. Rappaport ("Meinongian Theories and a Russellian Paradox," *Nous* 12 [1978]: 153–80) and R. Clark ("Not Every Object of Thought Has Being," *Nous* 12 [1978]: 181–88) argue that not for every property F is there a thing x that has F as its sole property, for F may be the property of lacking x's sole property. I go further to claim that no x can have a sole property, for if F(x), then x also has the properties of Being a Thing, of Having Properties, etc.; hence it has other properties in addition to F.

5. According to relativity theory it may be that a is timewise related to (hence interacts with) b and b is timewise related to c, though a is not timewise related to c. Yet a and c are in the same world.

too; a thing X and its occurrence O in world W are identical in W only. Occurrences O and O* are *incompatible* if conjoining their descriptions entails a contradiction. In a world, all occurrences are compatible, but a thing may have incompatible occurrences in distinct worlds: Jack is a bachelor in one world, and (if being single is not essential to him) he is married in others.

The thing that encompasses all things is the *universe*. If "X is red" is true in W, "X-in-W is red" is true in W and in the universe. X-in-W is red in the only world it occurs in, yet it is not necessarily red, for modal terms do not apply to what is barred from recurring in worlds. X-in-W *is* a possibility, so it *has* no possibilities, but this does not mean that it is necessarily as it is. Compare: I grow older, but my temporal occurrences do not grow older. This does not mean that they remain forever young! To age *is* for a thing to have a later occurrence, but a given occurrence cannot occur later than itself. Hitler-in-W_0 did not invade England in every world where he, Hitler-in-W_0, is, but that does not mean that he, unlike Hitler, could not invade England. Hitler-in-W_0 has no modal properties, just as a temporal occurrence does not age. There were no two *Führers* in reality, one (Hitler) who could, and one (Hitler-in-W_0) who could not, invade England. Rather, in W_0, Hitler is identical with Hitler-in-W_0, and in 1940, he is identical with his 1940 occurrence. The modal properties of things *are* their occurrences in worlds. To speak of the modal properties of worlds, or of occurrences in worlds, is sheer nonsense.

There are infinitely many ways to construct a set of worlds each of which consists of interacting compatible occurrences. The way that results in a set of *possible* worlds is based on two nonlogical conditions. Let me define. A world *specializes* in a property F iff every occurrence in it is F (a world specializes in Redness iff all things in it are red). A world is *exclusive* with respect to a property F iff only it contains occurrences that are F. We can choose a set of worlds in which one world (call it 'Redworld') is exclusive with respect to Redness: only in it and nowhere else can you find red things. Now, to get a set of possible worlds we require that one world specialize in *and* be exclusive with respect to the property Existence. That world, W_0, contains all and only occurrences that have that property. Worlds are mereological sums of the occurrences in them, so W_0 alone exists, and other worlds are only possible. Since W_0 is exclusive with respect to Existence, it includes all the real occurrences of all things; things have Existence in W_0 only. A thing that does not occur in W_0 is *fictional*. Hamlet has no occurrence in W_0, so *he* is a fictional thing.

Two things whose essences are incompatible with each other do not occur in the same world. Thus, not every thing occurs in every world: some worlds have things that do not occur in other worlds. To be incompatible with something in each world is not to be a thing, for it is to have an occurrence in no world. An occurrence O of X in world W needs to be internally consistent, and compatible with the other residents of W. Thus, not all things exist, because internally consistent occurrences may be incompatible with each other, and incompatible occurrences cannot reside in the same world. Yet all real things need to occur in the same world, W_0; so, not all things are real.

I sum up: (1) Things occur in worlds. (2) A world is a sum of interacting occurrences. (3) In a world all occurrences are consistent and mutually compatible. (4) In W_0 everything exists. (5) In other worlds nothing exists.

We use singular terms (indexicals, names, and rigid definite descriptions) to refer to things. We locate *real* occurrences of things by our method of referring to them: using indexicals, by linguistic rules (e.g., " 'I' refers to its utterer"); using names, by some causal chain (according to Saul Kripke) or by their sense (according to Gottlob Frege); using rigid definite descriptions, by their sense. No singular term provides, however, a strategy for locating non-real occurrences of its denotatum; nonexistent occurrences are untraceable by these methods.

A *target world* of a term is a world in which that term's sense is intended to be satisfied by its denotatum. Used as a rigid definite description, 'the Queen' refers, even in worlds where *she* is not a queen, to her who satisfies the description in W_0, the intended target world. That is how we explicate "The Queen might not have been a queen." In general, if the target world of 'the F' (rigidly understood) is W_0, we find the only F in W_0. If the target world of 'the F' is not W_0 (as when we use 'the Queen' to refer to Hamlet's mother), we chose a world where the intended denotatum of 'the F' occurs *and* is the only F. Unless the sense of 'the F' implies a contradiction, the intended thing is possible, so 'the F' refers to *it*. The target world of 'the F' is, then, a world in which its intended denotatum is the only F. By using 'the King of America' rigidly I intend to refer to one thing that satisfies that description in some world, and Charity stipulates that I succeed. Charity is moot and I fail to refer if my term is internally or externally inconsistent. 'The President King of America' is internally inconsistent, and 'the King of America in W_6' is externally inconsistent if America is a republic in W_6. For that reason 'the real King of America' ('the King of America in W_0') does not refer.

My theory preserves basic intuitions about existence. It lets us speak about fictional things and saves the intuition that "X exists," like "X runs," ascribes a property to X. This theory is also ontologically frugal, for it postulates neither infinitely many *real* worlds (as David Lewis does) nor infinitely many *real* unobtaining states of affairs (as Alvin Plantinga does). Can it be defended against the traditional attempts to discredit it?

8.2. The Actualist Objection

Actualists hold that what does not exist cannot exist. How, they ask, can there *be* things that *are* not?[6] I agree that there is no attenuated mode of being that falls short of Reality; mere *possibilia* do *not* exist. If X could exist, but does not, it exists in no mode or manner. One can refer to it, imagine it, describe it, but that does not make it exist. Actualists (Adams, Armstrong, Cresswell, Plantinga, Stalnaker) say that we can refer only to existents, but since God could make other things than those he has actually made, we can imagine a world that entirely consists of new things. We can refer to it; I just did. Since it does not consist of existents, we can refer to nonexistents.

Plantinga holds that a statement attributing Existence to Homer is about Homer only if it is true; if false it is about an existent essence, a haecceity; we attribute Actuality to *it* (we say that it is exemplified, not that it exists). So, if you hold that Homer is real and I disagree, then, if "Homer is real" does not express the same proposition when true and when false, the proposition you think it expresses is not the one I take it to express. You think you talk about Homer, while I wish to talk about some haecceity; so our disagreement is verbal. We disagree about the meaning of words and not about a matter of fact, that is, whether Homer exists. Surely that is false. The content of a thought cannot depend on its truth.[7]

According to Plantinga:[8]

6. See William Lycan, "The Trouble with Possible Worlds," in *The Possible and the Actual*, with an introduction by Michael J. Loux (Ithaca: Cornell University Press, 1979), 274–316.

7. Kendall Walton (*Mimesis as Make-Believe* [Cambridge: Harvard University Press, 1991], chap. 11) has the same problem.

8. Alvin Plantinga, "Self Profile," in *Alvin Plantinga*, ed. James Tomberlin and Peter van Inwagen (Dordrecht: Reidel, 1985), 92. Plantinga uses the letter alpha where I use "W_0."

1. In some possible world W there exist objects that do not exist in W_0

is true, but

1*. There exist some nonexistent things

is false.[9] How can (1) be true and (1*) false? Plantinga gives a special sense to (1): by 'objects' he means not objects but individual essences. Plantinga defines:

2. An object that does not exist exists in a world W iff its individual essence, E, is exemplified in W.

Does (2) help? If an essence is exemplified, there is some thing that exemplifies it; so (2) gets us back to (1*). But Plantinga uses words differently. For him a world, including the real one, is not a thing but a state of affairs, an abstract entity that exists whether it is actualized or not. By "A physical entity X is in a world W" Plantinga does not mean that X is literally *in* W, for concrete things cannot reside in abstract ones. He means that a state of affairs W entails the state of affairs *Something Has E*, which may be true even if W does not obtain. By "X is exemplified in W" Plantinga does not mean that W itself or some thing, X, in it exemplifies the haecceity E, but that E is a constituent of W. It can be that W exists, and X exists in W, and yet X does not exist. It can be that E is exemplified in W, and W exists, yet nothing exemplifies E. As used by Plantinga (1) and (2) only say that some abstract object has some property. In this way Plantinga hides the fact that he has changed the subject under discussion, substituting a nonconcrete existent E (Homerhood) for the concrete nonexistent X (Homer). To make the transition smoother and relate (2) to (1) Plantinga states,

3. Had W been actual, X would have existed.

That sounds right, but again the words do not carry their usual meaning. For Plantinga, Actuality is a property of states of affairs (not of things) akin

<hr />

9. Plantinga, *The Nature of Necessity*, 132.

to Truth.[10] Peter van Inwagen says that states of affairs *are* propositions,[11] making (3) tantamount to

3*. Had "X exists and . . ." been true, X would have existed

which is nothing more than

3**. If "X exists" is true, X exists.

The relation between possibility and reality degenerates into the trivial relation of a statement to its truth condition. This is wrong. Even if Plantinga rejects van Inwagen's interpretation (I think he accepts it) and takes Actuality to be another property, not truth, the view is implausible: how can some abstract thing's having some property imply that a real thing exists?

Actualists find nonexistents odd but claim odder things to exist: unexemplified states of affairs, worlds that include all worlds,[12] and haecceities. Plato's ontology is objectionable as it is; Plantinga's inflated Platonism, even more so.

Plantinga says that we understand the proposition "X does not exist" by grasping the elementary property E, which is the essence of X. Yet how can one grasp the elementary property E other than by imagining its exemplifier? (To grasp the property, Red, you need to imagine a red thing.) To do so, however, is to think of the *thing* X.[13]

Plantinga is right that no real thing could be Hamlet, but that does not imply that Hamlet could not be real. Had Shakespeare been a god, he could have made Hamlet a real, rather than a fictional, thing.[14] Fictional Hamlet *is* a possibly real Hamlet. You plan a house and then go ahead and build *it* or not build *it:* you build the house you imagined. The house you planned could be built in other ways too, but what of it? *That house* has

---

10. Ibid., 88: "Actuality for states of affairs is like truth for propositions."

11. Van Inwagen, "Two Concepts of Possible Worlds," 189: "Possible states of affairs are, or represent, ways things could be." (Is there no difference between being *a* and representing *a*?)

12. Plantinga, "Self Profile," 90: "Every possible world exists in every possible world." Such a vortex of infinities is mind-boggling.

13. See Kit Fine, "Plantinga on the Reduction of Possibilist Discourse," in *Alvin Plantinga*, 145–86, for a similar objection and a challenge to Plantinga's Discernibility Doctrine.

14. According to Jewish lore (*Bereshith Rabba*, 1) God consulted the Bible when he created the world; he made the world so as to make the Bible true.

qualitatively different occurrences at distinct worlds. That the real house is identical with a somewhat different possible house is no more problematic than the identity of your house now with the house you had a year ago. Your house has different-looking occurrences at distinct times, and different-looking occurrences in distinct worlds. How can that be objectionable?

Plantinga asks possibilists three questions:[15] (1) Is "Hamlet exists" true or false? (2) Is "Hamlet is blond" true or false? (3) Can *Hamlet* misdescribe Hamlet? I answer: (1) "Hamlet exists" is false. When used by a nonexistent, it means "Hamlet inhabits this world," which may be true. (2) "Hamlet is blond" is true in some worlds, false in others. (3) *Hamlet* cannot be wrong about Hamlet, for a statement about Hamlet is true iff it is true in *Hamlet*'s target worlds, and those are worlds where Hamlet occurs and satisfies what *Hamlet* says. In the following sections I deal with these issues in detail.

8.3. The Ontological Objection

'The golden mountain' is a consistent description; therefore its denotatum, GM, is in its target worlds a mountain and golden. 'The real golden mountain' is also logically consistent, so it, too, denotes a thing, RGM, that is real, golden, and a mountain, in that description's target worlds. Yet there is no golden mountain in reality. Russell thought that to block that move he must deny that Existence is a property.

Existence *is* a property; the culprit is another. 'GM' has many target worlds, but the target world of 'RGM' must be W_0, for things are real only in W_0. Now, things in W_0 have this property: no golden mountain occurs in their world. RGM would thus be incompatible with the other residents of its target world; hence 'RGM' does not refer. Definite descriptions that are internally consistent and contradict no descriptions of things in their target worlds are guaranteed to denote, but 'the only man in W_5' and 'the only two men in W_5' cannot both refer: Each of these statements is internally impeccable, but they cannot be satisfied together. Some world has only one man, some world has only two men, and some world satisfies 'GM,' but there need be no world that has a real golden mountain.

Were there a world, call it 'Goldworld,' that contained all golden occurrences, 'GM,' too, would fail to denote if Goldworld had no mountains.

---

15. Plantinga, *The Nature of Necessity*, 153–54.

(There can be no Goldworld in the possible-worlds model, for it requires all existents, including existent golden things, to occur in W_0, hence out of Goldworld.) If Being Golden is unessential to GM, GM also occurs in worlds where it is not golden. If Being Golden is essential to GM, it does not occur in such worlds, but this does not show that Being Golden is not a property: of course it is. So is Existence.

Many philosophers thought that if Existence is a property, the ontological argument is valid. Is it? Here is the argument:

1. God is the greatest being.

This is true by definition.

2. 'The greatest being' is noncontradictory.

This also seems true.

3. The greatest being is in the understanding.

I take this to mean that God occurs in some possible (conceivable) world. This is said to follow from (2).

4. One who is also in reality is greater than one who is only in the understanding.

True: to be in some possible worlds ("in the understanding") and not in reality is not as great as to also be in reality.

5. God is in reality.

This does indeed follow from (1), (3), and (4). Q.E.D.

The argument is flawed because (2) does not imply (3). A definite description may fail to refer if its purported denotatum is incompatible with other residents of its target world, and if God does not exist, that is the case. Step 4 shows that "X is the greatest being" implies "X occurs in W_0." Its target world is then W_0; but a description that specifies its target world may conflict with a true description of some item in that target world and so may fail to refer. Thus 'the greatest being' may fail to refer. The ontological argument is invalid.

8.4. The Modal Objection

I said that Hamlet could exist; I also said that Hamlet does not exist in any world. One may think that these statements are incompatible: "$\Diamond F(X)$" is true iff X is F in some world; thus, if Hamlet may have existed, he does exist in some world. So, either nonexistents cannot exist, or else Existence is no property.

My answer is that Thinghood is Existability: to be a thing is to be able to exist. That is why we can have a semantic model for modality. Why (one may ask) is "X is F in W" an analysis of "Possibly, X is F'? These sentences are not synonymous, so how can we explicate the latter by the former? How can Possibility, that is, Ability to Exist, be identified with Being in a World Other Than W_0? The semantic model does not say that W is a possible, not a remote, world, and that items in it are *possibilia*, not distant objects. The model says nothing of Possibility. How do we get this interpretation? Only by choosing Existence as the property with respect to which one world is exclusive and in which it specializes. Only if W is an unreal world can "X is F in W" shed light on "$\Diamond F(X)$." To be in a distant world is not to be possible.[16] A world is a possible world only if *a thing* is *an existable*, that which can exist. Things need not *exist* in a world to be possible; on the contrary, W is a *possible* world since it consists of existables. Substituting 'Existence' for 'F' in "$\Diamond F(X)$," the whole formula may be read either as "X may exist" or as "X is a thing"; in the possible-worlds model these two must be synonymous.

That objection can be formalized. I said that

1. X is Nonreal, but it could be Real

has the same logical form as

2. Y is Nonred, but it could be Red.

Sentence 2 means that the real occurrence of Y is nonred, but a nonreal occurrence of Y is red,[17] that is,

---

16. Hence a known objection to David Lewis's semantics: if other worlds are as real as ours, why is some object's being F in an alien world at all relevant to the possibility that *this* object here be F?

17. In Plantinga's ontology "*b* is red" is contingent, while "*b*-in-W_0 is red" is necessary (true in all possible worlds), so the former does not imply the latter. In my ontology *b* is

2a. Real(Y,W_0) and Nonred(Y,W_0) and $(\exists w)$[Nonreal(Y,w) and Red(Y,w)].

By parity of reasoning (1) means

1a. Real(X,W_0) and Nonreal(X,W_0) and $(\exists w)$[Nonreal(X,w) and Real(X,w)].

Since (1a) is rubbish, something must be wrong. If (1) means (1a), then (1) is false and actualism is vindicated. If that is what (1) means, it may be due to Existence's not being a first-order property; then, too, my view is refuted.

I answer that X need not exist anywhere for "X could exist" to be true; its being a thing, that is, a part of a world, is enough. Take a model where Redness does what Existence does in our model. Let R_0 be a world specializing in and exclusive with respect to Redness. A thing Y that is red in R_0 occurs in other worlds too, but there it is not red. Let "Y koud be F" mean that an occurrence of Y in some $R \neq R_0$ is F.

3. Y is nonsquare, but it koud be square

means

3a. Red(Y,R_0) and Nonsquare(Y,R_0) and $(\exists r)$[Nonred(Y,r) and Square(Y,r)].

So far, no problem; but if some nonsquare thing koud be square, some nonred thing koud be red; that is,

4. Y is Nonred, but it koud be Red.

If we treat (4) as we treated (3) we get this nonsense:

4a. Red(Y,R_0) and Nonred(Y,R_0) and $(\exists r)$[Nonred(Y,r) and Red (Y,r)].

---

identical in W_0 with its occurrence b-in-W_0, so if "b is red" is used in W_0 the implication is valid. Compare: "David" is not substitutable for "David on 1/1/90," but "David is sick" uttered on 1/1/90 implies "David on 1/1/90 is sick."

It is clear what went wrong. Statement 4a is false, not because Redness is not a property, but because, if Y is Nonred, then it is not in R_0. "Y koud be red" means that Y occurs in some r other than R_0. If Thinghood is possible Redness, then (4) means

$$\text{4b. } \neg(Y,R_0) \text{ and } (\exists r)[(r \neq R_0) \text{ and } (Y,r)],$$

and if Thinghood is possible Existence, what things have even if they fail to exist, then "X could be real" means that X occurs in some world other than W_0, not that its occurrence there is real. That is, (1) implies not (1a) but

$$\text{1b. } \neg(X,W_0) \text{ and } (\exists w)[(w \neq W_0) \text{ and } (X,w)].$$

8.5. The Causal Objection

Actualists, who hold that the only things that can exist do exist, find support in the causal theory of reference. On that theory my token 'N' names an object N only if a causal chain of kind K links it to a token that interacted with N in a rite of dubbing. Since my token 'Hamlet' is not linked in that way with Hamlet, my 'Hamlet' does not name Hamlet.

A fellow possibilist, Robert Howell, bites the bullet and says that there *is* a causal connection between our tokens of 'Hamlet' and Hamlet. When Shakespeare wrote *Hamlet* he saw Hamlet in his mind's eye and named him 'Hamlet,' thus starting a causal chain that connects our tokens of 'Hamlet' to Hamlet.[18] Yet we may refer to a possible entity even if no one "saw" it mentally; that is, it is not necessary that Shakespeare had a mental show of *Hamlet*. Moreover, if Shakespeare causally interacted with Hamlet, both are in the same world, and so Hamlet is real. But Hamlet is not real.

By contraposition, the causal theory of reference implies that if a token 'N' is not K-linked to any token used to dub N, then it does not denote N. Also, if an occurrence O of N has no ancestor dubbed by a token K-linked to 'N,' it is not denoted by 'N.' Thus, the causal theory requires that if 'N' names N, then all the occurrences of the name 'N' are K-linked, via the

18. Robert Howell, "Fictional Objects: How They Are and How They Aren't," *Poetics* 8 (1979): 129–77.

original dubbing, to all the occurrences of N. However, this requirement is *never* fulfilled: no causal route leads from Socrates' occurrences in other worlds to tokens of 'Socrates' that we use in reality. Then how can we talk about Socrates in other worlds? How do we discuss his unactualized possibilities?

Since there are no transworld causal chains, *possibilia* are referred to by terms to which they are not causally linked. A causal K-link is therefore not necessary for reference. If I can talk about the possibility of Socrates escaping from prison, that is, about an event that takes place in another possible world and has no causal link to my words and to Socrates in reality, then a fictional being such as Winnie the Pooh need have no causal link to his naming rite or to tokens that refer to him either.

Some philosophers answer that otherworldly occurrences of Socrates are related to the real Socrates "through identity."[19] Whatever that relation may be, it is not causal. Occurrences of Socrates in distinct worlds do not stand in causal relations to each other, for no causal chains straddle the abyss that lies between the infinitely many possible worlds. If a noncausal, nonphysical "relation of identity" can bridge the gap between distinct world occurrences of the same real thing, it can link the otherworldly occurrences of the same nonexistent thing too. That in one case one of these occurrences exists, while in the other case none does, is immaterial: the real Socrates does in no way indicate to us which items in other worlds are "related to him by identity." Identity is not a search strategy; we cannot use it like Ariadne's thread to lead us from the real Socrates to his occurrences in other worlds. Identity cannot be a physical relation, for no causal relations between occurrences can decide that they are *of one thing*. What occurrences are occurrences of the same thing is stipulated, hence a matter of intention *only*.

We talk of Socrates' unreal possibilities because we intend to talk about them; intention needs no vehicle to take it from world to world. Thus we can also talk about a fictional being, for no causal chain *can* lead us to the worlds where that being resides; our intention to refer to it will do. If our intention to talk about Socrates' possibilities is enough for our words to be about *them*, our intention to talk *about Hamlet* suffices to link *him* to our tokens of 'Hamlet.'

19. Alan Sidelle, "Rigidity, Ontology, and Semantic Structure," *Journal of Philosophy* 89 (1992): 410–30.

Actualists object to "ungrounded identity" (as Graeme Forbes calls it),[20] holding that if O is an occurrence of X and M is not, O must be distinguishable from M. That is to confuse identity with identification. A qualitative difference between O and M is needed if we are to *identify* O, but not for O *being identical with* X. Nothing, save being X, makes it true that O is X. The identity of X in W_1 with X in W_0 is not a natural relation such as Locke's Similarity or Grice's Causality. That we can talk about X, not about something else, if we intend to do so, is an a priori assumption, not based on our ability to identify X. If O is indistinguishable from M, we cannot tell which of them is X, but that hardly matters. The fanciful picture of us traveling among worlds, trying to *discover* whether O or else M is the one we talked about, is conceptually confused.

8.6. The Uniqueness Objection

The usual argument against possibilism is that we cannot refer to fictional beings, because singular terms intended to do so fail the uniqueness condition.[21] Take 'the golden mountain': distinct things are the only golden mountain in distinct worlds. Which one of them is the golden mountain? Shakespeare specified some traits of Hamlet, but infinitely many distinct men in distinct possible worlds have those traits. If X is a Danish prince whose father's assassin has married his mother (and who has all the other traits Shakespeare attributes to Hamlet) in world W_1, and if Y has these traits in W_2, who is Hamlet? X and Y cannot both be Hamlet, because they may cohabit a world W_3, where they are distinct. Thus it is not only that Hamlet does not exist, he *cannot* exist—he is not a possible being—for there is no way to single him out. A story mentions 'the policeman': what can qualify one possible thing and exclude all others as *that* policeman? Yet if 'the policeman' fails to single out a unique individual, it fails to refer.[22] So we cannot refer to fictional beings.

20. Graeme Forbes, "In Defence of Absolute Essentialism," *Midwest Studies in Philosophy* 11 (1986): 3–31; see 6–7.

21. The *locus classicus* is Willard Quine's "On What There Is," in *From a Logical Point of View* (New York: Harper, 1961). For restatements, see Saul Kripke, *Naming and Necessity* (Cambridge: Harvard University Press, 1980), 156–58, and D. Kaplan, "Bob and Carol and Ted and Alice," in *Approaches to Natural Language,* ed. K. J. Hintikka et al. (Dordrecht: Reidel, 1973), 490–518.

22. Forbes ("In Defence of Absolute Essentialism," 20) takes a middle position: "If a Holmes story says that Holmes nodded to a passing policeman on his way to Scotland Yard

Haecceitists invent a solution: each individual has one simple irreducible individual essence. Hamlet is the only one that has Hamleteity, and the said policeman has an essence too; whoever finds *it* can identify *him* in every world he occurs in. Yet to postulate a unique primitive essence for each thing is Baroque, and useless. Haecceities lack content, so how can one of them be distinguished from another? What is it about E that makes it the haecceity of Hamlet rather than that of Newton? Haecceitism is a pointless myth.

We need no mythology to overcome the uniqueness objection, for it is based on a conceptual error. To refer to a fictional being we need not be able to find it or distinguish it from others. Kripke should not have made that error, for he exposed a similar error about identification across worlds. How do I know who in a possible world W is Napoleon? I cannot tell Napoleon in another world apart from someone else there.[23] So how can I say that Napoleon occurs in other worlds? That problem may make one reject (as David Lewis did) the idea that things recur in many worlds: how can we identify Napoleon in a world where he is, say, a British sailor? Kripke saw that this question is based on misunderstanding. We do not search a possible world through a telescope, as it were, to find *who* an occurrence O in that world is. We do not, seeing that it resembles Napoleon, wonder whether it really is Napoleon. We *intend* 'Napoleon' to pick out Napoleon and no one else, in all worlds. You cannot tell Napoleon apart from others in other worlds, but you need not do that. To speak of Napoleon you only have to use his name. 'Napoleon' picks up all the occurrences of Napoleon in all worlds because we intend it to do so, not because in each world Napoleon carries a unique mark that identifies him as Napoleon.

The uniqueness of a nonexistent is, similarly, assumed and not discovered. We *intend* 'the policeman' to refer to that very policeman, not to others. It does not matter than we cannot tell Hamlet or the policeman from look-alikes who are not they; we intend to talk of *them*, not of others, and that is enough. "Who is Hamlet, O or M?" is a bad question. Hamlet is Hamlet, and Napoleon is Napoleon; a person is distinct from all others not because he or she has a unique haecceity, but because that person is a particular thing.

---

it seems excessive to regard 'that' policeman as a definite fictional character created by Conan Doyle, just on the basis of this one sentence in the story." But a hundred thousand sentences get no closer to unique characterization than one sentence, so if Forbes denies individuality to that policeman, he should deny it to Holmes as well.

23. As noted, e.g., in R. Chisholm, "Identity Through Possible Worlds: Some Questions," *Nous* 1 (1967): 1–8.

The Kripkean answer, "O and not M is Napoleon because O developed from Napoleon's gametes," is useless, for we know not which are Napoleon's gametes in that other world: are they J or the indistinguishable L? We have no way to know that, but we do not need to know it. We assume that Napoleon and his gametes occur in other worlds, and we refer to them. The uniqueness of reference is guaranteed not by interworld inspection but by the nature of names: a name is intended to denote one individual, no matter how that individual is individuated. Identity of origin *assumes* identity. The picture of Shakespeare searching worlds for Hamlet to hang the tag 'Hamlet' around his neck is preposterous. Shakespeare intended 'Hamlet' to name a possible individual, who, being possible, occurs in possible worlds, in some of which (*Hamlet*'s target worlds) he satisfies what the bard says about him.

Our intention in using a referring term is to speak about the same thing at various indexes. Nothing in that intention tells us how we are to reach that thing in all or any of those indexes. The latter is an epistemic, empirical problem that the use of names does not and need not resolve. It was such a confusion between epistemic and semantic considerations that produced the view that names are abbreviated definite descriptions, for philosophers thought that a name is useless unless it contains a strategy for reaching its referent. A name, however, is not a device for picking out an object; it is a device for referring to an object, *however* it is picked out.

Which occurrences belong together in one thing is a matter of decision. In reality, that decision may be made by a court of law. For example, if you are insured against Hurricane Andrew, the court decides, given our linguistic habits, whether it is more reasonable to say that the gale that damaged your house *is* Andrew or else is a spinoff *from* Andrew and therefore not Andrew. That decision can be appealed and revised in view of fresh evidence. Possible-world semantics, however, requires an ideal assumption that matters of identity have already been settled. When you talk about what Andrew could do, you *cannot* discover that what you talked about is not Andrew after all. You do not have to *show* that what you refer to is none other than Andrew. That in some worlds there occurs a thing who *is* Hamlet needs no proof: that is what possible worlds are for. They guarantee identity but not identification. Intending to refer to a possible being is enough to guarantee its occurrence in possible worlds. That it is an individual follows from the use of a singular term: my intention to refer does not have to "hook" some "preexisting" thing.

It is a (Lewisian) fallacy to forget that possible worlds are tailored for our referential needs. Unlike the real world, the identity of denizens of possible worlds is *given*, as if it had been predecided by an omnipotent court. Thus one such denizen is Napoleon, the other Hamlet, and there is no place for appeal or reconsideration of fact. Unless I sabotage my intention to refer, by attributing to the thing I intend to talk about internally or externally incompatible properties, I know that it occurs in some possible worlds; its status as an interworld possible being is stipulated and guaranteed a priori. That Kripke was taken in by the world metaphor and began to treat his model realistically, as if statements about Hamlet were true in virtue of empirical fact, as if it could be *discovered* that Hamlet is the one who occurs in them, shows that the seductive force of metaphor can lead even the best minds astray.

Haecceitism commits the same fallacy by conjuring a mythical feature that one thing only can and must have, thereby providing a way to identify it after all, in or out of this world. It is to Kripke's credit that he never fell for that myth. It is poor metaphysics to postulate real entities to mirror linguistic conventions for dividing the world into things. The haecceitists (Plantinga, van Inwagen, Adams, et al.) invent an occult entity to prop up a semantic convention. The predicate 'is Napoleon' denotes Napoleon only, but that does not mean that he has a trait that can be examined to verify that the said predicate is correctly applied. Verification is not here in question (verificationist habits die hard!). Similarly, the one predicate that only Hamlet satisfies is 'is Hamlet,' though not because it identifies a trait that enables one to "pick out" Hamlet in a pseudoempirical way. The "picking out" is semantic.

To conclude, it is not that 'N' denotes N iff 'N' specifies a condition C and a world W and the unique satisfier of C in W is N. Rather, 'N' denotes N iff 'N' is intended to denote a thing and specifies a noncontradictory condition C. It is assumed that in some worlds (the target worlds of 'N') N satisfies C.

8.7. The Creationist Objection

Kit Fine takes the creationist objection to be the "more fundamental" objection to views such as mine, a view he calls "internalism about nonexistents."[24] The creationist argument allegedly shows "not that the particular

---

24. Kit Fine, "The Problem of Non-existents," *Topoi* 1 (1980): 97–140. His other objections do not apply to my view, for I require things to manifest coherence and closure under standard rules of logic.

formulations are wrong but that the underlying conception is mistaken," requiring "not some modification in the existing axioms, but a totally new theory." Internalists deny that Hamlet is created by Shakespeare; but that, according to Fine, is wrong. Fictional beings do not "have being independently of the appropriate activity of the author. Rather, they come into being as the result of that activity, in much the same way as a table comes into being as the result of the activity of a carpenter . . . [I]t just seems false to say that Shakespeare discovered or first represented Hamlet."[25]

My intuitions are at odds with the creationist's. If 'to create' is to make something exist, then, had Shakespeare created Hamlet, Hamlet would have existed. Hamlet, however, does not exist, so he was not created, by Shakespeare or by anyone else. In reply to this objection Fine postulates grades of being: "[N]ot all actual objects are existent, at least on a creationist view of fictitious objects. For on this view, fictitious objects acquire their being through the appropriate creative activity . . . Thus these objects have their being in contrast to merely possible fictions that might have had such being but, in fact, do not. These objects are actual ones. On my view, then, there is a tripartite division within the realm of objects. There is the usual division between the actuals and the merely possibles. But among the actuals, there is a subdivision into the existents, and the non-existents."[26] Fine uses this baroque ontology just to make Shakespeare the creator of Hamlet. Yet how could Shakespeare create a man who lived many years before him? Hamlet was brought into his world by his parents, Gertrude and Hamlet, not by Shakespeare. Fine is wrong, then, but the issue he raises is basic in aesthetics. Shakespeare did not create Hamlet, but he created the play *Hamlet* that includes the role HAMLET. By creating *Hamlet* he created the character HAMLET. What is a character?

An artwork contains recurrent *motifs* as structural elements whose intertwined development forms the artistic fabric of the piece. Recurrent words, images, themes may all serve as motifs; for example, the image of disease and corruption is a central motif in *Hamlet*. Now, it is trivial, but nonetheless true, that Hamlet appears in *Hamlet*, so the role of Hamlet is a *motif* in *Hamlet*. A *character* is a person used as a motif in an artwork. HAMLET is a role, a recurrent motif; Hamlet is a man. The two are distinct. To each feature that a person manifests in a play there corresponds a feature of the character, but not vice versa. Hamlet speaks in riddles, so the role

25. Ibid., 130.
26. Ibid., 132.

HAMLET includes riddles; on the other hand, the character HAMLET alludes to Lord Essex and the Globe's financial problems, while Hamlet could do no such thing, not knowing Elizabethan England. Hamlet cannot be *played* (he can be *imitated*), but a role, a character, is *played by* a player. God can make Hamlet exist; Shakespeare, who created *Hamlet*, made the roles in it, including HAMLET, exist. A president can create an office, a role filled by his crony, but he cannot make that crony. He can create a role, the PRESIDENT'S ADVISOR, but he cannot create the president's advisor.

Hamlet is not only a description of some possible worlds; no literary work is so meager. *Hamlet* is much richer than the world it presents: that world can be presented in a flowery or in a terse style, in short or in long phrases, in natural sequence or in flashback. Such differences are in the artwork, not in its world. A character is *rounded* or *flat, central* or *peripheral, developed* or *sketchy;* none of that applies to the person the character presents. A character is a part of, a role in, a work; the person it presents is not.

Fine does not think that Hamlet antedated Shakespeare, but his alternative is less palatable. Fine holds that Hamlet's Actuality, but not his Being, is due to Shakespeare; so Hamlet would have had Being even if *Hamlet* had not been written. Fine's creationism, then, amounts to the view that Shakespeare promoted Hamlet in the ranks of Being. I find it incomprehensible. In my view Hamlet does not exist before Shakespeare, since Hamlet does not exist at all; yet he does antedate Shakespeare. To antedate Shakespeare one need not be in the same world with him, just as being fatter than Shakespeare does not make Falstaff real. Sherlock Holmes and Oliver Twist lived in the same place, London, but not at the same time. Since Shakespeare lived in England and Hamlet in Denmark, it is true, *in* the universe, that in W_0 and in W_H (*Hamlet*'s target worlds), Shakespeare's country in W_0 is west of Hamlet's country in W_H. It is also true, *in* the universe, that in W_0 and in some worlds of W_H, Shakespeare in W_0 antecedes Hamlet in W_H.

Let W_{S^*} be the worlds where Shakespeare is as he could have been and W_{H^*} the worlds where Hamlet is as he could have been. Hamlet does not occur in W_0, so there can be no $W_{0 \cap H}$ and $W_{0 \cap H^*}$ worlds. But $W_{S^* \cap H^*}$ and $W_{S^* \cap H}$ are possible worlds: Hamlet, whether as described in *Hamlet* or not, cohabits a world with the Shakespeare who never wrote *Hamlet*.[27] Fine's arguments against internalism involve cases where two things have

---

27. Forbes ("In Defence of Absolute Essentialism," 20–21) also admits fictional entities that are other than as described in their stories, but to do this he uses degrees of possibility

the same description. Let the story S mention twins and say nothing more about them. How can they be two when all that is said of the one is said of the other? It is a problem for Fine, who holds that the twins have only those properties ascribed to them in S,[28] but not for me. On my view each twin has the properties S attributes to him in every $W\varepsilon W_S$ (S's target worlds), but he also has in each $W\varepsilon W_S$ properties not mentioned in S (provided it is not the same property in all of W_S). Thus, the twins are different from each other in every world in W_S.

8.8. The Surrealism Objection

Can logically impossible stories be satisfied? Some writers (Meinong, Parsons, Castaneda) allow impossible worlds; I do not. What, then, is a surrealistic story about? Let a story S contain contradictions; does it have an interpretation? Worlds that obey paraconsistent logic can satisfy S,[29] but I think we should not use them. The point of S is to stretch comprehension beyond the pale; clever tricks that make S fully satisfiable violate its intent. Absurd literature is meant to be absurd, so the said story is not meant to be satisfied and should not be satisfied; to find a world that satisfies it after all is to mutilate it.

In conversation, Graham Priest argued that contradiction may be unintended. What if, at the time the story was written, people believed that there is a highest number and the protagonist of S is said to be a mathematician who found some of its properties? Should S not be satisfied? I think Priest is right: it should, but not in a paraconsistent model. By hypothesis, S is not a fantasy, so it should be interpreted as taking place in a world like our own, not in a bizarre paraconsistent world. My answer to Priest is that those who hold that there is a highest natural number have a different notion of

---

(lacking a feature that Conan Doyle attributed to Holmes "is possibility for Holmes to such-and-such a degree"), an unnecessary complication.

28. Fine ("The Problem of Non-existents," 116) says that Humbold, the hero of a story whose only sentence is "Humbold is a doctor," has one quality only, Being a Doctor. But if 'doctor' has its usual meaning, then Humbold has other properties as well: Seeing Patients, Having a Degree, etc. Fine's stipulation that the above story is in a genre that disallows features not explicitly attributed in the story makes that story meaningless.

29. G. Priest, *In Contradiction: A Study of the Transconsistent* (The Hague: Nijhoff, 1987).

number than ours. Perhaps they are strict finitists, and a number, for them, must be constructed from zero in actual consecutive steps. If 'number' means that, the number series is finite, and questions about the highest number are answerable. The worlds in which S is satisfied are standard, for the entity whose properties are researched by S's protagonist is not what *we* call 'the highest natural number.' The same holds for those in a story who are alleged to have invented a perpetual-motion machine, squared the circle, etc.

Let us return to surrealism. Can surrealistic stories have classical models? A story, S, contains explicit and implied statements $p_i, \ldots p_n$, satisfied in sets of worlds $W_{Pi}, \ldots W_{Pn}$, respectively. These are *partial target sets* of S. The set of target worlds of S, W_S, is their intersection, a set of worlds each of which satisfies all these statements. If S* contains a contradiction, W_{S*} is empty: there are no worlds in it. Still, S* has nonempty partial target sets. Maximal partial target sets are of special interest to us: if 'p and not-p' is the only contradiction in S*, it has two maximal partial target sets, W_{S*1} and W_{S*2}. The union of W_{S*1} and W_{S*2} is not the target set of S*. It is so only if S* leaves it open whether p; then, in some worlds in $W_{S*1US*2}$ p, and in others not-p. S*, however, is not silent about p; it says *that p* and *that not-p*. So its only interpretation is its two maximal partial target sets and its empty target set.

I have said that target worlds do not capture all that there is in a story. Style and level of language, order of narration, relation of explicit to implied statements, pace of depiction, rhyme and acoustic properties, tropes, graphic properties, etc. are all features of S but have no place in its worlds. No work is exhausted by the worlds in which it is satisfied; worlds are neutral to the means of presenting them, but these means are central to the work. A contradictory statement contributes to S by ensuring that no world satisfies it. That S cannot be satisfied, that all attempts to envisage its world fail, is an effective literary device that creates irony, anxiety, or cynicism, as the case may be, thus giving S its atmosphere and effect.

In an ingenious argument intended to undermine the realistic conception of interpretation, Margolis shows that, like absurd stories, realistic literature does not fit the possible-world model.[30] A person in a possible world can be either alive (p) or else dead (not-p), but not both: 'p and not-p' is unsatisfiable. Yet a story may leave the life-or-death issue open. It may open

30. Joseph Margolis, "The Logic of Interpretation," in *Philosophy Looks at the Arts* (New York: Scribner's Sons, 1962), 108–20.

both options and have the reader vacillate between them. How can that be realized in a possible world? The evidence that p is as good as the evidence that not-p, but it cannot be that both p and not-p. Margolis's solution is that 'p' and 'not-p' do not say what *is* the case in W, but what is plausibly assertible about W. Contradiction is avoided: 'Plausible(p) and Plausible(not-p),' unlike 'p and not-p,' can be true. W cannot be F and not-F, but it can be plausibly F and plausibly not-F.

To defend realism I use the notion of interpretation. If both possibilities, *that p* and *that not-p*, are relevant to the story S, it has two *augmented* target sets: W_{S1} is $\{W_S \cap W_p\}$, W_{S2} is $\{W_S \cap W_{not\text{-}p}\}$. The target set of S is, again, $\{W_{S1}, W_{S2}\}$, only this time W_S is nonempty. Suppose that it is an essential feature of the story S that it leaves it open whether the hero survives a car crash. It will not do to say that in some worlds in W_S the hero is killed and in others he lives, for that is true of every trivial detail not mentioned in the story. Rather, S itself specifies two significant augmented target sets; these sets are *interpretations* of S. Whatever is true in every world in W_S is true in them too. However, W_{S1} is such that in every world in it, p, and W_{S2} is such that in every world in it, not-p. The set $\{W_{S1}, W_{S2}\}$ of augmented target sets of S is of special interest to us because each of its members has a high aesthetic value. There is a set of worlds $W_{H \cap p}$ complying with *Hamlet* plus a random sentence 'p,' but if 'p' does not illuminate *Hamlet*, $W_{H \cap p}$ is not an interpretation. Classical works of art are those that have many valuable augmented target sets, that is, many interesting interpretations.

9

TRUTH IN ART

9.1. Real Referents

This, the last, chapter discusses the thesis

> TA: Art reveals significant truths; its epistemic merit is an aesthetic virtue.

To examine whether statements in art are true, we need to know when statements, in general, are true. Take the sentence

> P: Chicago is big.

Is it true? To know what statement is expressed by a given token of P, you need to know at which index it is intended to be evaluated—that is, what world, or time, P's utterer talks about. Evaluated in a world (or time) where Chicago is big, the statement expressed, hence the token-sentence used to express it, is true; evaluated where Chicago is small, it is false; evaluated where Chicago does not occur, it is truth-valueless. Thus, if in uttering P you mean to talk of the real world at the present time, the token of P you use to make your statement is true *simpliciter*.

When you say, "The king is cruel," it is usually clear from the context which country it is whose king you claim to be cruel. The statement you make is not true at some countries and false at others; it is true or false *simpliciter,* depending on whether the king of the nation you meant is or is not cruel. An actress playing the queen in act 4, scene 7, of *Hamlet,* who says, "Your sister's drown'd," is not saying that the actor's sister drowned, which is false or truth-valueless. Her intended addressee is Laertes, and she talks about *Hamlet*'s target worlds. In these worlds Laertes' sister, Ophelia, did drown, so what she says is true *simpliciter.*

Statements made in fiction, for example, "Ophelia drowned," are, then, usually true (unless made by unreliable protagonists or under other transparent discrediting conditions). Yet that is not enough to support TA. TA does not state the truism that *Hamlet* is satisfied in some unreal worlds but that it is, somehow, satisfied in reality. We think that art reveals a true face of reality. Is that right?

To express a true statement about reality, a sentence needs to refer to real things. That seems an easy condition to meet; surely 'London' in *Oliver Twist* refers to the real city of London? Yet that is contested by many. If 'London' refers to the real London, they say, then Oliver Twist, a fictional being, has never set foot in it. Thus the statement that Oliver Twist lived in London is untrue. Since Dickens, who makes this statement, knows that it is untrue, he is a liar! Therefore, some philosophers deny that 'London' in *Oliver Twist* refers to London. Dickens does not refer to London, they say,[1] for he does not intend to refer at all; he only pretends, makes believe, as if he were referring.[2] Sentences in fiction express no statements, and in uttering them the author states nothing. Among those who hold that view some hold that fiction writers perform an illocutionary act other than assertion;[3] others maintain that fiction writers perform no illocutionary

---

1. See John Searle, *Expression and Meaning* (Cambridge: Cambridge University Press, 1979), 58–75, and Kendall Walton, *Mimesis as Make-Believe* (Cambridge: Harvard University Press, 1991), 218ff.

2. Searle argues that Dickens pretends to refer to Oliver Twist but cannot refer to him "because there was no such antecedently existing character" (*Expression and Meaning,* 71). On the other hand, readers can refer to Oliver Twist, since Dickens has created that fictional character. Yet Dickens, too, introduces Oliver only at the beginning of the novel; then he proceeds to talk about Oliver. Thus Searle's view oddly implies that the *first* occurrence of 'Oliver Twist' in the novel fails to refer, though subsequent tokens of that term, made after the character is presented, do refer!

3. For this suggestion, see Richard Gale, "The Fictive Use of Language," *Philosophy* 46 (1974): 324–39; Nicholas Wolterstorff, *Worlds and Works of Art* (New York: Oxford University Press, 1980), 219–34; and George Currie, "What Is Fiction?" *Journal of Aesthetics and Art Criticism* 63 (1985): 385–92.

act at all, that they only pretend to perform one.[4] Still others maintain that terms in fiction do refer, but not to real things. Ingarden says that in Henryk Sienkiewicz's *Quo Vadis* 'Rome' does not denote the real Rome: "Rome itself—the capital of the Roman Empire—does not belong to the given work."[5]

Take first the view that in writing fiction one performs a special fictional illocutionary act. John Searle showed that this cannot be right: to change the illocutionary force of a sentence is to change its meaning, so a sentence in fiction cannot mean what it means in everyday contexts; it differs in meaning from its everyday counterpart as a question differs from an order. That would make fiction strictly incomprehensible.

Next, examine the view that sentences in fiction carry *no* illocutionary force: novelists assert nothing; they only pretend to assert. Searle holds that this exonerates authors from the charge of lying, for one lies only if one intends, by making a false statement, to deceive the hearer into believing that it is true.[6] I think Searle is wrong here: consider a secretary who brazenly says, "Mr. Bossman is out," when you know, and the secretary knows that you know, that Bossman is in his office and does not want to see you. The secretary does not intend to deceive you, yet he surely lies, for he says what he knows is untrue.

The pretense ploy misfires. When you pretend to A you go through the motions of A-ing, but something external is missing. For instance, pretending to brush your teeth you make brushing motions without a toothbrush. So, to pretend to refer to Hamlet you must go through the motions of referring: you say 'X' intending to use it as a proper name. But then, when you say 'X,' you *do* refer to X. 'Hamlet,' used as a name, names Hamlet; so by saying 'Hamlet' you refer to Hamlet, not pretend to refer to him.

---

4. Walton's view, that artworks are props in a game whose point is to authorize imaginings, also implies that sentences in fiction have no illocutionary force. The sentence 'p' in a novel, he says, does not state *that p,* but helps us imagine *that fictionally p.* Thus my argument against Searle applies to Walton too.

Walton's own criticism of Searle (*Mimesis as Make-Believe,* 82–83) is that Searle's definition of fiction does not apply to the visual arts. But Searle never intended his definition to apply to anything but fiction. Walton writes as if it were common use to call paintings and statues 'fiction'; that use, however, is quite uncommon.

5. Roman Ingarden, *The Literary Work of Art* (Evanston, Ill.: Northwestern University Press, 1973), 25.

6. Searle, *Expression and Meaning,* 65.

Kendall Walton construes 'fictionally' and 'make-believedly' as intensional sentential operators. I think that is correct. Intensional logic is lame, however, without Truth. "Fictionally, X is a house" is true iff, evaluated in the assumed fictional world, "X is a house" is *true*. Yet Walton denies that "X is a house" is *true* at some world. He limits truth to reality only. Walton uses " 'p' is fictional" to *replace*, not to abbreviate, " 'p' is true at an assumed fictional world." That robs his formulas of meaning. If "It is fictional that 'p' " does not mean that 'p' is true at a possible world, what does it mean? "At [blank] 'p' is [blank]" is meaningless.

Does Iris Murdoch, in writing a novel, pretend to make statements? A comedian may pretend to make statements by uttering gibberish, but what you find in Murdoch's novel is not gibberish. She is not "pretending to recount to us a series of events";[7] rather, she recounts a series of events that she does not believe took place in reality. To tell stories *is* to recount events. Murdoch does not pretend to talk about those events; she talks about them. Her statements are about fictional events and are true at the novel's target worlds (those that satisfy what is stated in her novel).

Ingarden's suggestion is also unacceptable. If 'Rome' in *Quo Vadis* does not denote the city of Rome we know, what should we believe about its denotatum? How many heads, hands, and legs does a Roman have? The novel does not explicitly say that. We assume that these Romans are human beings, but that depends on attributing to the denotatum of 'Rome' in *Quo Vadis* what we know of the real Rome. The justification for believing innumerable such statements is only that the term 'Rome' in *Quo Vadis* refers to the real, historical Rome.

I conclude that 'Rome' in *Quo Vadis* and 'London' in *Oliver Twist* refer to Rome and to London, the very cities we know. Yet Ingarden is partially right: since the real world is not among the target worlds of *Oliver Twist*, the London-occurrence that Dickens refers to is not the real occurrence of London; the *real* occurrence of London has no Oliver Twist in it. London occurs in the real world and in other worlds as well, and Dickens tells us of a possible world where London is not quite as it is in reality. In his novel, Dickens describes that occurrence of London. His statements are therefore true, since in the intended target worlds London (the very London we know) is as he describes it to be. Thus, he does not lie.

7. Ibid.

An artwork's reference to reality may be indirect. For example, the power of Henri Moore's small-headed humanoids is partly due to their being *distorted*, not conforming to the real human anatomy. To appreciate them one needs to know how real people look and what the proportion of real heads to real human bodies is. Moore's sculpture is, therefore, indirectly mimetic. We need to keep in mind the shape people are in reality to see the brutality and threatening nature of these statues, where a tiny head sits on a huge body. A Martian who does not associate the head with the mind (Martians have their brains in the big toes) cannot understand Moore's work. Apes cannot understand it either, if due to their physiognomy they will not see the proportions in Moore's sculpture as grotesque. Thus, although people in the target worlds of this statue do have these odd proportions, Moore illuminates such worlds by requiring that we compare them to reality, where people do not look that way. The real world is referred to, nevertheless.

9.2. What Are Artworks About?

A notorious difficulty of the semantics I use, taking art to be true about possible worlds,[8] is the problem of clutter. If a story describes a world that differs from the real one only in details implicit in the story,[9] and if the content of a story includes all that is true about that world, then stories are about very odd things indeed. It is hard to believe that *Three Blind Mice* tells us about molecular biology. Walton bites the bullet: he is ready to "admit Marco Polo, the San Francisco Earthquake, Watergate, and all the rest into the world of *Three Blind Mice*."[10] His answer to the clutter problem is to "de-emphasize" these details. How do you de-emphasize a thing in a world? What is it to emphasize blind mice and de-emphasize Marco Polo if both are equally denizens of the *Three Blind Mice* worlds? To say that the text is

8. For a systematic, rigorous presentation of such semantics, see David Lewis, "Truth in Fiction," in *Philosophical Papers* (Oxford: Oxford University Press, 1983), 1:261–80.

9. See Monroe Beardsley, *Aesthetics: Problems in the Philosophy of Criticism* (Harcourt, Brace & World, 1958), 242–47; John Woods, *Logic of Fiction: A Philosophical Study of Deviant Logic* (Hawthorne, N.Y.: Mouton, 1974); M. L. Ryan, "Fiction, Non-Factuals, and the Principle of Minimal Departure," *Poetics* 9 (1980): 403–22.

10. *Mimesis as Make-Believe,* 149.

"more" about the mice and "less" about Marco Polo is to assume a notion of content for which no semantics is given. In Chapter 8, I examined the view of writers (Parsons, Fine) who avoid that problem by reckoning from a story's world only things explicitly mentioned in the story, and from a thing only properties explicitly ascribed to it in the story. That, we saw, is absurd: one whose *only* property is Being a Doctor is certainly not a doctor!

I suggest that the various target worlds of *Three Blind Mice* differ with respect to the San Francisco earthquake and Marco Polo: some include them, some do not, but the blind mice occur in all of them. A work is about what occurs in *all* its target worlds, so *Three Blind Mice* is not about Marco Polo. Kripke and Putnam will not be impressed: you got rid of Marco Polo, they may say, but not of necessary facts such as the genetics of mice; those occur in all worlds, including all target worlds of *Three Blind Mice*. I reply that mice might have had other genetic traits than those they really have. We have every right to call creatures (say, on another planet) who look and behave like mice, but are not mammals, by the name 'mice.'[11] Mice in distinct *Three Blind Mice* target worlds do not share the same genetic features, which therefore make up no part of the content of the nursery rhyme. Truths of logic obtain in all worlds, hence in all *Three Blind Mice* target worlds, so I eliminate them from the content of *Three Blind Mice* by stipulating that a text is about a noncontingent fact iff it is explicitly referred to in the text.

According to the neo-Millian semantics, natural-kind words ('tree,' 'water,' 'gold,' etc.) name substances. In Chapter 7, I accepted and extended that construal to all categorematic expressions: they all name recurrent things (types). 'Napoleon' names Napoleon, 'milk' names Milk, 'chair' names The Chair, and 'blue' names The Blue, in all its occurrences, thus all blue things, whether existent or not. In fiction, names retain their usual denotation: 'London' in Dickens's novels refers to London, just as 'sad,' 'sand,' and 'man' in Dickens refer to The Sad, Sand, and Man, respectively, whose occurrences abound in the real world. However, the occurrence of Man referred to by a token-word 'man' in a work of fiction is not a real-world occurrence of Man, and so it may differ from real-world men in some details that do not jeopardize its identity as Man. The same is true of 'London' and all other

---

11. See my "Putnam's Theory on the Reference of Substance Terms," *Journal of Philosophy* 73 (1976): 116–27.

names. Fiction, then, is mostly about things that occur in reality, as they are in other worlds.

In Walton's view, a man who points to a picture and says, "This is a ship," *does not refer*: "He only *pretends* that there is something which he refers to and calls a ship."[12] That man, says Walton, does not refer to the blotch on the canvas, which is clearly *not* a ship; so he is referring to nothing. Walton concludes that the said token of "This is a ship" expresses no proposition. I wonder: if such a paradigm of reference (the man says "this," pointing his finger at something!) is not referring, nothing is.

Walton could say that the picture-ship on the canvas is *fictionally* a ship, so by "this" in "This is a ship" we refer to that picture-ship. Walton declines. Like Goodman, he holds that a picture-ship is no more a ship than the word 'ship' is a ship. Saying "This is a ship" we are "merely *pretending* to refer to something and to claim it to be a ship."[13] I think that is very wrong. By "*This* is a ship" one refers, first, to the picture-ship on the canvas and, second, to the (unreal) ship represented by it. In the painting we see a picture-ship, and through it we can, and most often do, directly see some real or unreal ship.

Wittgenstein taught us that a picture-ship is a blotch of paint *seen as a ship*.[14] I add that we see a blot of paint as a ship if, through it, we see a ship. In our case the ship we see is not in the real world. It is in the target worlds of the said picture, and the picture is a device that enables us to see it. We can see things in other worlds through things in the real world (the latter being representations of the former) in the same sense that we see a man by looking at his picture. In modern times, we are accustomed to seeing things by using various devices, via optic, electronic, or photographic images. What makes X the image of Y, I believe, is not a privileged "causal route" (whatever that is) that connects them. Optic, electronic, and photographic images, for instance, are generated by radically different causal means. Thus it is not X's causal relation to Y that makes it a device for seeing Y; instead, it is our native, culturally enhanced ability to see X *as* Y that makes it possible for us *directly* to see Y (e.g., the president) through X (electronic flashes on a television screen). The nonexistent ship that the painting represents can

12. *Mimesis as Make-Believe*, 219.
13. Ibid.
14. "When I see a picture of a galloping horse—do I merely *know* that this is the kind of movement meant? Is it a superstition to think I *see* the horse galloping in the picture?" (Wittgenstein, *Philosophical Investigations* [New York: Macmillan, 1953], pt. 2, xi, 63 [202e]).

therefore be referred to, and seen, via a blotch of paint *iff* the latter is seen *as a ship*.[15]

9.3. Talking About Interworld Things

Oliver Twist refers, then, to real things and is true about them; but that still fails to support TA, for I have established only that what *Oliver Twist* says of those things is true in virtue of the way they are in unreal worlds. That falls far short of TA, which claims that art tells important truths about reality as it is. A critic may say that novel X is good because it vividly depicts the life of migrant workers, that poem Y is good because it captures the feeling of unrequited love, etc.; aesthetics should explain that basic idiom of literary criticism.

To say that X is F in some world is tantamount to saying that X is possibly F. *Othello* refers to Jealousy, describing a world in which it causes a man to kill the woman he loves. Thus, *Othello* describes what Jealousy, a real thing, can do: it can cause a man to kill the woman he loves. Thus, fiction describes modal properties of real things. Even fantasy refers to real things, such as Jealousy, Sorrow, and Hope. That is also true of painting, including nonfigurative painting, and music: all works of art represent real emotions as they are in the target worlds of these artworks, so they say what these emotions could be. No artworks fail to describe the modal properties of *some* such real things, so all art is representational.

Even that conclusion falls short of TA. TA says that good art is *deep:* it reveals important truths about reality. That claim is much stronger than the tepid one I just made, that a work of art implies truths of the form "X is possibly F." Such truths are shallow: it is logically possible that Jealousy would move one to murder, but it is also logically possible that it would not. It does not take a Shakespeare to tell us *that!*

John Hospers, a detractor of the *mimesis* view of art, says that literature does require mimetic accuracy; "it is of its correspondence with reality (truth) that we must be convinced." Hospers holds that "human beings in fiction . . .

---

15. For more on seeing nonexistents, see my "Look, This Is Zeus," in *Interpretation, Relativism, and the Metaphysics of Culture,* ed. Michael Krausz and Richard Shusterman (New York: Humanities Press, forthcoming).

must behave, feel and be motivated as actual humans behave, feel, and are motivated."[16]

> On examining major characters in admittedly great works of literature I cannot think of any flagrant violation of human nature. Hawthorne's requirement of all great fiction that it be "true to the human heart" seems always in one way or other to be fulfilled. This strongly suggests that it is a necessary condition for great literature—since the latter never occurs without it—even though it is not a sufficient condition . . . If one is convinced that in works of art no reference to the world of life outside the work of art is required, that a work of art is entirely "self contained," serenely independent of the world outside and to be evaluated without regard to any relation to it, then this fact about characterization will indeed be inconsistent with his doctrine.[17]

Morris Weitz, another opponent of the mimesis view of art, also upholds TA for literature. Tolstoy and Dostoevski, he says, are great because they saw something deep in human nature that Proust and Eliot did not see.[18] I feel so too. That feeling, however, is suspicious. How do I know that Dostoevski is right about human nature? Weitz and I are not psychologists, and our claim that Dostoevski reveals a truth about human nature is not based on research that confirms Dostoevski's descriptions.[19] When a novel is hailed for psychological insight, the praise is based on reading it: critics conduct no empirical research and cite no scientific journals. How can that be a valid procedure of verification? Is it not irresponsible to extol as true and profound, without conducting any tests, a view about such an immensely complex matter? That question may not bother those who, like Schopenhauer, Maritain, or Heidegger, hold that the truth revealed in art is a truth of a higher order, beyond the ken of science. I have no idea what that

16. John Hospers, "Art and Reality," in *Art and Philosophy,* ed. S. Hook (New York: New York University Press, 1966), 126. See also his "Implied Truths in Literature," *Journal of Aesthetics and Art Criticism* 19 (1960): 37–46.

17. John Hospers, "Literature and the Nature of Man," *Journal of Aesthetics and Art Criticism* 17 (1958): 51.

18. Morris Weitz, "Truth in Literature," *Revue Internationale de Philosophie* 9 (1955): 116–29; reprinted often.

19. Cf. Arnold Eisenberg, "The Problem of Belief," *Journal of Aesthetics and Art Criticism* 13 (1955): 395–407.

truth may be, but Hospers and Weitz do not say that; they speak of ordinary truth, claiming that great art captures it. How can that be?

Some modal statements are about the essence, that is, the nature, of things: what a thing must be and what it cannot be. That nature is more apparent in some worlds than in others; so one can learn more about X by getting to know it in a world where its essence is evident. We cannot learn a great deal about Jones in a world where he leads an uneventful life; in the target worlds of a novel, however, he undergoes adventures that bring his nature to a sharp focus. A survey of such worlds may be instructive. We may find Jones's essential traits by contemplating what he would do in some nonreal world. Fiction, then, conducts a simulated experiment: it shows how X would react in situations that reveal its nature. The work's target worlds are experimental conditions set up to check the nature of X. *Othello's* target worlds are laboratories in which we observe how Ambition, Love, and Insecurity interact. Experiments conducted under controlled conditions can reveal important truths about the world outside the laboratory, and a thought experiment in fictional worlds reveals important truths about reality.

9.4. Thought Experiments and Catalysts

It is not true that artists conduct no experiments and thus cannot discover empirical truths. There is a kind of experiment we all perform every day and therefore ignore, yet it is a perfectly genuine experiment: thought experiment. Each person has a vast data base that can be probed, mined, and rearranged, given the right "search" commands, with surprising results. A good way to tease new findings out of old data is to introduce hypothetical conditions into it and compute the result. Working out permutations in extant data is the core of thinking: we consider a possible scenario and use our data base to derive significant conclusions and predictions. Artists do it best.

Overlooking the similarity of fiction to thought experiments is due to bad ontology. One who holds that fiction refers only to fiction, or to nothing at all, naturally would not expect to learn anything valuable from it. But if works of fiction refer to real things about which we already know a lot and of which we wish to know more, things such as Love, Ambition, Jealousy, The Family, Old Age, etc., then fiction's thought experiments have an obvious cognitive role. Artists find more about these things by using the familiar method of chemists: mix substances to see how they interact.

Chemists do it with samples of the substances themselves, whereas artists use a mental simulation of those things, yet both kinds of experiment may result in illuminating findings and reveal significant truths.

What, then, is the cognitive use of fictional beings, things referred to in works of fiction, which do *not* exist? If *Hamlet* is about Truth, Love, Treason, Power, and other real things, what is Hamlet doing in *Hamlet?* What do we need him for? The answer is that he is a catalyst. Due to his presence the real elements interact and undergo accelerated processes, revealing what they are and what they do to each other. The fictive agent exposes what under normal conditions stays hidden. Fiction puts a familiar thing in simulated conditions that make it show what it is and what it can be, that is, its essence. For instance, *Hamlet* shows that a frantic quest for truth and justice, untempered by compassion, destroys the innocent (Ophelia) with the guilty (Claudius) and with those one should protect (Gertrude), and rewards the worst villains (Fortinbras). The real database unfolds under the influence of the fictional catalyst: the play catches the conscience of the thing.

Philosophers of science show that scientists often focus on data they deem significant and extrapolate from them, ignoring counterevidence.[20] Similarly, a reader immersed in a L. F. Celine world W_C may become convinced that people are contemptible, but that decision is due to the diet of data Celine dishes out, expunging all else from his W_C. Scientists and artists try to make sense of experience by weaving it into aesthetically good yarns; the aesthetic appeal of the story vindicates its way of formatting data. Nancy Cartwright demonstrates how science explains not X's actual behavior but an ideal behavior of a Y from which X deviates under some conditions. Analogously, artist A portrays a world W_A that illuminates the behavior of a fictional Y, implying that we shall better understand a real X if we see it as a W_0 variation on Y.

What is the cognitive use of fiction? What segment of reality is *Hamlet* supposed to illuminate? May we fault it if it fails to fit an average American? No, for Hamlet is not an average American. Should we use *Hamlet* to understand nonaverage Danes? Which ones? Need the real X explained

---

20. See Thomas Kuhn, *The Structure of Scientific Revolutions,* 2d ed. (Chicago: Chicago University Press, 1970); Paul Feyerabend, *Against Method* (London: New Left Books, 1975); idem, *Philosophical Papers* (Cambridge: Cambridge University Press, 1981), vols. 1 and 2; Larry Laudan, *Progress and Its Problems* (Berkeley and Los Angeles: University of California Press, 1977); and Nancy Cartwright, *How the Laws of Physics Lie* (Oxford: Oxford University Press, 1983).

by the fictional Y be exactly like Y? There is no such X. So, how much should X resemble Y for Y to be applicable to X? We have no idea how to measure likenesses, so the project seems hopeless. So why do we say that art illuminates reality?

No rule tells us how to apply a story. Yet that is no cause for alarm, because, as Kant and Wittgenstein showed, no rule is needed.[21] No rule can tell us how to apply a model, for if we need a rule, we get caught in a vicious regress of rules for applying rules to rules for applying rules, etc. Wittgenstein's Kantian answer is that you realize you applied a rule when you see things in terms of that rule. We cannot be told how to fit fiction to fact, but if historical reality makes sense, if it is a compelling story, more often than not that story is the work of an artist. We understand a situation through *Othello* though no rule told us how to format experience by it. The shoe fits, so to speak, after we wear it for a while.

9.5. Significant Form

Another problem for TA is that we seldom expect artworks to mimic the thing they represent; mimesis is often not an aesthetic virtue. A musician using a folk song need not reproduce it; a painter need not faithfully copy his model; a dancer need not duplicate the motion of the object he depicts. So why do we praise fiction for truth? We criticize a novel, saying, "Farmers do not talk that way" or "The farmer character is phoney; the author knows nothing about farmers." Why is truth aesthetically relevant here?

There are formal reasons why aesthetic value is enhanced by truth. The above comments about the representation of farmers may be construed as purely structural: the novel is criticized not for lacking truth but for lacking coherence. Part of the meaning of 'farmer' is what we know or believe about the behavior of real farmers; so if farmers behave F-ly, the sentence "X is a farmer and behaves non-F-ly" is problematic. Fact guides use, hence meaning; gross misrepresentation of facts verges on the meaningless. For example, it is not clear what "The farmer flies from flower to flower" means: how do you envisage the truth-condition of that sentence? Wittgenstein noted

21. Immanuel Kant, *KdU* 169. For Wittgenstein's solution of this problem, see my "Meaning, the Experience of Meaning, and the Meaning-Blind in Wittgenstein's Late Philosophy," *Monist* 78 (1995): 480–95.

that sense disintegrates if we depart from common judgment. On that explanation, literature must be true to the human heart because psychological facts are important to us, therefore essential to the fabric of meaning. To use sentences that seem to violate them is to be incomprehensible.

That formal reason is helpful, yet it alone cannot explain why we believe that works of art are aesthetically better for being true. A fuller account starts by noting that a big chunk of reality is incorporated into every artwork. The matter that art forms is usually taken from mundane experience. Rendering its material comprehensible by molding it into a story, art makes a chunk of life aesthetically valuable and epistemically clear. The medley of life that the artist shapes, making it a unified whole, includes many of our actual beliefs. A portion of life is rearranged, perhaps revolutionized, by art. Art restructures our cognitive maps; thus, it has an epistemic value.

Art uses material that has high value for us, things we deem important. Formalists cannot explain why art typically treats topics of high human interest. If beauty is a perfect form, the material the artist uses should be irrelevant, yet art addresses itself to things that we value in real life. Literature is about fear, death, love, ambition, sex, God, etc., and no novels or poems develop mathematical theorems, although these may be given a complex formal structure and solutions that are both varied and unified. A novel about a mathematician may describe the problem he works on, but no artwork deals with a mathematical problem as such. Art uses themes of *immediate* and *general* human interest. No poem expounds laser physics; no novel elaborates on electronic themes; no lyrics portray protein syntheses; no ballet depicts particle mechanics; no drama exposes the battle of cell and enzyme. A story about molecules or stars will anthropomorphize them and endow them with emotion, intention, and desire. *Pace* formalism, art requires valuable material: artists give form to already significant matter.

Art, then, uses fictional catalysts to elaborate significant data into aesthetically valuable self-explanatory wholes. Even nonfigurative art needs significant matter: its protagonists are emotions and moods expressed by colors and shapes. The types Despondent, Lighthearted, Morbid, etc. that abstract art presents are all real things. To better understand them we observe them in worlds where they occur in well-structured event sequences that give them sense and make us grasp what they essentially are (i.e., what they can and cannot become).

I summarize: artists take significant items, real things we care about, and in controlled thought experiments place them in circumstances that occur in unreal worlds, to reveal their (man-made) nature. Perfecting matter that is of no significance to us is not art. Insignificance is an *aesthetic* demerit: to reach aesthetic excellence, art forms significant matter. Unity in variety is good design, but significance makes it into art. Good art is, then, significant form.

9.6. Emotion and the Fictional

Sam watches a movie in which a green slime seems to slither right at him. Sam shudders, his stomach sinks, he perspires profusely and feels an urge to escape; he clutches the armrests of his chair so hard his knuckles turn white. Why? My answer is simple: because he is afraid. Anita feels a clog in her throat and tears stream down her cheeks when she reads of Anna Karenina's suicide; she says, "Poor Anna." I take that as evidence that Anita pities Anna. Now, to fear X one needs to believe that X is dangerous to one, and to pity X one needs to believe that X unduly suffers; I therefore hold that Sam believes that the slime endangers him and Anita believes that Anna is an innocent victim. That is, I take what we say about fictional beings (that we fear them, pity them, etc.) at face value.

Many aestheticians think that such a simple account cannot be true. Sam and Anita know that the slime and Anna do not exist; hence Sam knows that the slime does not endanger him in reality, and Anita knows that Anna does not suffer in reality; so how can they have the beliefs necessary for fear and pity? Among those who take that objection as decisive and therefore hold that Sam and Anita experience no emotion, the most sophisticated is Walton. He holds that emotion consists of beliefs that cause certain sensations, and he calls the latter "quasi-emotions." Thus the sensation caused by a belief that one is in danger is quasi-fear; the one caused by believing that a victim deserves help is quasi-pity. Walton would therefore say that Sam and Anita in the above examples experience quasi-fear and quasi-pity, not fear and pity. However, Walton will add, Sam and Anita play games of make-believe in which quasi-fear or quasi-pity are used as props. A rule in these games stipulates that these sensations are to *count as* fear or pity, just as a tree stump may count as a bear in some children's game. Walton's account is that Sam "experiences quasi fear as a result of realizing that fictionally the slime threatens him. This makes it fictional that his quasi fear is caused by a belief that the slime poses a danger, and hence that he fears the slime."[22]

---

22. *Mimesis as Make-Believe*, 245. See generally 240–89.

Let 'Fic(p)' abbreviate "It is fictional that p." Walton's argument is, then, as follows:

1. Fic (Sam believes that the slime threatens him).
2. [Fic (Sam believes that the slime threatens him)] makes Sam feel quasi-fear.
3. Fic [(Sam's belief that the slime threatens him) makes Sam feel quasi-fear].
4. Necessarily, if [(Sam's belief that the slime threatens him) makes Sam feel quasi-fear] then Sam is afraid.
5. Fic (Sam is afraid).

That is an ingenious account. To get (3) from (2), however, you need importation:

IMP: If *Fic(p)* causes *q*, then Fic(*p* causes *q*).

'Fic(p)' can be read as 'in some game p.' Suppose that I bet that Karpov will sacrifice a bishop in some chess game. So I believe that if Karpov sacrifices a bishop, I shall make money:

6. B{[Fic(sacrifice)] → I make money}.

Yet

7. Fic{[B(sacrifice) → I make money]}

(in words: fictionally, if I believe that Karpov sacrifices the bishop, I'll make money) does not follow. The bishop's sacrifice is fictional, but my making money is real. Furthermore, it is false that to make money I only need to *believe* that Karpov will sacrifice the bishop. Thus, IMP is invalid.

Do (3) and (4) imply (5)? Only by transitivity:

TRA: [Fic(p) and □(p → q)] → Fic(q).

But TRA is not valid either: to sacrifice a bishop is to commit murder; fictionally, Karpov sacrifices a bishop. Does it follow that, fictionally, he commits murder? Of course not. Further, Walton explains that Fic(p) is an injunction to imagine *that p*, so TRA mandates that *Alice in Wonderland* requires us to imagine everything, and if in monopoly a boy owes

$120, he has to imagine that he owes \$5! (five factorial). Surely that is wrong.

Let us forgo the argument and accept (5) as an axiom. Can it explain why Sam and Anita behave as they do? No, 'Fic(x)' is too trivial. Sleep can count as Fic(fear), yet sleep cannot explain Sam's involuntary behavior. Fic(pity) may be true of Anita in virtue of Sam's blowing his nose, but Sam blowing his nose cannot explain Anita's tears.[23] Contrast this with a genuine explanation by reference to rules: the rules of chess do explain why Karpov behaves as he does (moves a piece of wood on a board). Nothing similar takes place with Sam and Anita: there is nothing that they do *because* their quasi-emotions count in some game as emotions.

Walton may be aware of that objection, for he says that what counts as Fic(fear) should incline us to count it as Fic(fear).[24] That is asking too much, for no sensation inclines you to count yourself as fictionally afraid; why would you do a strange thing like that? Your sensation may incline you to think that you *are* afraid, but even that is doubtful, since sensations when in the throes of a given emotion are not specific to that emotion. Feeling warm all over (a feeling you also have when in love) does not incline you to count that sensation as fictionally being in love, nor would you naturally take a chest pain as Fic(pity).

Walton may answer that besides quasi-emotion we have the fictional belief. Sam does not believe the slime attacks him, yet Fic(Sam believes the slime attacks him); that and the quasi-fear incline Sam to make the quasi-fear count as Fic(fear). I reply that having a Fic(belief) is again trivial: my sitting may count as my Fic(believing the slime attacks me). Anything may count as Fic(believing that p), so it cannot explain Sam's apparent fear. Further, *what* counts here as Fic(Sam believes that the slime attacks him)? What prop does Sam use to stand for so believing? Perhaps his beliefs about spots on the screen. But while watching the movie, Sam has no beliefs about spots on the screen! Are these beliefs unconscious? If so, how can Sam use them as props to generate fictional beliefs? He needs to decide that beliefs about the screen count as fictional beliefs about the slime! I doubt that Walton can extricate his theory from these difficulties.

Other writers admit that we emotionally react when we face fictional beings, but claim that the objects we react *to* are not fictional; they are

23. Walton says (ibid., 251) that fictionally detesting Iago may be generated by quasi-hate, but that is trivial: Fic(detests Iago) may be generated by anything whatsoever!
24. Ibid., 252.

real beings that resemble the fictional ones. Reading *War and Peace,* Nat believes he loves Natasha, but the true objects of his love are real women who resemble her.[25] That, however, is counterintuitive. In cases of repression and self-denial one may think one loves *a* though it is really *b* that one loves, but most of us are not so out of touch with our feelings as not to know who it is that we love. Is Nat deluded? If he does not love Natasha, why does he think of her? It is odd that Nat pictures Natasha, calls out her name, etc. *because* he loves other women. And how can Nat love millions of women he has never met? Perhaps Nat loves not Natasha but her traits only; but who can love traits? Indeed, it is due to her traits that Nat loves Natasha, but it is a person he loves, not traits. The same is true of Sam and the slime: Sam fears *that* slime (he points at it), not some real monster that resembles it. No such monsters exist, and even if there were some in jungles, Sam has no reason to fear them![26]

Noël Carroll thinks that the slime evokes genuine horror, but the horror, he says, is caused not by a belief that the slime is here but by a mere thought whose content is the slime.[27] That is impossible: as I write this, and when you read it, we think about the slime; that is the content of our thought. Yet surely we experience no horror.

Unlike these writers, Colin Radford admits that we emotionally react to nonexistent beings, but contends that our reaction is irrational.[28] Sam knows that the slime does not exist and that he is in no danger; since nonetheless he is afraid, he is irrational. Nat is irrational, since he knows that Natasha is an

---

25. See M. Weston, "How Can We Be Moved by the Fate of Anna Karenina?" *Proceedings of the Aristotelian Society,* supp. vol. 49 (1975): 81–93. B. Paskins ("On Being Moved by Anna Karenina and *Anna Karenina,*" *Philosophy* 52 [1977]: 344–47) concurs: we feel "pity for those people if any . . . are in the same bind as the character." W. Charlton ("Feelings for the Fictitious," *British Journal of Aesthetics* 24 [1984]: 206–16) says: "The analysis of 'We feel for Anna' which I am proposing here is not that we categorically pity hypothetical persons; it is that we hypothetically desire to benefit real persons. Our state of mind is expressible by, 'If any of my friends has a husband like Karenin or a lover like Vronski, would that I might be able to help her.' " See also D. Mannison, "On Being Moved by Fiction," *Philosophy* 60 (1985): 71–87.

26. Bijoy Boruah, in his *Fiction and Emotion* (Oxford: Oxford University Press, 1988), claims that the emotion we experience is real but that our putative beliefs about fictional beings are insincere, not genuine beliefs. But if Anita does not sincerely believe that Anna Karenina is a victim, she cannot pity Anna; her feeling is then also insincere. I can pity you only if I think you are really hurt; if I fake believing you are hurt, my show of pity is a fake too.

27. Noël Carroll, *The Philosophy of Horror* (New York: Routledge, 1990), 60–88; see esp. 80–83.

28. "How Can We Be Moved by the Fate of Anna Karenina?" *Proceedings of the Aristotelian Society,* supp. vol. 49 (1975): 67–80, and several later publications.

imaginary being, and yet he falls in love with her. The aesthetician therefore has a dilemma: either hold that we are rational and conclude that we do not emotionally react to bogus beings, or else admit that we emotionally react to them and conclude that we are irrational. I reject both horns of the dilemma. Fictional beings do move us, which implies that we hold the relevant beliefs about them (that they are in danger, that they endanger us, etc.), yet having those beliefs is perfectly rational.

9.7. Emotion and Rationality

Otto hates Iago because he believes that Iago is a villain, and that belief is true, for in the *Othello* target worlds, where Otto means his belief to be evaluated, Iago *is* a villain. Hating a villain is not irrational: on the contrary, it is the right reaction. Iago's lack of existence does not lessen his villainy, and Anna's innocence is not compromised by her fictionality. Since "Iago is a villain" (intended for evaluation in the *Othello* target worlds) expresses a true statement, Iago should be hated. What reason is there for hating someone other than for being a villain? Some philosophers say that "Iago is a villain" is false because 'Iago' does not denote. That is an error: by all linguistic criteria 'Iago' is a name, and for any name 'S,' " 'S' denotes S" is an axiom. Thus Iago (in the intended index) *is* a villain and should be hated. Not to react emotionally to a villain is a flaw of character.

If Sam is afraid of the slime, why does he not escape? If Anita pities Anna, why does she not try to help her? One reason is that in rational adults emotion does not cause action; rather, it gives them a reason to act. Reasons are weighted against each other and are defeasible, so emotion need not lead to action. A given emotion makes a certain course of action seem appropriate. For instance, love makes you consider right a gift that otherwise you would have considered excessive; anger makes you see an attack as eminently justified; etc. Emotion causes an action to seem prima facie justified, but that justification may be defeated by other considerations.

That justification is defeated does not mean that there was none to start with. On the contrary, defeasibility is essential to justification. Anna Karenina is truly miserable, so Anita is justified in pitying her. This does prima facie justify Anita's helping Anna, but the justification is defeated by the fact that Anna does not exist. It would also be defeated had Anna lived too far away for Anita to come to her aid. Anita has a good reason to help

Anna, but a better reason to do nothing. Events in other star systems, in the past, and in other possible worlds do not lead to action, not because they do not prima facie justify action, but because that justification is defeated. Again: Anna deserves to be helped. Karenin, Anna's husband, and Vronski, her lover, are contemptible because they could have helped Anna but did not. Anita, on the other hand, cannot help Anna. Anita exists, Anna does not exist, and in reality the twain shall never meet.

Sam's fear justifies his taking certain action, say, escaping. Should he escape? That depends on whether the justification is overridden or not. It is overridden, for example, if Sam has a duty to stay despite the danger or if running exacerbates the danger. The justification for escaping is also defeated if Sam knows that although the slime is dangerous, it does not endanger him. One reason for that can be that the slime does not exist, in which event escape is silly. To be afraid is to see one's state as prima facie justifying escape, but if the justification of flight is defeated, then, for rational people, no flight ensues. Rational agents would not initiate an action unless they believed that it had a chance of bringing about the desired result, and in Sam's case that chance is nil.

The justification is genuine: Anna needs help, and Iago should be stopped; unless that is so, the stories in question make no sense. What Iago does is wrong, which implies that he should not be allowed to do it. However, we are exempt from so acting, since Iago is not real and there is nothing we in reality can do to stop him in *Othello*'s target worlds; so we just sit back, let ourselves be engulfed by fear and pity, and, since nothing can be done about it, enjoy the complexities of the unfolding plot.

That Stalin is dead and can do no more harm is a reason against trying to stop him, but not a reason against hating him; the death of a person you love is not, by itself, a reason not to love that person. Nat's belief that Natasha is charming justifies his love for her, and that justification *is not* defeated. It also gives him a prima facie justification to court Natasha, but that justification *is* defeated by his belief that she is not in the real world.

9.8. Belief Dossiers

Otto believes that Iago is a villain, and does not believe that Iago is not a villain. Sam, on the other hand, believes that the slime endangers him, but also believes the slime does not endanger him. Is Sam irrational? Can rational people have contradictory beliefs? There is a reason to think they cannot: avoiding contradiction is a mark of rationality. Rational people make decisions in view of their beliefs: if I believe that it will rain, I do A, and if I believe that it will not rain, I do not do A. What should I do if I believe that it will rain and that it will not rain? No action can be indicated. So it seems that having contradictory beliefs should be avoided. Yet we all hold some contradictory beliefs; not being omniscient, we often fail to see that 'p' implies 'not-q' and believe both *that p* and *that q*.

If Sam believes a contradiction, does he believe all that follows from it, that is, everything? Some writers get out of this difficulty by denying that believing is closed under *modus ponens;* they deny that '(Bp and Bp→q)' implies 'Bq.' If we do not attribute to Sam all that follows from his beliefs, he may have contradictory beliefs without believing everything.[29] So, may we maintain that 'B(p and not-p)' does not imply 'B(q)'? I cannot accept that. *Modus ponens* is a hallmark of rationality; a belief system not closed under *modus ponens* is not rational. If Jane believes that she has $10 and that 10 > 5, then, if she is rational, she also believes she has more than $5. The rule that sanctions that conclusion is '(Bp and Bp→q)→Bq,' so how can it be invalid? To abandon it is to forsake reason.

Why, then, are we not perfect reasoners? I answer that belief systems are closed under *modus ponens*, but (as I have argued elsewhere)[30] a person has more than one such system, more then one belief dossier (the latter term is due to Grice). To use *modus ponens* all the premises must be mutually accessible, they must all be in one dossier. If they are not, if, when one premise occurs to you, the others elude you, deduction cannot take place. (As in relevance logic, inference is valid only from identically indexed premises.) *Modus ponens* across epistemic dossiers is invalid, just as it is invalid across persons: if I believe *that p* and you believe *that p→q*, neither of us need believe *that q*. That holds for conjunction too: '(Bp and Bq)' implies 'B(p and q)' only if both 'p' and 'q' are in the same dossier; if they are not, one may hold *that p* and *that q*, but not *that p and q*. Though I believe all Peano's axioms,

---

29. In *Philosophical Explanations* (Oxford: Oxford University Press, 1981), 172–78, 197–227, Robert Nozick shows that Knowledge is not deductively closed either: Kp and K(p→q) do not imply Kq. Jonathan Dancy (*Introduction to Contemporary Epistemology* (Oxford: Basil Blackwell, 1985) agrees but says (p. 11) that deductive closure of Justified Belief is more acceptable. That is clearly wrong: if I have twenty beliefs, each of which is 90 percent justified, their conclusion is only 10.9 percent justified, i.e., hardly justified at all.

30. In "Transparent Belief," *Australasian Journal of Philosophy*, 60 (1982): 55–65.

I do not believe all the truths of arithmetic, for if the resulting theorems are lodged in distinct files, no further beliefs are generated.

Joe owns a few shares; when the market goes up, he is glad, for he has shares; when the market goes down, he is glad, for he practically has no shares. Does Joe believe that he has and does not have shares? No; the belief that he has shares and the belief that he practically has no shares are lodged in distinct dossiers. Such doublethink is very common; our beliefs are not entirely integrated, and we are better off for it.

Usually, a person acts on the beliefs in one privileged dossier, but other dossiers have their field day too. When Sam sees the slime, his dominant dossier contains the belief that he is not in danger, and that belief motivates his staying in the theater, but the thrill comes from the fact that another dossier contains a belief that he is in danger, and the fear and panic it calls forth are felt, tasted, and enjoyed for their aesthetic quality. Research in neurology, psychiatry, and toxicology and studies of hypnosis and linguistics all indicate that a person has more than one belief system. Studies of corpus callosum lesions (commissurotomy), dissociation, and aphasia and psychoanalytic studies of hysteria, dreams, and hypnotic states all indicate that the human mind contains many semi-independent centers of belief whose methods of belief acquisition and processing differ (Freud's primary versus secondary cognitive processes) and whose outputs may be mutually incompatible.[31] Were we unitary, seamless souls rather than complex minds with more than one system of belief, we could not have played our distinct belief centers against each other for aesthetic profit.

Let me name a belief whose content is *that p* '[p].' My claim is, then, that Sam has the belief [p and q] only if [p] and [q] are in the same belief dossier in his mind. If [p] and [p→q] are not lodged in one dossier, Sam will not have [q]. Like sheep, beliefs procreate only if put in the same enclosure.

One reason a person has more than one belief dossier is economy. Beliefs come in droves: when one is activated, a host of others trails it, and it is wasteful to have a belief call too many others to mind. Yet if the belief [p] is not there with the belief [q], arguments that need "p and q" as a premise will not run through. Another reason for having multiple dossiers is that

31. A bibliography of studies of the modularity of the conscious mind could take a whole volume. For a good but outdated bibliography on the split-brain issue, see Charles E. Marks, *Commissurotomy Consciousness and Unity of Mind* (Cambridge: MIT Press, 1981). I discussed the multicenteredness of the mind in "Unconscious Mind or Conscious Minds?" *Midwest Studies in Philosophy* 10 (1986): 120–48.

not all truths are good for us to believe. Freud maintained that an internal mental mechanism (the censor) keeps harmful beliefs out of the system Cs (later, the ego). I think that such beliefs are shunted to another dossier. If the censor finds that [q] is harmful to me, given my having [p], it may put [p] and [p→q] in different doxastic dossiers to prevent their generating [q]. I then have [p] and [p→q], but not [p and (p→q)]. Thus, by depositing [p] and [p→q] in distinct dossiers, I avoid having [q] without giving up either [p] or [p→q].

Self-deception is a glaring example of that strategy: Jane holds [p], a belief about her husband's behavior; she is rational enough to hold [p→q], [q] being the belief that her husband has a lover, yet she does not have [q]. She deceives herself. The censor deems [q] too dangerous for Jane, so it puts [p] and [p→q] in distinct dossiers. That is not irrational: if the choice is between emotional breakdown and deductive incompleteness, it is rational to sacrifice the latter. It may be rational to hold logical acumen in check.

Sam's two beliefs [p] and [not-p] may be due to distinct doxastic strategies, where Sam can ill afford to discard either one. It is rational to keep a doxastic stratagem that usually yields true beliefs at the cost of acquiring a few false beliefs too. It is rational to keep incompatible beliefs if both can be used (say, one for good times, one for bad). Some beliefs we know to be false are beneficial, so we induce them in ourselves and file the knowledge that they are false in another dossier. Examples are setting the watch ten minutes ahead, cultivating "positive thinking," overestimating one's abilities, and so on.

Thousands of years of hard-gained experience taught us to trust our eyes and believe visual data; we learned that what we see is in our immediate vicinity. These maxims are false. For example, we see stars that are not in our vicinity, and some of them no longer exist. Is it rational, then, to discard these maxims? No, for most of the things we see are near us, and our life depends on prompt reaction to them. If I deliberate whether what I see is or is not in my vicinity, by the time I reach a conclusion, it may be too late to act. The doxastic strategy, seeing is believing, is thus worth keeping, though it generates false beliefs.

Another ancient doxastic maxim is that I know only about what is crucial to my survival, so if I know that X bodes ill, I must attend to it by fight or flight; there is no such thing as having information about X that has nothing whatever to do with me. That maxim is false, but too useful to discard. Now, Sam, who sees the green slime on the screen, has information about it; therefore he acquires the belief that the slime is right there in front of him. Consequently, he is afraid. Reading a novel, Anita gets to know in great detail the world it portrays, and thus she believes that the described events take place in her own sphere and that she is present in that world, whether in her own persona or in the persona of a protagonist. Believing she is in that world, it is rational for her to fear or to hope for certain events in it. To avoid contradictions, however, these beliefs are placed in a dossier other than the one where she has her beliefs about the real world.

Some emotions about nonexistents are caused by true beliefs: "Anna is innocent" is true, and so is "Iago is a villain." On the other hand, Sam's belief that the slime is real and Otto's belief that he is Othello are false. Sam *also* believes that the slime poses no danger to him, and Otto believes that he is not Othello, but these true beliefs do not expunge their false opposites. Sam holds the true belief [p] and the false belief [not-p], but not the absurd belief [p and not-p].

9.9. Emotion and Interworld Travel

One serious problem with the rationality of emotions generated by false beliefs remains: it seems that some of those beliefs are not only false but *necessarily* false. It is true, in the movie's target worlds, that the slime feeds on human flesh; but the statement that the slime has come to the real world to attack Sam is not only false but also (I maintain) impossible. It is impossible for a resident of one world to visit another. The slime in the movie's target worlds can slither out of its world and show up in reality no more than the number five can become the number six. But if it is *necessarily* false that the slime attacks Sam and that Nat meets Natasha and that Anita helps Anna, because these scenarios require interworld travel, then Sam, Nat, and Anita are irrational, for they wish for or believe the impossible. That means that some emotional reactions to fictional beings are, after all, irrational.

Plantinga does not share my misgivings about interworld commerce. In Chapter 8, I discussed his (and others') view that Anna-in-W has possibilities of her own. I argued that this is absurd: things (Anna Karenina, Socrates, Tolstoy, et al.) have possibilities, but not their occurrences in worlds. The latter *explicate* what it is for things to have possibilities. The ability of a thing to be otherwise *is* its occurrence in another world, so that world-bound occurrence cannot occur in yet another world. Possibilities have no possibilities.

My answer to the question about Sam's or Anita's rationality is that the imagined scenarios do not require interworld travel and therefore are quite possible after all. In the usual (not Lewis's) semantics for modality individuals occur in many worlds, so real individuals such as Sam inhabit not only the real world but countless other worlds too, and on my semantics the same is true of nonexistent beings. Natasha inhabits many worlds other than the target worlds of *War and Peace,* and the slime inhabits worlds other than those that satisfy the movie Sam is watching. Nat does not inhabit any of the *War and Peace* target worlds (he is neither mentioned nor implied in *War and Peace*), so he cannot meet Natasha there, and Natasha is absent from reality. Natasha, however, occurs in other worlds too, for she has possibilities that are not realized in the *War and Peace* target worlds. For example, in the *War and Peace* target worlds Natasha is engaged to Prince Andrei but does not marry him; yet she could have married Andrei. So, in other worlds she does marry him. In some such non–*War and Peace* target worlds Nat and Natasha do both occur; in some of them they meet; and in some of those worlds they, yes, fall in love. So Nat does not wish for the logically impossible: it is possible that he meets Natasha. The same is true of Sam and the slime: the slime need not come to the real world to attack Sam, for there is a possible world where both it and Sam occur and where it *does*— how horrible—attack Sam. Similarly for Anita, who does, in some possible world, manage to comfort Anna Karenina and save her from death. There is even a world where all of the above meet and merrily party: they need no interworld travel for that.

9.10. Emotion and Realism

Anna Karenina herself is not present in *Anna Karenina:* in that book you find only words that denote her (the words 'Anna Karenina'). To see Anna herself you must envision her in a possible world where she occurs. Painting is different: seeing a painting of Anna you say, "That is Anna Karenina!" so you do see her by looking at her picture; the picture is a device by means of which you see Anna Karenina as she is in a world satisfying that picture. When you see a photograph of Sam, you see Sam, and seeing a picture of Anna Karenina is a way to see Anna herself. So, paintings are more realistic than words. Anna's painting is not entirely realistic, however, for it reveals only one frozen aspect of her face. A movie is more realistic, yet it has its limitations too: it shows Anna Karenina from outside, but that is not the most important facet of her. Her feelings are much more important. Anna's feelings are represented by words, and therefore they are not represented realistically. Thus, although more realistic than literature, pictures are not very realistic either.

Music achieves a higher degree of realism. The first movement of Mahler's Second Symphony does not denote Despair by conventional means as the name 'Anna' denotes Anna, and it does not show the looks of Despair from the outside, as a picture of Anna does. It shows the essence of Despair: it is ponderous, meandering, muted, hesitant; it breaks down, throbbing and crying, as desperate people do.[32] Many aestheticians (e.g., Peter Kivy)[33] argue that the kinship between the music and the emotion it represents justifies saying that the emotion is itself present in the music. If that is so, then, when Molly listens to Mahler, she not only learns something about Despair but also meets it face to face. Of course, a symphony is not a despairing person, no more than the picture is Anna, but as looking at the picture is a way to see Anna, Mahler's music is a device through which you sense the thing Despair. In Mahler's music Despair is more fully apparent than Anna is in her picture, for the aspect of Despair with which you come in perceptual contact through the music is more essential to Despair than the aspect of Anna (her exterior) that you directly see through her picture. Mahler's music represents Despair in a more realistic way.

Further, music is more like a movie than it is like a still picture, for it shows emotion as it changes. The music shows Despair as going through various adventures, as the movie shows the adventures of Anna. In the music the protagonist, Despair, vies with other emotions: fear, courage, hope, and bitterness. The set of target worlds of that work of music is, then, a set of worlds in all of which these emotions are experienced in that order. The person who experiences those emotions differs from world to world (as those worlds differ in other details), yet a world where exactly *that* emotional drama occurs is a target world of that piece of music. Since target worlds satisfy a work, Mahler's Second Symphony is true at those worlds.

---

32. The idea is originally due to O. K. Bouwsma ("The Expression Theory of Art," in *Philosophical Essays* [Lincoln: University of Nebraska Press, 1942]). For a contemporary analysis of emotion in a piece of music, see, e.g., Jerrold Levinson, "Hope in *The Hebrides*," in *Music, Art, and Metaphysics* (Ithaca: Cornell University Press, 1990), 336–76.

33. Peter Kivy, *Sound and Semblance: Reflections on Musical Representation* (Ithaca: Cornell University Press, 1984).

Works of music are true in reality too. Paintings may, but need not, be true in reality: Rembrandt's painting of Saskia is satisfied in the real world because Saskia exists, but a picture of the slime is not satisfied in reality. Music has no fictional characters: the emotions, its protagonists, really exist. Is the drama that a given work portrays, the emotional adventure that shuttles between joy and despair, also true in reality? It is: music evokes in the listener the emotions it presents, so it guarantees its own satisfaction in reality. Music is, therefore, the most realistic of the arts.

In Mahler's music we meet Despair, a thing found in many places in the real world. Today it is in Bosnia, in Sudan, in India. Despair is present wherever there is someone who is desperate.[34] Through music you sense it as it really is.

34. Cf. chaps. 1–3 of my *Types: Essays in Metaphysics* (London: Brill, 1992).

Index of Names

Adams, Robert, 171, 183
Aldrich, Virgil, 37
Alexander, Samuel, 162
Andersen, H. C., 61
Aquinas, Thomas, 12, 17, 106
Aristotle, 62, 102, 164
Armstrong, D. M., 171
Augustine, 110
Ayer, Alfred, 3

Bach, C. P. E., 72
Bach, J. S., 29, 60–61, 72, 137, 153
Bacon, John, 145–46, 162
Bailey, George, 91
Barnes, Anette, 121
Barnes, Barry, 123–24
Battin, Margaret, 57
Beardsley, Monroe, 24, 26–32, 38–39, 129, 132, 193
Beethoven, Ludwig van, 140, 144, 146, 151–52, 162
Bell, Clive, 30–31
Berkeley, George, 162
Berlyne, D. E., 106
Blackburn, Simon, ix, 120
Bloom, Judy, 89
Bloor, David, 123–24
Bonaparte, Napoleon, 181
Borges, J. L., 40, 90–91, 96
Boruah, Bijoy, 205
Bosanquet, Bernard, 162
Bouwsma, O. K., 213
Brueghel, Pieter, 82
Bullough, Edward, 35–36
Byron, George Gordon Lord, 72

Cage, John, 85
Carnap, Rudolf, 143
Carroll, Lewis, 126
Carroll, Noël, 205
Cartwright, Nancy, 198
Cassirer, Ernst, 37
Castaneda, H. N., 186
Celine, L. F., 198
Cervantes, Miguel de, 90
Charlton, W., 205
Chisholm, Roderick, 181
Chopin, Frédéric, 82, 92
Churchland, Paul, 63
Clark, Romane, 168
Coleman, Francis, 33
Colleghan, William, 98
Collingwood, R. G., 36, 162
Cresswell, M. J., 171
Croce, Benedetto, 23, 36–37, 162
Currie, Gregory, 151, 190

Dancy, Jonathan, 208
Danto, Arthur, 84, 96–97, 118, 159–61
Davidson, Donald, 5, 46, 69, 121
Derrida, Jacques, 122
Descartes, René, 49–50, 75
Dewey, John, 23
Dickens, Charles, 190, 192, 194
Dickie, George, 32–33, 35, 84, 127
Donatello, 162
Donne, John, 83
Dostoevski, Feodor, 197
Doyle, Conan, 181, 186
Duchamp, Marcel, 84, 159–60
Dufrenne, Mikel, 162

Index of Subjects

Eddy M. Zemach is Ahad-Ha'am Professor of Philosophy at The Hebrew University of Jerusalem. He is the author of *Types: Essays in Metaphysics* (1992) and *The Reality of Meaning and the Meaning of "Reality"* (1992).

Breinigsville, PA USA
27 June 2010
240657BV00001B/65/A